The Political Morality of the International Monetary Fund

The Political Morality of the International Monetary Fund

Ethics and Foreign Policy

Volume 3

Edited by
ROBERT J. MYERS

Published for the Carnegie Council on Ethics & International Affairs

Transaction Books
New Brunswick (U.S.A.) and Oxford (U.K.)

Published by Transaction Books.

Library of Congress Catalog Number: 86-16098
ISBN: 0-88738-143-X (cloth); 0-88738-674-1 (paper)
Printed in the United States of America

Library of Congress Cataloging in Publication Data

The Political morality of the International Monetary
Fund.

(Ethics and foreign policy ; v. 3)
"Published for the Carnegie Council on Ethics & International Affairs."
Bibliography: p.
Includes index.
1. International Monetary Fund. 2 International finance—Moral and ethical aspects. I. Myers, Robert J. II. Carnegie Council on Ethics & International Affairs. III. Series.
HG3881.5.I58P65 1985 332.1′52 86-16098
ISBN 0-88738-143-X ; 0-88738-674-1 (pbk.)

Contents

Contents

Introduction

Robert J. Myers

The Carnegie Council on Ethics and International Affairs (formerly the Council on Religion and International Affairs) was founded in 1914 by Andrew Carnegie, and is an independent, nonpartisan, nonsectarian, and tax-exempt organization. Since its beginnings, the Carnegie Council has asserted its strong belief that ethics, as informed by the world's principal religions, deontological theories, or utilitarian calculations, is an inevitable and integral component of any policy decision, whether in the realm of economics, politics, or national security. The interrelationship of ethics and foreign policy is thus a unifying theme of all Carnegie Council programs.

In this particular study, we have chosen the deontological method, the normative point of view, that is, to propose what ought to be as opposed to what is. To do this in a responsible and constructive way, it is necessary to describe the "is" and the "ought" from a number of perspectives and to determine what lines of reform are the most promising.

If one applies this approach to the world of international economic affairs, a larger number of factors come into play—the world economy is indeed larger than the sum of its parts. The primary actors in the economic realm, particularly the major industrial powers—the United States, Japan, and the European countries—are the decisive influence. Some claim that the United States, by virtue of its economic might and by its pursuit of economic policies on its own, forces the rest of the world to trail in its wake. This charge has most recently been leveled at the Reagan administration, particularly over its internal deficits, which are said to be responsible for high interest rates worldwide, for one example, and which, in turn, exacerbate the difficulties of the debtor nations.

At other times, the scale of international economics goes beyond the ability of any one nation to exert effective unilateral control. Oil is a good example. Over the past ten years, the wildly fluctuating price of oil has alternately raised and dashed the economic prospects of the producers and the importers, the rich and the poor.

Another factor determining the international economic reality has been the question of exchange rates. In September 1985, the Group of 5, at U.S. urging, embarked on a program to lower the value of the dollar against European currencies and especially against the Japanese yen to help correct the huge U.S. trade deficit ($150 billion) and to bring down interest rates.

These recent developments demonstrate again the reason for international economic cooperation, a need first recognized in an acute way as the end of World War II came into sight. At that time, the malfunctioning world economy of the 1930s, marked by mutually high tariffs and "beggar thy neighbor" trade policies, was considered to be a significant source of global tensions. Clearly there was a requirement to provide an international mechanism to help rehabilitate the war-torn world, through loans and stable, dependable exchange rates, as well as to address anticipated short-term balance of payments and current account imbalances. Very briefly, then, these were the principal impulses behind the Bretton Woods meetings in 1944, which provided the way for the creation of both the World Bank and the International Monetary Fund (Mason and Asher 1973).

The dollar as the international currency was taken almost for granted in the postwar period; as Henry Luce had proclaimed, this was the "American century." In contrast to the United Nations General Assembly system of "one nation, one vote," membership in both the Bank and the Fund was determined on the basis of contribution, like buying shares in a credit union. U.S. and Western domination of these institutions seemed assured. And, as to this day, the U.S. preferred to control its more ambitious economic/security programs (at that time, the Marshall Plan) on a unilateral basis.

The postwar demand for the resources of the Bank and the Fund soon tested the resources of both institutions. (Sir John Maynard Keynes's appeal for a larger initial capital outlay was prescient.) The old order fell away under the impulse of anti-colonialism, with former colonies joining the U.N. as new nations in a continuing stream. (The number of countries in the U.N. has risen from 44 at the founding in 1945 to 151 today.)

Beyond the explosion in the number of new nations, all of which were demanding financial assistance, the other crucial event was the decision in 1971 by the U.S. to detach the dollar from gold. After this, currencies floated against the dollar, adding to the uncertainties of world financial markets and adding to the willingness of these organizations and private banks to lend money for economic development and for balance of payment requirements.

The magnitude of the economic dilemma facing the new nations was eloquently described by Gunnar Myrdal in his study *The Asian Drama: An Inquiry into the Poverty of Nations* (copyright 1968, the Twentieth Century

Fund). Dr. Myrdal further elaborated on this thesis during 1969 in the Cristian Herter Lectures delivered at the Johns Hopkins University School for Advanced International Studies, in Washington, D.C. These were published as *The Challenge of World Poverty, a World Anti-Poverty Program in Outline,* a summary and continuation of *Asian Drama.* A lineal descendant of this study was published in 1980, *North-South: A Program for Survival,* by the Independent Commission on International Development Issues, chaired by Willy Brandt. This latter work very heavily promoted the idea of a redistribution of world resources from the generally wealthy "Northern" states to the generally poor "Southern" states. At the time, certainly in the U.S., this kind of message was falling on deaf ears.

The Brandt report had not, to be sure, pioneered this view all on its own. To try to promote the redistributionist view of the world, the Third World nations organized two associations. The first, the Group of 77 (actually about 120 countries), was formed to urge a New International Economic Order. The program of choice was a worldwide conference to bring about these economic changes, now. As a corollary, these same disadvantaged countries also established another new instrument, the New Information Order. Only by creating a new system that could tell the economic story from their perspective could they possibly expect to influence the wealthier nations to understand the reality of their plight and the justice of their demands.

Neither new order went over well in the developed industrial societies. A whole development literature had begun to arise in the 1960s, challenging the causes of poverty in the Third World nations and more profoundly considering the elements in play in the complicated process of modernization and economic growth. (See, for example, two World Bank studies published by Oxford University Press: Blitzer et al. 1975; Chenery 1979.) The evidence seemed to point more toward faulty and corrupt government structures, poor economic policies, downplay of markets and private initiative, and so on, rather than to only a lack of resources. Agricultural policies in Africa, for example, were cited as turning previously food-exporting countries into nations of famine. Growth, not redistribution, showed greater promise. The situation was compounded by the accumulation of huge loans by Third World nations, especially in Latin America, which threatened the stability of international banking and the Bretton Woods system.

It is against this general background that the idea of taking a fresh look at the Bretton Woods arrangement was first considered. How suitable was this system to a world its originators could hardly imagine? This then was to be our general line of inquiry, first into the International Monetary Fund, then the General Agreement on Tariffs and Trade (a voluntary association dedicated to freer trade established in 1949, and now part of the triad of international economic institutions), and finally the World Bank.

The IMF was selected as the first subject for study because it has recently become something of an international fire horse, rushing in to solve crisis situations all over the world, many of which are of a character beyond its original mission (see Dam 1982). As the debt crisis worsened in 1985, the IMF appeared to be the only actor on the scene offering an overall approach to improve the situation. IMF assistance uniformly involved a "conditionality" plan for the financially troubled government that emphasized financial austerity. Key ingredients usually required currency devaluation, an increase of exports, and a lowering of imports (also see Killeck 1982; Muns 1984). The Carnegie Council was drawn to investigate alternative strategies in part because if this was all that can be offered to Latin American countries, as Pedro-Pablo Kuczynski writes his paper, "it means the end of economic development." The Baker Plan announced in 1985 and the anticipated revitalization in 1986 of the World Bank under the leadership of its new president, Barber Conable, may improve that bleak prognosis.

The separate chapter headings in this volume indicate the thrust of each article, and the different perspectives of the authors present a stimulating and challenging analysis of what the International Monetary Fund is doing and possible means of improving the effectiveness of its operation.

Finally, I would like to thank again the General Service Foundation of St. Paul, Minnesota, for providing the initial funds to begin this twelve-lecture study, and Irving Louis Horowitz, a specialist on Third World development strategies at Rutgers University. Meetings were held at Carnegie Council's headquarters, Merrill House, in New York City; in Washington, D.C.; Indianapolis; Chicago; and San Francisco. A partial list of those attending one or more meetings and contributing to the general discussion of each paper appears at the back of this book.

The views expressed herein are those of the authors and do not represent those of the Carnegie Council on Ethics and International Affairs.

References

Blitzer, Charles R., Peter B. Clark, and Lance Taylor, eds. 1975. *Economy-Wide Models and Development Planning*. New York: Oxford University Press.

Chenery, Hollis. 1979. *Structural Change and Development Policy*. New York: Oxford University Press.

Dam, Kenneth W. 1982. *The Rules of the Game: Reform and Evaluation in the International Monetary System*. Chicago: The University of Chicago Press.

Killeck, Tony, ed. 1982. *Adjustment and Financing in the Developing World: The Role of the International Monetary Fund*. Washington, D.C.: International

Monetary Fund, in association with the Overseas Development Institute, London.

Mason, Edward S., and Robert E. Asher. 1973. *The World Bank Since Bretton Woods.* Washington, D.C.: The Brookings Institution.

Muns, Joaquin, ed. 1984. *Adjustment, Conditionality, and International Financing.* Washington, D.C.: International Monetary Fund.

1

Reforming the IMF: Different or Better?

John Williamson

No human institution is perfect, and the IMF has certainly never given any cause to doubt that trite proposition. It is therefore possible to conceive of proposals for its improvement. I have endeavored to develop such proposals in the past (Williamson 1982a, 1982b, 1983), and return to the quest later in this paper.

The first section contains a critical discussion of a series of proposals that would fundamentally alter the nature of the institution. Finally, I will examine possible ways to pursue certain objectives more effectively without risking the destruction of what is valuable in the Fund.

What Is the IMF?

The IMF is an international institution which currently has 151 countries as members. In dealing with its members, the Fund's operative rule is that the government of the day *is* the state (a contention of the prosecutor and the judge in the recent Ponting trial in Great Britain). The Fund does not ask whether a government is democratic, whether it respects human rights, whether it is capitalist, or whether it is color-blind; it asks only whether the government controls the country and is capable of implementing an economic program.

The IMF has a limited set of goals which are explicitly defined in its Articles, and its limited set of policies are geared to the achievement of those goals. The goals of the institution are specified in Article I, which reads as follows:

Purposes

The purposes of the International Monetary Fund are:

1. To promote international monetary cooperation through a permanent institution which provides the machinery for consultation and collaboration on international monetary programs.

2. To facilitate the expansion and balanced growth of international trade, and to contribute thereby to the promotion and maintenance of high levels of employment and real income and to the development of the productive resources of all members are primary objectives of economic policy.
3. To promote exchange stability, to maintain orderly exchange arrangements among members, and to avoid competitive exchange depreciation.
4. To assist in the establishment of a multilateral system of payments in respect of current transactions between members and in the elimination of foreign exchange restrictions which hamper the growth of world trade.
5. To give confidence to members by making the general resources of the Fund temporarily available to them under adequate safeguards, thus providing them with opportunity to correct maladjustments in their balance of payments without resorting to measures destructive of national or international prosperity.
6. In accordance with the above, to shorten the duration and lessen the degree of disequilibrium in the international balances of payments of members.

The IMF has interpreted this statement of purpose as giving it responsibilities in three major areas: surveillance of the world economy; provision of temporary balance-of-payments support; and maintenance of a system of multilateral trade and payments. As overseer of the international monetary system and the world economy, the Fund publishes statistics and analyses (notably in its *World Economic Outlook*), provides a forum for multilateral discussion, and conducts confidential discussions with the major countries whose policies are critical to the system. The IMF's multilateral surveillance is generally rated as ineffective, and the usual explanation for this is that the Fund has no sanctions to wield as a means of influencing countries that do not need to borrow from it.

The Fund can exercise considerably more power and influence in its second role, as provider of temporary balance-of-payments support. Over the years, the Fund has come to demand specific actions from its member countries that need to take advantage of the Fund's resources in some way. The Fund provides almost automatic credit and attaches very few conditions when the financial support required is modest or where support is needed to deal with certain temporary factors like low export prices. But when it can be presumed that the balance of payments will not return to a sustainable level unless the country institutes macroeconomic policy measures, IMF drawings are subject to conditionality, which means an agreed adjustment program.

In the past, the Fund has normally agreed to an adjustment program only if the recipient government institutes measures to limit internal demand (credit ceilings and fiscal discipline), to promote exports and efficient import substitution (devaluation), to improve efficiency (price liberalization), and to avoid the intensification of controls over trade and payments. The Fund may also seek to limit short-term capital inflows that might subvert the planned program of credit constraint, although it normally encourages the country to welcome long-term capital in order to increase the sustainable capital inflow. Some of these measures are customarily formalized in performance criteria, notably credit ceilings, limitation of short-term foreign borrowing, and nonintensification of controls over trade and payments. Violation of these performance criteria gives the Fund the right to suspend disbursements.

It is worth noting that the Fund has a financial structure like a credit union (Kenen 1985). Each member country has a quota which determines the member's voting weight, the amount of its expected contribution to the credit union under normal circumstances, and how much the member can withdraw (subject to approval) when the need arises. The assumption is that any member may need to borrow from the Fund at some time to offset the ebb and flow of payments imbalances, but that no member should be a permanent borrower. In other words, the Fund provides short-term balance-of-payments finance on a revolving basis; it is not meant to become the intermediary for long-term development finance from one group of countries to another (which is the task of its sister institution, the World Bank). Until recently, the Fund has indeed operated that way: the two largest borrowers from the Fund over the years have been the United Kingdom and the United States, not Brazil, India, or Mexico. Admittedly the advent of floating exchange rates and extensive international capital mobility may have changed this; it is not certain that industrial countries will borrow from the Fund in the future. If there is a segregation of the Fund's membership into borrowers and lenders it may profoundly change the character of the institution, although to what extent remains to be seen.

The Fund's third role is to foster a multilateral system of payments. The original inspiration for this was the desire to avoid the economic waste and the potential for naked power politics of bilateralism (as exemplified by Nazi Germany). To fulfill this objective the Fund includes pledges not to intensify trade and exchange controls in the performance criteria. (The stronger pledge to liberalize is often ruled out in the case of a balance-of-payments crisis, which is the only time the Fund has much muscle to influence policy.) However, the recent sharp increase in countertrade makes one wonder how effective these conditions are.

Radical Proposals for Change in the Fund's Objectives

Many proposals offered for reforming the IMF involve broadening the Fund's role beyond the limited goals now embraced by its Articles. As a prelude to discussing such proposals, it is useful to inquire into the logic of compartmentalizing problems, that is, of assigning one international institution one range of issues and insulating it as much as possible from other questions.

There seem to be two justifications for compartmentalization. The first is the desire for effectiveness. There is simply too much diversity in human values to give hope of assembling a majority who agree on everything, so cooperation for limited ends among those who agree on that issue is most beneficial. Hence we form coalitions to pursue various mutually beneficial objectives with those whose actions in other areas we may deplore. The second justification is that to demand that others share all our values would be to directly threaten some values that we hold most dear: pluralism, the right to freedom of thought, and the right to dissent. A refusal to participate in coalitions dedicated to limited ends is a big step toward totalitarianism.

The first justification for compartmentalization is totally pragmatic. Linkage between two different issues or objectives would be admissible if such linkage offered the possibility of a gain in one that outweighed the possible costs in the other. For example, an American threat to cease exchanging weather information with the Soviet Union would be beneficial if such a threat would force the Soviets to end human rights abuses. The cost of such a threat would simply be a loss of the benefits of exchanging weather information.

The IMF, then, is a coalition of those countries that see mutual gain in cooperating for limited monetary purposes. Some propose that the IMF's objectives be broadened beyond that limited area, to include political objectives like promoting democracy, human rights, and racial equality.

An attempt to convert the Fund into an instrument for overtly advancing the cause of democracy or human rights would seem to be misconceived. Not only would many of the Fund's current members clearly be disqualified, but there would be potentially endless disputes as to whether particular countries did or did not qualify for membership. Once the offending members had been identified, they would presumably either be expelled or would withdraw voluntarily once they realized that they were to be denied the benefits of membership. There is even the possibility that some Third World countries would withdraw from the Fund in sympathy (even some that do respect human rights), on the ground that the ethical principles being imposed are those for which the West's record is good, while other ethical concerns on which the West's record is appalling—such as a willingness to redistribute income to the poorest—are ignored.

When the size of the Fund had shrunk to include only the righteous, its ability to fulfill its present monetary objectives would inevitably be circumscribed. For example, with membership limited by such criteria, the IMF would have been unable to deal with the debt crisis. A decision would also have to be made whether to help excluded countries (which may actually serve to reward countries for being undemocratic or abusing human rights), or whether to abandon such countries to their fate. The position of the technocrats in the excluded countries, who are generally the element most sympathetic to liberal values, would be compromised by their inability to invoke the support of the Fund, and the reduction in working contacts with the West would weaken one of the long-term forces for liberalization. The only possible gain to be set against these losses would be that some countries may be bribed into democratic forms of government or the termination of human rights abuses by the possibility of drawing on the Fund's resources.

Others have proposed that the Fund be used to combat apartheid. This differs in one respect from proposals to use the Fund to advance democracy or human rights: there is only one country in opposition to the international consensus against apartheid. There is, then, much less danger of compromising the Fund's monetary objectives by denying access to Fund resources to all countries practicing apartheid. The objection that such a move would weaken the position of the technocrats and reduce potentially useful contacts would still apply. The critical question is surely whether any payoff can be expected in return (just as in the example of the Soviet Union and meteorological cooperation). Given the evidence that countries do not abandon what they conceive to be their vital interests because of economic sanctions, even when these are much more severe than loss of the benefits offered by Fund membership (Hufbauer and Schott 1983), any formal use of the Fund to combat apartheid would seem counterproductive.

Rejecting the proposal that the Fund should refuse loans to countries practicing apartheid does not, however, necessarily imply that the Fund should ignore the subject. While it is surely not the major reason that most of us condemn apartheid, one effect of apartheid is to create artificial rigidities in the labor market that are responsible for shortages of skilled labor that, in turn, impede the growth of the South African economy. Elimination of such rigidities is the sort of technical measure often demanded by the Fund as a supply-side element in an adjustment program. In fact, the Fund made a minor move in this direction in the South African program of 1982, when the Fund stated that

> . . . the authorities will ensure that training . . . programs designed to ease medium-term constraints on growth will be less affected (i.e., reduced) than other public expenditures. (Press Release No. 82/52, reprinted in *IMF Survey*, November 15, 1982)

The other broad political issue that has been raised in discussion of IMF reform is whether the Fund should be neutral on the issue of capitalism versus socialism. Neutrality should be favored for all of the reasons cited above. These reasons are supplemented by the ethical consideration that the choice between capitalism and socialism is on an order of magnitude less important than that between democracy and authoritarianism, between respect for human rights and suspension of the rule of law, or between racial equality and apartheid.

It follows from the preceding arguments that the entry of the Soviet Union and East European nonmembers to the IMF is to be welcomed, provided that this poses no danger to the Fund's monetary role. In light of the Soviet Union's mediocre economic performance in recent years, and given the relegation of gold (on which Soviet views are archaic and strongly held) from monetary base to speculative toy, there is no reason for the West to be defensive on this point.

The argument that membership in the Fund or the right to borrow from it should not be conditioned on a country's performance with regard to democracy, human rights, apartheid, or free enterprise raises the question of whether the Fund has exhibited such neutrality in the past. While the Fund has very rarely, if ever, been accused of positively favoring regimes that suppress human rights or practice apartheid, it certainly has been accused of favoring authoritarian regimes and of being hostile to socialism. There have indeed been instances when the Fund showed indecent haste in sending a mission to negotiate with the authoritarian successor to a democratic regime, but the last instance of this was in Chile in 1973, and one hopes that the Fund has now learned its lesson. The accusation of anti-socialism does not seem to be supported by the scale of Fund lending to socialist governments in recent years (Williamson 1982b, 55–56), although Cheryl Payer has suggested that the fund gives "special introductory offers" to entice countries to enter its "trap" (1985, 6).

In addition to the suggestions that the Fund should embrace a political mission, there are proposals that it extend its economic objectives, for example, to include trade liberalization, security of food supply, or encouragement of economic diversification. A common call in the past has been for the IMF to temper the impact of its programs on the poor and to pay special attention to basic human needs.

Again, many of those proposals seem misconceived for the pragmatic reason of maintaining an efficient division of labor between international institutions more than any other. Trade liberalization is handled primarily by the General Agreement on Tariffs and Trade, food supply by the Food and Agriculture Organization, and diversification of production by the World Bank. The Fund does not have the expertise to play the leading role in these areas, and for it to seek such expertise would be inefficient given that those other organizations already exist.

This is not to say that the IMF should take no account of these issues. On the contrary, in negotiating programs with member countries the Fund already seeks to prevent the erosion of liberal trade because this is perceived to be in the interest of both the country and its trading partners. In principle, the Fund also works with the World Bank to make its programs consistent with the needs of development, although some observers are skeptical of the effectiveness of this cooperation. In this general area of designing programs to achieve adjustment while respecting other economic objectives lies perhaps the greatest latitude for improvement in the Fund's operations.

Proposals for Improving the Effectiveness of the Fund

The major critics of the IMF have traditionally focused on its role in designing adjustment programs. Many of the complaints registered have been naive or even intellectually dishonest. A country goes to the Fund because it has a payments deficit that (usually) cannot be financed in the private market. If the IMF lent money to an uncreditworthy borrower to enable it to go further into debt it would do no service to anyone. The Fund therefore aims to lend enough money to enable a country to finance an orderly adjustment program, but insists on evidence that the adjustment program is adopted and implemented. The measures that can help achieve adjustment are fairly standard: fiscal and monetary restraint to limit domestic spending, devaluation to switch expenditures at home or abroad to domestic goods (or *ersatz* devaluation measures like import controls, to which there are other objections), and supply-side expenditures to improve resource allocation, of which the main one the Fund understands is price liberalization. So the family resemblance of Fund programs is to be expected, given that most often it is the same disease being treated. Those who claim otherwise have the duty to describe the type of program they favor and demonstrate that it would be consistent with observance of the foreign exchange constraint.

The Fund is also right to concern itself with the "internal" dimensions of economic performance as well as the balance of payments. The Fund should attempt to achieve a full utilization of capacity, a satisfactory growth rate, and low inflation. True, improvement in the balance of payments is the underlying objective of the exercise, but improving the balance of payments is in itself trivial. A sufficiently brutal deflation will always eliminate a payments deficit. The essence of successful adjustment is to achieve a sustainable balance of payments with minimal cost to other objectives. Hence the Fund's practice of negotiating a complete program and attaching performance criteria to policy variables like fiscal and monetary ceilings should be supported.

My criticisms of the Fund's programs are less fundamental than those mentioned above, but are nonetheless important. They focus on four areas:

the speed of the adjustment process, the effect of Fund programs on overall income distribution, the inflexibility of performance criteria, and the issue of the Fund's relations with social forces other than the government in power. These are treated in turn.

Speed of Adjustment

Measures which are intended to improve competitiveness and switch resources into the balance of payments, like devaluation, are slower-acting than other austerity measures designed to cut imports by reducing demand. Given this economic fact, rapid elimination of a current-account deficit almost inevitably requires a more brutal cutback in income than is necessary with a measured pace of adjustment. This has been vividly illustrated in Latin America in the past two years: the dramatic reduction in the current-account deficit was bought at the cost of depression on a magnitude that rivaled, and in some cases exceeded, that of the 1930s. (This was the price of the West's decision to reduce inflation in the debtor countries to a level no greater than that borne by the industrial countries themselves.) Export-led growth is only now beginning to reduce the excess capacity that was created during this time. Export growth may actually have been impeded by the severity of the contractionary measures adopted, which resulted in real interest rates of over 30 percent in most countries, a level that is bound to discourage the investment needed to expand and create new exports.

A measured pace of adjustment is particularly important in countries with a narrow economic base. In such countries, which are generally the poorest, the production structure has little flexibility to respond to a change in the price incentives with additional exports or import substitutes. Responding to changed price incentives typically requires structural adjustment, including new investment, sometimes in sectors in which the country has no established expertise. Export expansion is therefore bound to be a lengthy process.

To avoid excessive output contraction ("overkill") during the transitional period while resources are being switched into the balance of payments, the current-account deficit must be financed during this period. The magnitude of this financing depends on the resources the Fund can lend or induce others to lend. The Fund accepted the principle that where adjustment must deal with structural problems, larger sums must be lent over a longer adjustment period when it created the Extended Fund Facility in the mid-1970s. Unfortunately, the full potential of this innovation was never realized due to the limited, ad hoc nature of cooperation between the IMF and the World Bank, its sister institution which has expertise in supply-side programs. To remedy this I have suggested that countries facing a structural payments problem should be expected to approach the Fund and the Bank simultaneously to negotiate a joint loan (Williamson 1982b).

In the case of Latin America, the Fund had neither the necessary cash nor sufficient muscle with the bankers, whose arms it twisted to continue lending modest sums "involuntarily," to finance a more measured pace of adjustment. If the Fund is to have the flexibility to allow the speed of adjustment to match the circumstance of the country (and to avoid unnecessary waste), then it must have the means. That involves persuading Congress to vote for much larger IMF quotas.

Income Distribution

Fund programs are often criticized for hitting the poor. The Fund denies that there is any systematic tendency for the poor to carry the inevitable burden disproportionately, and also asserts that the distribution of the burden of adjustment is not the responsibility of the Fund, but is an internal matter for the borrowing country. (In support of the first claim, the IMF points to research studies examining the distributional impact of four Fund programs, particularly Johnson and Salop 1980.) Fund spokesmen have also pointed to the fact that while elimination of food subsidies—a frequent feature of Fund programs, as critics point out—is indeed likely to hurt the urban working class, it often benefits the rural poor, who are invariably much poorer (Finch 1983). This is a valid point, as is the claim that there may be no systematic tendency for Fund programs to hurt the poor disproportionately. But is that good enough, or does morality require an active concern to spare the poor and to safeguard the provision of basic needs?

There will undoubtedly be occasions when restoration of external equilibrium will require a reduction in real wages and a shift of income to profits. To obstruct those changes would be to negate the prospects of achieving adjustment. Nevertheless, it is possible to influence the design of the adjustment programs to take account of distributional objectives. The greatest area of flexibility is in the choice of where to direct cuts in public expenditure. For example, the macroeconomic impact will be much the same whether a reduction in public expenditure is achieved by cutting food subsidies or military spending, but the distributional impact is quite different. (And food subsidies need not necessarily be at the expense of the rural poor, which happens when imported food is subsidized but not when domestic producers receive deficiency payments.)

Any proposal that the Fund concern itself with the allocation of cuts in public expenditure runs straight into the Fund's second claim, that this is an area where it should not interfere. The IMF is dealing with sovereign countries. As a matter of fact, many of them resent the intrusion on their sovereignty implicit in having to negotiate with the Fund in the first place.

There are compelling reasons why the Fund should impose conditionality. The exceptions are the limited sums available under facilities like the compensatory financing facility, where the entitlement to borrow arises from temporary factors outside the country's control. The Fund needs to be assured of repayment, especially when it is lending to countries deemed uncreditworthy by the private sector. The Fund also needs to avoid moral hazard, "tempting" countries to create payments problems for themselves so as to qualify for IMF loans. And of course the Fund needs to help reestablish a country's creditworthiness with the private market. In principle, the IMF's attitude is: show us a program that will produce payments adjustment, commit yourself to it in a Letter of Intent, and we will then approve *your* program. In practice, however, the Fund rarely judges the country's program to be adequate, and so it then negotiates for changes—or is even perceived to be dictating a program. The Fund does try nevertheless to draw the line at deciding *where* spending will be cut, presumably because this is such a politically sensitive issue.

The practical consequence of this concession to sovereignty is that expenditure cuts are most likely to focus on those programs that are easiest to cut, capital expenditure of the more mundane sort (roads rather than nuclear power stations) and programs that benefit the politically weak. Clearly there are limits to the extent to which sovereign countries will accept foreign management of their economies. The most feasible method of expanding the IMF's influence would be to include an analysis of the expected distributional impact of proposed programs, including the impact on basic needs, when these are submitted to the IMF Executive Board. This should at least sensitize the IMF staff to the importance of these issues, and hopefully would also cause governments to think twice before sacrificing agricultural extension programs or family planning rather than military buildups.

Inflexible Performance Criteria

Fund programs usually include performance criteria such as credit ceilings and budget deficits which are stated in nominal terms and include no provisions for adjustment to subsequent developments. The Fund's wish to avoid excessive flexibility is understandable, since this could eliminate any incentive to fulfill the agreed program, but contingent criteria are possible which would be adjusted automatically in the light of developments outside the country's control. A first step in this direction would be to list the major exogenous assumptions made when a program was drawn up and to indicate the impact that deviations from those assumed conditions would have. (See Williamson 1982b, section 5, for elaboration.)

Social Contract

As mentioned earlier, the IMF has traditionally dealt exclusively with the governments of its member countries (CRIA 1984, 6). The suggestion has been made that governments might be required to consult with "internal opposition groups, labor unions, and other internal political entities" before a program was approved, with a view to establishing a social contract. Any formal requirement of this sort would pose major difficulties: appropriate groups to be consulted may be difficult to identify in some IMF member countries, and policing the sincerity of the member government's consultation efforts would be an invidious assignment. Perhaps the Fund itself should seek the views of other responsible social actors within the country.

Conclusion

The preceding discussion of possible improvements in the IMF's effectiveness has focused on Fund relations with countries that wish to borrow under the high-conditionality facilities. These loans have often, but not always, left a bitter legacy in the borrowing country. Perhaps the most successful Fund program in recent years was that with India, which was agreed to in 1981 and terminated a year before it was due, having helped to foster the desired payments adjustment. India had been pursuing a rational macroeconomic policy when it applied for its loan, and the performance criteria essentially served to guarantee that it would continue to do so. Certainly this is the ideal toward which the Fund should strive. Sadly, the Reagan administration opposed the Indian loan on the ground that India had not exhausted its creditworthiness with the commercial banks, and although it was overruled on that occasion, it is very doubtful indeed whether any similar program would be approved today. In fact, the major priority of the moment may be to prevent emasculation of the Fund, rather than to improve it.

There is scope for improvement in the effectiveness of the IMF in other areas. For example, it would be desirable to have the Fund lend more, *ceteris paribus*, during a world recession than during a boom, mainly because it seems right that the international community give greater help to its weaker members when their difficulties are being compounded by developments outside their control. But this would be a modest contribution to global anti-cyclical policy. This is a direction in which the Fund could make a big contribution if its surveillance of the policies of the major industrial countries was more effective. A technical step that might help to achieve this would be to focus discussion around quantitative targets for such critical components as current-account balances and exchange rates.

Overall, however, the fundamental obstacle to the IMF exerting influence on the major countries is that the current leaders of these nations recognize neither a moral responsibility to take account of the impact of their policies on other countries nor the possibility that events and conditions in the world have a major impact on them. It is not difficult to understand the developing countries' resentment of the contrast between the fact that they must accept Fund "dictation" and the fact that the U.S. Treasury Secretary complains if the Fund so much as dares to criticize the U.S. budget deficit.

References

Council on Religion and International Affairs (CRIA). September 4, 1984. "Review of the IMF from Both Operational and Moral Perspectives" (mimeo). New York: CRIA.

Finch, C. David. 1983. "Adjustment Policies and Conditionality," in *IMF Conditionality*, edited by J. Williamson. Washington, D.C.: Institute for International Economics.

Hufbauer, C. Gary and Jeffrey J. Schott. 1983. *Economic Sanctions in Support of Foreign Policy Goals.* Washington, D.C.: Institute for International Economics.

Johnson, Omotunde, and Joanne Salop. March 1980. "Distributional Aspects of Stabilization in Developing Countries," *IMF Staff Papers.* Washington D.C.: IMF.

Kenen, Peter B. January 1985. "Financing, Adjustment, and the International Monetary Fund," paper presented to a conference of The Brookings Institution, Washington, D.C.

Payer, Cheryl. 1985. "The IMF in the 1980s: What Has It Learned; What Have We Learned About It?" *Third World Affairs 1985.* London: Third World Foundation for Social and Economic Studies.

Williamson, John. 1982a. "The Economies of IMF Conditionality," in *For Good or Evil,* edited by G. K. Helleiner. Toronto: University of Toronto Press.

________. 1982b. *The Lending Policies of the International Monetary Fund.* Washington, D.C.: Institute for International Economics.

________. May 1983. "On Seeking to Improve IMF Conditionality," *American Economic Review.*

2

The International Monetary Fund: A Founder's Evaluation

Irving S. Friedman

Introduction

I was in the U.S. Treasury during the war years when the proposals for an international monetary organization were analyzed and formulated. Although I was overseas during the time when the Bretton Woods Conference was held, I resumed my work on the Fund and the Bank in the subsequent months, and as a consequence, joined the Fund in July 1946, and the World Bank eighteen years later in 1964.

A consideration of the International Monetary Fund raises many ethical questions. Questions of equity, justice, and humanity arise in all human situations, and the Fund deals with the conditions and problems of human beings throughout the world. I have long tried to point out that even highly technical questions, like exchange rate adjustment, affect the well-being of all people in major ways and to differing degrees.

I have had the opportunity to have a major role in the evolution of the Fund's policies, practices, and procedures. In this leadership role, I know that I have been deeply influenced by many value systems. It was this value system that led me to join the Fund in 1946 and the World Bank in 1964. I have lived for decades with the assumption that these institutions embody values I cherish: improving the material well-being of people, promoting the preconditions for social mobility and personal freedom, and strengthening the bases for orderly and peaceful domestic and international human relations. I have tried to use my positions in the Fund and Bank to improve the ability of the Fund and Bank to serve these objectives. There is no practical or theoretical question or approach which is not based on a prior philosophical or religious view. Thus, every issue raised by the Fund's activity can be analyzed by seeking to answer the question of what philosophy or ethical view underlies the actions.

I will not evaluate Fund activities using ethical criteria, although such an exercise is indeed worthwhile. My comparative advantage as a commentator on the Fund lies elsewhere. I will try to bring a historical perspective to these lectures. We have come here not as technicians, but as social philosophers and concerned citizens. The IMF is not an abstraction or a theory, or an autonomous entity with a separate life of its own. It is a collection of countries represented by an ever-changing kaleidoscope of governments. The Fund today can only be understood by knowing what it was intended to be and what it has been hitherto. I will not try to present a formal or chronological history, but rather to give my interpretation of the Fund's past, my understanding of how it has evolved. Having done this, I will make some suggestions as to how its role in the world economy can be improved in such ways as to serve the ethical values I tried earlier to summarize very briefly.

The Setting

World War II wreaked incredible destruction in Europe, the Pacific, and North Africa. Total destruction was experienced in many places. Tens of millions of people died in and out of uniform. Hundreds of years of progress in humanizing the conduct of war were wiped out. The horror was universal. At the same time, there was hope: the war would end; the Allies would win; most of mankind would remain to rebuild. People could plan to avoid the conditions which had nurtured the seeds of world war, and nations, even former enemies, could work together. This was not utopian or millenium thinking. The causes of general war were man-made and could be man-remedied by practical steps. The key was the willingness to limit national sovereignty. In the United States, isolationism began to give way to internationalism. Wendell Willkie, a highly respected businessman, carried the banner of the Republican party with the inscription "One World" vividly inscribed. Franklin D. Roosevelt, the President, had long been an internationalist. The other allied leaders, Churchill, Stalin, and de Gaulle, were not philosophical internationalists, but the war crises had forged a new acceptance of international collaboration.

The International Monetary Fund and the World Bank were offspring of these conditions. They were paralleled by other efforts to create international institutions: the Food and Agriculture Organization, the World Health Organization, the ill-fated International Trade Organization, and the United Nations itself. The causes of the war were not seen simply as nazism, fascism, and Japanese militarism; deeper causes were sought and found. The roots of these developments were the stupidities of the Treaty of Versailles, the intransigence of the victors of World War I, the nationalism of the former Allies, the failure to create a strong international political institution witnessed by the repeated failures of the League of Nations, the inability to prevent the rise and spread of Nazi power, and the breakdown of the world economy in the 1930s, the Great Depression.

The aftermath of World War I had taught the lessons of the futility of laying all blame on the vanquished nations, and of trying to keep them down while getting from them the means to restore the victors. Yet the Marshall Plan, in essence, also expressed the convictions which prevailed during World War I, and the Soviet Union was hard to fit into this philosophy. Views varied sharply on what to expect from the Soviet Union after the war. During the war, however, the fact of alliance dominated, and, with the many fingers crossed, efforts for the postwar world rested on the assumption that the Soviet Union and her wartime Allies would continue to collaborate.

The Bretton Woods twins, the IMF and the World Bank, were never seen as existing by themselves, but were part of the new host of international organizations. Their special responsibilities would be international monetary and financial cooperation within the context of broad international cooperation. Of great importance to them would be international cooperation in international trade. Without comparable international trade rules, the rules to govern international monetary relations could be useless or worse. The thorny area of international capital relations was left untouched; the World Bank would be a source of international financing, but not a manager of agreed international rules of conduct governing capital movements. For this and other such reasons, it was never as complicated or as difficult to envisage and secure agreement on the Bank as it proved to be on the Fund.

IMF and the Industrial Nations

The International Monetary Fund was given the responsibility to manage and enforce a code of international behavior regarding exchange rates, exchange systems, and use of governmental restrictions on international payments for goods and services. It was an extraordinary code in that its purpose was to achieve the *elimination* of governmental restrictions, usually referred to as exchange controls. The goal of the code was to reestablish and maintain the functioning of free markets in currencies and to eliminate the multiplicity of exchange rates introduced by governments through their central banks. There was a strong presumption that exchange rates were to be kept stable, as stable as possible. On the other hand, this stability was *not* to be achieved by using exchange restrictions or equivalent trade restrictions, but rather by domestic management of the economy. Occasional intervention by central banks in foreign exchange markets was envisaged, but only to counter temporary disturbances in the supply and demand for currencies. The Fund was given a pool of currencies to enable member countries to obtain foreign currencies needed for such market interventions.

To monitor the process and assure that governments did not manipulate currencies to the disadvantage of other countries, changes in exchange rates needed IMF approval. Because the code of international monetary behavior was essentially designed to avoid exchange restrictions, it could be essentially simple.

Originally, in the earlier years of the Fund (the first fifteen years), its activities were concentrated on trying to achieve the removal of exchange restrictions and equivalent trade restrictions, which were introduced by the industrial countries in the depression years of the 1930s and the war years of the 1940s. By the end of the 1950s, the industrial countries had largely achieved the elimination of these restrictions and restored the so-called convertibility of their currencies.

In the meantime, as free foreign exchange markets were re-established, exchange rates became adjusted to market conditions. The pound sterling proved most difficult to adjust because sterling had long been an international currency used by many central banks to hold international liquidity as well as to make international payments. The sterling-area countries also tended to follow similar international trade practices. The management of an international currency, in this case sterling, proved difficult, as the Americans were to learn later. What suited the immediate interests of the United Kingdom as a national economy often conflicted with the longer-run interests of the United Kingdom as the manager of the sterling area. They also often conflicted with the immediate interests of other sterling-area members, whose balance-of-payments positions often differed markedly from that of the United Kingdom. These countries also had vested interests, as holders of sterling, in avoiding the devaluation of sterling in terms of other currencies, particularly the U.S. dollar. Until North Sea oil became a major foreign exchange earner for the U.K., sterling was repeatedly devalued, but only after much soul-searching and costly delays. The IMF played some role in these devaluations, especially in providing additional intervention funds and in counseling (and at times insisting on) the need for economic policies to defend the newly established exchange rates.

The transition to convertible currencies by industrial countries took many years despite the assistance of the Marshall Plan and the cooperative efforts of the European countries in the European Payments Union, the OEEC (which became the OECD), and the European Monetary System. Yet it was accomplished. Exchange rates did not become the vital issue in international trade and payments which it had been in the 1930s. Instead of needing to prevent countries from devaluing their currencies to achieve stronger export competitiveness, countries had to be urged to devalue to overcome balance-of-payments weaknesses. Nor did the industrial countries return to the widespread use of bilateralism or exchange restrictions characteristic of the 1930s. In the most recent world recession, international trade suffered its worst years in half a century, but the system of international trade and payments proved resilient and sturdy. Indeed, it is probably very difficult for people today to think of general wars caused by breakdowns in the economic systems of the Western industrial countries. The roots of fears of general war are found elsewhere. The U.S.-USSR relations embody these fears, but not because of international economic or commercial rivalries.

The industrial countries are, however, still concerned with exchange rates. The overvalued dollar is widely decried, although it has given great commercial advantages to other exporting nations. Still, more concern is felt for the implications of the U.S. dollar position in strengthening inflationary pressures in other countries, the converse of constraining inflationary pressures in the United States. Attention is also focused on U.S. interest rates, their pull on foreign savings, and their impact on international debt and its servicing costs.

All of these issues are important, but they are not generally critical in that they have not upset international political/military relations. Thus, the fact that the IMF is a weak authority in relation to the strength of the U.S. dollar exchange rate does not rock the international system. It causes vibrations, waves, and even storms, but the emotional attitudes of the 1930s and 1940s are no longer relevant and present. If the international monetary and trading system were to collapse because of another world depression, the critical signs would be the destruction of the political rapport which has characterized the relationships of the Western industrialized countries, including Japan. This has not happened, nor does it appear likely. Technicians will continue to be fascinated by analyses of exchange rates, balance-of-payments behavior, and the ingredients of "sound" economic management in the industrial countries—for example, fiscalist arguments versus monetarist; forecasters versus simulators; free market proponents versus interventionists. Yet, the International Monetary Fund, being an organization of governments, is likely to find that although it spends much time on these technical issues, its most significant role lies elsewhere, i.e., with the developing countries.

The international monetary system remains the primary responsibility of the IMF. In this sense, what happens in industrial countries continues to be more important for the IMF than what happens in developing countries.

However, as long as the present floating-rate system prevails and convertibility of the U.S. dollar and other major currencies remains intact, most of the Fund's activities are likely to consist of activities with developing countries. If the industrial countries constituting the Fund, particularly the United States and the major industrial nations, decide that the Fund must be the mechanism for judging exchange rates and for bringing about realistic exchange rates, the activities of the Fund with industrial countries will again become of key importance.

Thus, it may be said that the reduced activity of the Fund in relation to industrial countries reflects the success of the international convertibility system, which has provided the international monetary framework for the pursuit of domestic policies and the accommodation of domestic structural changes. The system has minimized the international friction arising out of international competition among the industrial countries. The rise of Japan has been difficult to accommodate, but accommodations have been made. Various forms of protectionism, including so-called voluntary constraints on Japanese exports, have been necessary to avoid more obvious and objectionable forms of protectionism. Brazil, Korea, and others also have become rigorous competitors of the older, established industrial countries in international trade. A major structural transformation is happening requiring painful adjustments, but national economic and social policies, rooted in the views prevalent during World War II and its aftermath, have made these adjustments sufficiently tolerable to avoid the repeat of the deep, disruptive, and destructive events of the 1930s. The continued overvaluation of the U.S. dollar is an overhanging threat to the functioning of the international monetary system and, thus, to the orderly functioning of the world economic system. The overvalued dollar has helped the export earnings of many countries, but the disruption in many countries, which could be caused by a sudden drop in the dollar, could dramatically alter the world economic scene. The unique ability of the U.S. to finance a huge balance-of-payments deficit is a great benefit to other exporting nations, but the abnormality of this situation renders it essentially unstable and unpredictable. Thus, the IMF must regard the position of the U.S. dollar as its key concern, even while it devotes most of its energy and time to the problems of the developing countries. It is in this area that the Fund is finding itself confronting modern problems which shake nations to their foundations and are the roots of civil and international conflicts.

IMF and the Developing Countries

The Fund, which was founded with a primary concern for the relationships among industrial countries and at most secondary concern for the

behavior of developing countries, is experiencing a 180–degree shift in its global role. Today, the IMF is playing a key role in monitoring or controlling the economic management of developing countries, especially those which have required the restructuring of their external debt, and a relatively lesser role vis-à-vis the developed countries.

Developing countries have always been active members of the Fund. In the years of discussions prior to Bretton Woods and afterwards, representatives of such countries, including Mexico, Cuba, Chile, Peru, Brazil, Egypt, and India, took an active part in the deliberations. For these developing countries, issues of convertibility and the role of sterling were also of major importance. Their patterns of international trade and payments were greatly influenced by the convertibility of currencies used in international payments and by the usage of sterling held by a number of developing countries as international monetary reserves. Their own national currencies were usually inconvertible with widespread use of restrictions, and, in the case of a number of Latin American countries, were part of highly complex multiple currency schemes with different import and export rates of exchange.

These developing countries had the same obligations under the Articles of Agreement as the industrial member countries. From the beginning, the Fund has operated with the principle of universality. Because of this principle, the Fund's annual consultations with members on their exchange rate practices, balance of payments, and related matters have been essentially uniform in procedures and scope. The criteria for judging a country's behavior or management have been about the same. A successful country, from the Fund viewpoint, is a country moving in the direction of achieving the preconditions for having a realistic, unified exchange rate system without reliance on exchange restrictions on current international payments. From these goals or criteria came the emphasis on such questions as balance-of-payments behavior, inflation, monetary and fiscal policies, income or wage policies, subsidization, and the financial performance of publicly owned enterprises. These criteria were incorporated into the conditions for having access to the financial resources of the Fund.

At the time, universality of the Fund code seemed quite sensible. Mexico and Cuba, for example, had convertible currencies and did not use exchange restrictions. It was assumed that developing countries would be able to manage their balance of payments without recourse to multiple currency devices or restrictions on international payments. Balance-of-payments deficits would be limited by inflows of foreign exchange from primarily private sources. Economic growth would be automatically constrained to what was possible with available domestic and external resources. Some members of sterling-area countries, e.g., Egypt and India, had accumulated large international monetary reserves in the form of sterling as Britain paid for war materiel procured in these countries. It was presumed that these countries would have convertible currencies when Britain achieved this goal.

The dynamics of post–World War II development were not yet clearly visible. Accelerated social and economic change, made possible by large inflows of official capital on concessional terms and encouraged by government intervention in markets, became a common objective of the developing countries in the late 1940s and 1950s. The resulting dynamics of population explosion, rapid urbanization, demands for modern consumption goods, and social and personal mobility created very different conditions in the developing countries than anticipated during the war years and earlier. In the newly established countries in Asia and Africa, as well as in Latin America, economic and social objectives were combined with strong nationalism and anti-foreign sentiments. In particular, anti-foreign business sentiments often became virulent in Latin America and elsewhere. The combination of these factors was explosive and created unstable political and social conditions and erratic and difficult balance-of-payments behavior. The international monetary rules embodied in the Fund's Articles of Agreement could not be followed by most of the developing countries. The Fund recognized this fact, and, within the general principle of universality of its rules, actually gave much leeway to the developing countries as long as they followed agreed procedures. In this way, the Fund's industrial member nations tried, as they were doing in other fields like development assistance and trade, to accommodate the developing countries. The Fund did not give up the objectives of achieving unified, convertible currencies in all countries, but was most patient in giving developing countries as much time as they required to achieve these objectives and in being understanding and tolerant of repeated backsliding.

For the industrial countries whose currencies constituted the international monetary system, the Fund criteria proved adequate and valid. They provided the basis for judging whether countries were moving towards convertibility of currencies and realistic exchange rates. By 1960, this progress was formally recognized as these countries accepted fully the convertibility obligations of the Fund. The establishment of the convertibility of the Japanese yen in the early 1960s completed the process of establishing an international monetary system based on convertible currencies, as envisaged in the Fund's Articles of Agreement.

The experience with the developing countries has been very different. For these countries, great difficulties were experienced in establishing the desired preconditions. Balance-of-payments deficits persisted. Inflation in many countries was only temporarily constrained. Exchange restrictions were repeatedly reduced and then intensified. Overvalued exchange rates were frequent occurrences. Repeated programs failed to produce lasting results as they had in the industrial countries. Only a few developing countries could live up to the criteria being met by the industrial nations.

Many of the developing countries did not become part of the international monetary system as originally envisaged in the 1950s. The fact that the developing countries could not, and did not, meet the criteria and goals of the Fund was, however, of relatively minor importance for the functioning of the international system. Their currencies were not used internationally, and their balance-of-payments problems had only small impacts on the general international system or the world economy. The Fund could, and did, take a lenient attitude towards these countries, working with them and providing financial assistance from time to time. The major issues of the international monetary system as such were with the industrial nations. Although developing countries obeyed the procedures of the Fund, but could not fulfill the substance, this was not fatal for the system.

It was persistent inflation in the industrial countries, especially the United States, that eventually undermined the system. By the early 1970s, the goal of stable exchange rates was abandoned in favor of floating exchange rates determined by market conditions with a minimum amount of governmental intervention. Fortunately, the practice of convertibility of the major currencies was maintained despite difficulties like the oil price increases in the 1970s and the world recession of 1981–83. Because convertibility was maintained, the world economy did not slide back into widespread trade discrimination and bilateralism. The world economy was hit, but not shattered. If this had happened, the Fund would again be centering its activities on the currencies of the industrial nations, if it could even have survived such major setbacks.

In the meantime, the developing countries have become the sick countries wherein deep modern crises are being nourished. Most of these countries have not been able to achieve the preconditions for domestic or international monetary stability. In the midst of adjustment programs agreed with the Fund, many of these countries have inflation rates of hundreds of percent per year, and exchange rate systems which are complex, exchange rates which are overvalued, and they use exchange restrictions extensively. Nevertheless, commercial bank lenders have turned to the Fund to achieve the preconditions necessary for these countries to be acceptable international borrowers, or, at least, to be able to service external debts restructured with much longer maturities. National and multinational development assistance agencies are also insisting that recipients of their help obtain "good housekeeping" seals of approval from the Fund. All capital flows into the developing countries now have to go through the sieve of Fund approval of a developing country's balance of payments and domestic management. Even new foreign equity investors are asking whether the host country has a program endorsed by the Fund. The role of the IMF has become a major issue in the politics of many developing countries, as the Fund has become the major "foreign" influence in their affairs. This is new.

During the 1960s, the developing countries turned largely to the official development assistance agencies for help in financing their chronic balance-of-payment deficits. These agencies—national, like the U.S. aid program, and international, like the World Bank—had great influence on the economic management of the borrowing developing countries, more influence, in fact, than the IMF. The development finance agencies were keenly dedicated to helping development. Their criteria of success, like identification and execution of major public projects to increase hydroelectric power or modernize roads or improve health, could be met by the developing countries. The development finance agencies brought improvements in economic policies and practices, for example, improved utility rates, more efficient administration of public investment, more thoughtful choices of investment projects, honest administration of these projects, encouragement for modern export industries, and so forth. Borrowing countries were also able to satisfy the criteria of these development finance agencies.

In turn, these agencies, often under the leadership of the Development Assistance Committee of the OECD (DAC) or the World Bank, felt justified in urging more development assistance to these countries. Consortia and consultative groups were formed to mobilize external public resources for these countries on concessional terms. Grant funds became an increasing proportion of the total assistance. The IMF, with its emphasis on short- and medium-term balance-of-payments management, played a useful but relatively minor role. New important development finance institutions came into existence in the 1960s, notably the International Development Association (IDA) in 1960, followed by the Inter-American Development Bank, the African Development Bank, and the Asian Development Bank.

Thus, while the Fund was building the international monetary system with its work with the industrial countries, the developing countries were under the tutelage of the development finance institutions. It was their criteria of successful development that dominated economic policymaking in the developing countries in the 1960s. The private banks were deeply interested in what these development institutions thought and did with regard to the borrowing developing countries. Unfortunately, the events of the 1960s increasingly caused the industrial countries to become more restrained in providing official assistance. The magnitudes of such assistance increased, but not sufficiently to meet needs or absorptive capacities.

When the adverse events of the 1970s occurred, the development finance institutions could not respond in the magnitude and manner needed. Their reaction times were slow as the bulk of their lending was for projects and because the international community had not given them a major countercyclical role as it had given to the Fund. Appropriate official finance was not available to meet the emergencies of the 1970s. The response of the international community to the oil crises of the 1970s was to increase the resources of the IMF. Thus, the emergency compensatory role was left to the Fund. It could have been given to the development finance institutions, but they did not vigorously seek this role. The IMF was already deeply experienced in balance-of-payments problems and financing, and willing (even eager) to expand its role—vis-à-vis the developing countries.

The Fund, however, could not be a source of development finance. It had to safeguard the revolving character of its limited pool of currencies. It could lend for medium-term periods, but could not commit itself to rollovers or to new lending exceeding in magnitude the repurchase or repayment obligations of its borrowing members. To do so, its own resources would need to be greatly expanded beyond what its members were willing to contribute. Nevertheless, the Fund began to have more influence in the economic management of developing countries during the early 1970s because, through its special "oil facilities" and other measures, it was the principal source of emergency balance-of-payments support needed to deal with the oil crises. The development finance institutions declined in relative importance and have not yet regained the general influence they had in the 1960s.

The Fund influence, however, was limited because it could not perform the essential developmental role, either conceptually, analytically, or financially. It was not established for these purposes. Yet it had learned much about developing countries, especially that they often followed policies which did not result in manageable balance-of-payments positions. The Fund did know how to reduce inflation and reduce balance-of-payments deficits; it could advise on better monetary and fiscal management, urge more realistic exchange rates, and explain how appropriate exchange rates could be calculated. The Fund could not, however, provide the supplemental savings needed for long-term development. It could not insist on the preconditions for satisfactory development. The Fund performed a useful but limited role, both in scope and time. The developing countries emerged from the crises of the 1970s with larger balance-of-payments deficits needing continuous financing, and the Fund could not provide this financing. Thus, the value systems which were embodied in the purposes and practices of the World Bank and the IMF declined in influence in the 1970s.

The developing countries turned instead to the commercial banks as a major source of development finance. As a result, during the 1970s, the views and criteria of these commercial banks became a major influence in the economic management of the developing countries. Profit-making and avoiding losses had to be their principal guides. For commercial banks, credit and country risk analyses are the screening devices. Maturities were not a serious problem because borrowing nations could increase their total foreign-currency indebtedness as long as they defended and retained their creditworthiness. *De facto* rollovers, or the equivalent, made it possible to use medium-term credits for longer-term purposes. The ever-present danger was the loss of creditworthiness. Mexico and Brazil lost their creditworthiness in 1982, and the process of using commercial bank credit for developmental purposes experienced a sharp setback. The era of widespread debt restructuring was opened.

The commercial banks then turned to the IMF to set the preconditions for debt restructuring and for renewed lending by them. In so doing, the banks greatly reduced their own influence on the economic management of borrowing countries. The banks made some overtures to the development finance institutions in this respect, but these institutions could only respond very partially to the needs of 1981–83. Instead, these development finance institutions also tied their lending to the Fund.

The criteria of the Fund in judging domestic economic management and balance-of-payments performance became virtually the entire play, not just the center stage of international financing for the developing countries. Individual developing countries, not important for the functioning of the world system, have become the centers of attention and activity. African, Asian, and Latin American countries now get the attention reserved in the 1950s and 1960s mostly for the industrial nations. Fund missions to Brazil, Mexico, and elsewhere are reported on the front pages of the press in industrial countries.

The adequacies, inadequacies, or suitability of the Fund in relation to developing countries became and is a central world issue, and rightly so. Those reacting to this situation have cited ethical values, like equity in income distribution and consumption, or social justice in employment, to criticize Fund policies and practices. Economics and technical reasons are thoroughly intermingled with ideology and values.

Fund approaches to economic management had to become increasingly pragmatic, but still compatible with the fundamental purposes and mandate of the Fund. The Fund's international mandate was not changed—it was not asked to become a development finance institution or a private commercial bank. It was asked to be what it was, but with the other lenders now having virtually adopted the Fund's lending criteria as their own. With this very broadened responsibility vis-à-vis the developing countries, Fund "conditionality" became a red flag for politicians in developing countries to raise and "waive."

The development finance institutions remained of secondary importance and remained unable to influence and unable to provide a practical alternative to the problems of borrowing developing countries. The development finance institutions were not prepared to defend development—even the development they financed—during prolonged cyclical downturns. The developing countries had no effective champions of development in the international financial arena. The Fund was not hostile to development; the policies it recommended could be compatible with development, but were too often not central or feasible in the environments found in developing countries. The Fund was widely seen as not being keenly concerned with developmental objectives.

The Fund definition of good economic management encourages a certain kind of development: export orientation, reduced protectionism, less forced import substitution, more efficient public corporations or parastatals, reduced public sector deficits, more realistic interest rates, and more self-financing of investments. Developmental criteria would, however, add more specific concerns about the magnitudes of investments and their composition, the relative roles of the public and private sectors, the availability and adequacy of external sources of development finance, and other factors entering importantly into structural change. With the need to meet developmental criteria as well as monetary criteria, the content of all policies would change and would become more realistic. Credit restraints, for example, would often still be needed, but with the recognition that governments are not interest-rate sensitive—high real interest rates do not inhibit governments the way they inhibit private investment. To channel more savings into productive investments in the private sector, certain conditions must exist simultaneously in the public sector. Thus, from a monetary point of view, higher interest rates may be regarded as sufficient for an adjustment program. From a developmental point of view, higher interest rates which do not accompany measures to inhibit inappropriate investment will be seen as not meeting the criteria of a successful adjustment program.

Similarly, in setting targets for monetary expansion, how the money supply is used becomes of key importance. Monetary expansion to finance inefficient public sector enterprises, like the state railways in Argentina, is at the expense of development. Monetary expansion to finance the introduction and adaptation of new technology to achieve more efficient and diversified export industries helps development. What constitutes sound investment for a country's development can be better judged by a developmental institution than by the IMF, though the Fund staff member, as an individual, may have very good ideas and may be able to comment usefully on views expressed by his colleague from the development finance agency.

Similarly, on exchange rates, a monetary approach stresses the accompanying measures needed to keep an exchange rate realistic in the short run: reduced inflation, flexibility in the mechanism for changing exchange rates like using floating exchange rates, and the availability of a fund of foreign currencies to intervene in the market in the case of temporary disturbances. From the viewpoint of development, it is not enough to be concerned with the general shift of resources into export industries and away from inefficient import-substitute industries, or to end capital flight. Conditions must exist to shift resources into export industries which have the necessary ingredients for success, in addition to an attractive relationship between the national currencies and foreign currencies. These other factors include the necessary infrastructure for the new or expanded export industries, and marketing, financing, technology, management, and the like. As Brazil and South Korea are demonstrating, creating export capacity is creating a new economy. Indeed, it may be demonstrated that it means creating a new society. Even if monetary and development experts agree on the magnitude and form of an exchange rate adjustment, they will have different views on what are the appropriate accompanying measures. Such changes in the content of adjustment programs will affect all its important aspects. (Perhaps it is unnecessary to add that similar observations could be made if the starting point is a proposed development program.)

A chronic weakness of economic management of developing countries is the dichotomy frequently found between monetary and development policies and practices. Often their objectives are seen as hostile to each other; often as subordinating one to the other. Both views are wrong and lead to wrong policies. In practice they merge, but they can be merged politically in a hodgepodge of political compromising, or they can be merged thoughtfully using the economic and social well-being of people and the national interest as the deciding factors in making judgments. In practice, this can be done domestically by making adjustment policies the combined responsibility of monetary, fiscal, and developmental authorities and individuals, and internationally by making it the combined responsibility of the IMF, the World Bank, and the appropriate regional development bank. I will return to this suggestion later.

The Fund has always understood the need for realism, gradualism, compromise, and patience, but in its newly enhanced world role, it was in the midst of crisis management and needed to take firm, concise, drastic, urgent positions and to stubbornly insist on performance or else—a condition it had only very occasionally experienced in the past. The burden of responsibilities placed on the Fund is mammoth. It is, in effect, trying to serve the needs of others with different purposes and objectives while performing its own responsibilities. Leaving aside possible conflict of purpose, it is in the danger of losing its flexibility in dealing with member countries in difficulties. Like Gulliver, it may become tied down by many ropes and become unable to perform its own responsibilities in the manner it would prefer. At the same time, it blunts the need for other lending institutions to examine their own policies to see how they might play a more constructive role in development finance.

Suggested Changes in Fund Practices

In light of its experience and the needs of its member countries, I would suggest some changes in Fund practices and, incidentally, in the practices of the World Bank and the regional development banks.

First, the Fund's ties with the GATT should be strengthened as should its activities to help assure that the rising tide of protectionism does not lead to intensification of trade restrictions by industrial countries. Quotas on imports and subsidies on exports are examples of this. The Fund has long been involved in the process of international consultations in the GATT on the use of such trade restrictions for balance-of-payments purposes. This responsibility may well become more acute during the next world recession. In addition, the Fund may need to go well beyond certifying that intensifications of trade restrictions are or are not justified for balance-of-payments reasons. It may need to insist that such restrictions are internationally unacceptable, even if balance-of-payments reasons exist. In effect, it would need to insist that other ways be found to deal with a country's balance-of-payments difficulties. Otherwise, the world can slip back to widespread use of restrictions on international trade and inevitably to widespread bilateralism. "Beggar thy neighbor" policies could again become the order of the day. In addition, the Fund may find it increasingly necessary to play an active role in cases of pure protectionism, i.e., protection of domestic industry and employment not related to balance-of-payments reasons. The Fund has a major stake in helping to prevent the revival of strong protectionism, especially in the United States and other industrial nations. Brazil, for example, could not be experiencing its present return to external financial acceptability in an environment of protectionism. Korea would now be in serious balance-of-payments difficulties if strong protectionism had prevailed during the recent worldwide recession. European countries would not have been able to avoid the conditions which in the past have led to competitive exchange rate depreciation and bilateralism.

Second, Fund-endorsed programs which are accompanied by access to the Fund's financial sources—mostly in the form of stand-by arrangements—should include developmental policies, practices, and criteria. To achieve the necessary professional expertise and to enhance the program's credibility in the developing countries, these programs should be the joint responsibility of the Fund, the World Bank, and the appropriate regional development bank.

It is essential that in this collaborative effort, each institution maintain its identity. The purpose is not to make all three institutions experts on the same areas of economic management, but to ensure that all aspects benefit from the views of others. Because the need will essentially be for improvement in the short- and medium-term balance-of-payments outlook, the lead role would be taken by the IMF. When a domestic program seeking international endorsement and support emerges, it would be labeled as a program of the country endorsed by the three institutions.

The financial support for the agreed program could come from all three institutions, but not necessarily at the same time and surely not on the same terms. Each institution would maintain its own lending criteria, but, again, their application would benefit from the viewpoint of others involved. Thus, it is quite conceivable that the three institutions would at times agree that one or two of them could proceed with certain lending, while a third did not until certain conditions existed. The aim would not be rigidity or uniformity but rather flexibility and diversity—made sensible and credible to the borrowing country and to the international community because the three institutions had collaborated in the country assessments and in evaluating and monitoring the economic management of the borrowing country.

As a consequence of its preoccupation with the problems of developing countries, the Fund may well find that the industrial countries will become more reluctant to substantially increase their financial support of the Fund in the future. In a sense, the Fund could find itself faced with the same reluctance as now exists to increase official development assistance. This possibility is enhanced by the perception that the problems among developed countries are being increasingly handled bilaterally or in small groups and by the fact that international liquidity in U.S. dollars is being increased by large amounts because of the U.S. external deficits. The Fund may be seen as unnecessary to create international liquidity. In dealing with the developing countries, it will continue to be an important provider of liquidity, but the magnitudes required may be much more than the Fund can provide. It is in concert with other lenders, public and private, and as the leading institution in dealing with emergency and cyclical balance-of-payments difficulties that the Fund will continue to be of major international importance. For the developing countries, it will remain—like the central bank—the international lender of last resort and the institution able to mobilize additional support, if needed, with accepted credibility as a judge of country economic management.

The third major change, directed to improve the quality and timing of financing of a developing country in balance-of-payments difficulties, the financial support to a developing country could include four *interlinked* layers of financing:

The first layer should be the Bank for International Settlements (the BIS), which provides immediate balance-of-payments assistance given under conditions previously specified by the BIS. Closely related, and a possible substitute, is central bank support by the industrial nations, again under conditions previously specified. Such funds would be short-term, say up to three months, and renewable only once. They could be made conditional on the willingness of the country to enter into discussions and negotiations on an adjustment program with the three relevant international institutions acting together. The central banks might act as guarantor of assistance obtained from the BIS. The central banks and the BIS would expect to be repaid promptly and fully with, if needed, drawings from the IMF.

The immediate role of the IMF in this first layer would be to judge the viability of the exchange rate. A realistic exchange rate—and so judged quickly by the Fund because of its continuing relationship with the country—would be the prerequisite for any assistance from the BIS or central banks. If major capital flight is in process, the Fund would recommend immediate remedial steps, again being ready for this contingency by its ongoing work with the country. If the country was not a net debtor of the Fund, the Fund drawing facilities could be used up to the gold tranche and so-called first credit tranche, or a special issue of SDRs could be used, instead of the BIS and central banks, but always assuming that the needed changes in exchange rates and the measures to stop the capital flight have taken place. Such measures might well be only temporarily and partially effective until the adjustment program is in place, but Fund and country would agree on what is worthy of international support.

The second layer of financing would be the credit tranches of the Fund. These would be subject to conditionality agreed by the three institutions involved. If such practice were to be adopted, the three institutions would soon be cooperating closely enough in their ordinary activities to assure the ability to act cooperatively, efficiently, and in a timely manner when contingencies arose. The endorsement of the program would be made by the three institutions combined. Thus, the adjustment program and the preconditions for assistance would be jointly made and agreed with the country. The country work of each institution would become increasingly a collaborative product, and the missions to the country for this purpose would probably become joint missions.

The third layer of assistance would be the multilateral development banks. Lending by them would be conditional on agreed adjustment programs in which they had played a vital role and shared responsibility. Lending could be in nonproject forms. If the balance-of-payments conditions and outlook of the country warranted, the Fund drawings could be refinanced by the development finance institutions into long-term loans.

The IMF and the multilateral development banks would need to have the necessary financial resources. The Fund could obtain the resources from its members by the normal increases in the quotas of members, SDR allocations, or borrowings from members under pre-arranged agreements, like the General Agreement to Borrow, first put together around 1960 to help defend the newly established international convertibility system. If necessary, the Fund could make arrangements to augment its financial resources by borrowing from the private financial or capital markets. Whether in borrowings from governments or private lenders, the form of borrowing could be committed stand-by lines of credit instead of drawn-down borrowings. The multilateral development banks could borrow from the private capital markets, based on their capital structures. This need for additional lending could be taken into account when member governments consider the desired capitalization of these banks. Fortunately, these resources can be obtained with very small budgetary expenditures by the shareholder countries.

It is the ultimate guarantor role of members which creates the creditworthiness of the multilateral development banks. The forms of their assistance, such as general balance-of-payments support, project loans, general impact loans, structural adjustment loans, and supplementary finance, could be suited to the borrowing countries and conditions. In all cases, however, they would serve developmental purposes and have maturities suitable to a developing country. The feasibility of this proposal would largely depend on how much the banks knew about the countries, and how well they could keep up to date on the development process and programs. In any case, the developmental aspects might well take more time to investigate than the monetary aspects. In practice, as noted earlier, the adjustment program might well require financial support from these institutions at differing times.

The fourth layer of potentially interlinked financing would be private sources of finance plus other official sources of development finance, like export-credit schemes. These sources would presumably usually be more risk-averting. With this approach, other sources of finance might well not go again into the state of hysteria and near paralysis witnessed from 1982 to the present. Instead, earlier resumption of lending by commercial banks would facilitate the ability of countries to meet their financial obligations to the IMF and to the multilateral development banks.

The fourth overall suggestion for reform of the IMF is that, in case of need for external debt restructuring, the existing mechanisms would come into action, though hopefully in a more simplified form. The essence of the international action would be to defend the creditworthiness of borrowers. If debt restructuring were nevertheless deemed necessary or desirable, the programs of adjustment evolved with the help of the three international institutions could be linked to the debt restructuring. The process would be similar to the present process, but with some important changes. Those involved in the debt restructuring could decide at what stages in the adjustment process they wished to act in restructuring debts, or even decide not to tie them to the agreed adjustment program. It need not be uniform for all debtors. Hopefully, the lending institutions would have the ability to make their country assessments, separately or jointly, and act on them. Linking to agreed adjustment programs would be made on other grounds. The Fund and the development institutions would not have the *de facto* responsibilities of having their relations with countries determine the relations and actions of other creditor institutions. This link has been useful in the past. Some links may continue to be found desirable, but these links should arise out of future conditions and not be merely the imitation of past and current practices.

It is hoped that the private lenders would have more confidence in the longer-run creditworthiness of developing countries if this practice is adopted. However, this does not necessarily involve the strict linkages which have been found useful to meet the conditions of the last few years. The practice of the major international lenders of tying their lending to implementation of Fund-agreed programs has made rigid the system of capital flows to the developing countries. The international financial system needs variety and flexibility. Crisis management may justify the present rigidity, but only until better ways are found and used.

Conclusion

I have dwelled on institutional changes, not on the ethical considerations of the various possible programs evolved with active Fund participation and support. Questions of ethics are inherent in the workings of any socioeconomic system. The twentieth century has seen the worldwide acceptance in political and social practice of an old ethical and religious belief, namely, the dignity of *all* people, the right of *all* people, not just a fortunate few, to be regarded as persons entitled to aspire and strive to change and improve their social positions and economic well-being, and the right of *all* people to be treated by all others in societies as human beings. We do not try to rationalize poverty and distress as inevitable conditions of economic life. We have come much beyond the prevailing ethical views of the nineteenth century. We look to science and technology to provide the means of improving the well-being of all. We expect modernization in the developing world to avoid the distresses of the commercial and industrial revolutions. We support institutions, at every level, devoted to the abolition of poverty. We expect the wealthier among us to accept the philosophy, in practice, that all should share in the benefits of modernization.

We are not unrealistic in our assessments of the difficulties and the length of time needed to realize this philosophy, but we still have a profound belief in the feasibility of general progress, though we no longer believe it is inevitable. This belief in progress was the prevailing social philosophy in the United States and other countries in the World War II period. The international organizations which emerged from World War II remain our chosen instruments to help achieve these social and economic objectives which embody our ethical value systems. I am convinced that these institutions continue to merit the support of people of goodwill everywhere. The strengthening of their international role is desirable and I heartily support their strengthening. At the same time, it does not follow that either the country programs recommended by them or their management of the international monetary system are above criticism. As in our lives as citizens of our countries, we must judge what the Fund does in particular cases by our own standards of equity as well as by our standards of efficiency and feasibility. I often find myself in disagreement with what the Fund is doing or advocating, but not in my conviction of its usefulness for the welfare of the world.

3

IMF Conditionality: Incomplete Theory, Policy Malpractice

Lance Taylor

More often than not, a developing country with balance-of-payments problems ends up requesting a line of credit or a "stand-by" loan from the International Monetary Fund. The reason is that under present arrangements in the global macroeconomic system, the IMF is the final source of cash—the lender of last resort—for economies to which commercial banks or aid donors no longer care to lend. In exchange for the loan, the borrowing country pledges to reform its economic policies to meet the requirements of the Fund; it can draw on the credit as long as the promised policy changes are instituted and macroeconomic indicators behave according to pre-specified performance criteria. The policy revisions and the criteria together amount to "conditionality."

Conditionality has a complicated history. As recounted by Sidney Dell (1981), its juridical rationale developed over two decades after the founding of the IMF at Bretton Woods, and its strictness fluctuated over time. The variations were due at least in part to shifts in the resources of the Fund relative to the demands placed upon them. In other words, conditionality may get tougher when the global economic situation worsens. For reasons spelled out below, the poorer countries are forced, through tight conditionality, to respond to global shocks with reductions in their economic activity and most likely with a worsening of their income distributions. The reasons why conditionality has such effects on developing economies is the topic of this paper.

The design for Fund interventions is well-established. It comes from an article published in the *IMF Staff Papers* in 1957 by the Dutch economist Jacques Polak, then a member of the research staff (Polak 1957). Since this paper has guided the practice of Fund missions in scores of country interventions, it is one of the most important pieces of macroeconomics done after Keynes. The IMF's policy recommendations look remarkably similar over space and time. Such uniformity says much for Polak's vision, as well as the hermetic nature of the institution which carries it on.

Conditionality along Fund lines is almost certain to "work" by improving the balance of payments, as we will see shortly. However, its efficacy is strictly limited both in duration and in the aspects of the economy addressed. How else can one explain the fact that Fund programs are applied in one- to five-year cycles in economies all around the world? Countries may have chronic stabilization crises because of the way that the international economic system is organized—a topic we cannot address here—but they are also afflicted by the character of the Fund staff, its institutionally sanctioned narrow vision, and an occasional lack of competence. The fact that the IMF holds the purse strings to international credit explains why sovereign states call for its advice; the fact that the advice does not lead to long-run structural adjustment explains why the Fund is called upon again and again. To see what goes wrong, we have to look at the recommendations and their theoretical basis in some detail.

The Content of Conditionality

An agreement between a country and the Fund about a stand-by loan subject to conditionality takes the form of a "Letter of Intent" from one to the other. The contents and language are hammered out in negotiations between an IMF mission of perhaps five people and the authorities of the country concerned. Letters of Intent are not released officially, but are frequently leaked. Similarly, the Fund's internal "Recent Economic Developments" reports are stamped confidential, but circulate among cognoscenti in Washington, D.C. and the countries concerned. From such sources, one can make a good judgment into what comprises conditionality.

The package is usually made up of some combination of the following four policies:

- Restrictions on credit to be made available from the domestic banking system, especially to the central government and public enterprise.
- Specific targets for the public sector deficit to back up credit restrictions, sometimes with agreements about which programs are to be cut (or revenue sources increased) so that the deficit targets can be attained.
- A program for depreciation of the local currency (either gradually or once-for-all in a maxi-devaluation). and
- An agreement to "liberalize" by removing restrictions on external trade or capital movements, or on internal prices and transactions.

The goals these policies are supposed to achieve are threefold. The first and most important is improvement of the balance of payments—either the trade deficit is to go down or external capital is to flow in. Second, restrictive monetary and fiscal policies may be aimed at making inflation run slower. Finally, the liberalization exercises are meant to clear the economy for steady growth along classical laissez-faire lines. Of these three, improvement in the balance of payments is most often attained; the inflation target is less frequently met, and steady growth is by no means a guaranteed outcome. The IMF's success or failure in achieving these goals can be understood by examining in some detail simple macroeconomic accounting identities.

Both the IMF and the economic-policy team of the borrowing country work with three sets of interlocking accounts: the sources and uses of national income, the flows of funds within the financial sector, and the economy's transactions with the rest of the world. In developing countries, these accounts do not capture much of what goes on in the economy, especially in urban informal sectors and rural sectors. The total effect of any policy is necessarily misjudged because so large a share of economic life is not reflected in the official numbers. Much criticism of IMF-type policy is based on its alleged effects on the poor, but these are extremely difficult to quantify. Here, we concentrate on the incomplete data that are actually recorded—as do the Fund staff and the finance minister of the country in question.

The accounting is set up in the form of double-entry bookkeeping balances that the numbers are constructed to satisfy. The balances or equations are presented here in simplified form, and minor (but sometimes important) items are omitted. The first is for the consolidated banking system, made up of the central bank, commercial banks, savings and loans, and other similar institutions.

Equation 1

Increase in Money Supply = Increase in International Reserves
+ Increase in Credit to the Private Sector
+ Public Sector Deficit

"Money" in any economy is made up liabilities of the banking system: deposits at commercial banks plus currency issued by the central bank. The total liability must be balanced by assets—foreign-reserve holdings and loans from the banks to persons and firms (usually from commercial banks) and to the public sector (usually from the central bank).

A second identity shows where international reserves come from:

Equation 2

$$\text{Increase in International Reserves} = (\text{Exports} - \text{Imports}) + \text{Net Capital Inflow}$$

If there is a trade surplus or net lending to a country (total lending minus repayment of debt), then its reserves go up. For specific countries, other items may be important in equation 2 as well—interest payments going out, for example, or emigrant workers' remittances coming in—but these are ignored for the sake of simplicity.

The first two equations reflect the monetary and foreign balances, respectively. Equations 3 and 4 are based on national income relationships. First, there is the balance between national saving and investment (the latter interpreted as formation of physical capital, such as machines or houses).

Equation 3

$$\text{Saving by the Private Sector} = \text{Investment} + (\text{Exports} - \text{Imports}) + \text{Public Sector Deficit}$$

"Saving" to an economist means acquisition of assets. Equation 3 shows that the private sector's assets can take the form of physical capital or financial claims on the public sector or on the rest of the world, since an excess of exports over imports means the country is gaining access to foreign exchange which can be converted to assets abroad. A detailed description of asset and liability changes appears in flow-of-funds accounts, which can be linked directly to equation 1 by means of equation 3.

The final relationship shows that the value of domestic production is paid out to diverse recipients

Equation 4

$$\text{Value of Output} = (\text{Wage Income} + \text{Income of Small Proprietors}) + \text{Profits of Firms} + \text{Interest Paid to Banks} + \text{Costs of Imported Production Inputs}$$

"Wage income" and "income of small proprietors" reflect payments to humble people—workers and operators of small enterprises, such as farmers or peddlers. "Profits" refer to incomes of large and/or incorporated firms, while the "interest paid to banks" is due on loans for investment or working capital. The "costs of imported production inputs" does not appear in standard presentations of the national accounts, but is included here to reflect the fact that production activity in many poor countries is strongly dependent on materials imported from abroad (think of fertilizer for agriculture, "kits" of components which are assembled in the manufacturing sector, and petroleum for the whole economy).

The genius of the Polak model is to concentrate only on balances 1 and 2, although that is the source of the problems with many IMF packages as well. A Fund program is designed through computations based on these equations; the procedure is called "financial programming." Polak's omission of equations 3 and 4 from his framework made sense in his time, since few countries had national income accounts in the 1950s but did keep banking and trade records. The same is not true today.

Financial Programming

Like all monetarist economists, Fund staff members start their analysis from a fifth relationship called the equation of exchange.

Equation 5

$$\text{Money Demand} = (1/V) \times \text{Value of Output} = (1/V) \times \text{Price Level} \times \text{Quantity of Output}$$

Here, V is a number called "velocity," which is supposed to stay roughly constant. Since V is the ratio of the value of output in some reference period (say a year) to the stock of money, it measures the speed at which money is used to finance transactions. A low ratio indicates a slow turnover of cash and hence low velocity.

To undertake financial programming, assume that the increase in output in a given year is known, from supply considerations. If V holds still, then the increase in money demand will depend only on increases in price. These may be partly determined from rises in costs, but are also supposed to respond to the money supply, i.e., lower money supply will reduce the amount that can be demanded, or, in other words, price increases will be held down.

The money supply figure in equation 1 depends on credit to the private sector and the fiscal deficit. Suppose that these are restricted. Two things may happen.

First, since demand for money must equal supply, restraining the latter will force down the output price index in equation 5. However, given the exchange rate, the prices of goods traded within the country will be determined by the world market price. For example, domestically produced wheat cannot sell within the country for more than the local currency cost of freely imported grain from the U.S. or Argentina. This postulated equality of domestic and international commodity prices is sometimes called the "Law of One Price." If economy-wide average prices go down while those of traded goods stay constant, then prices of nontraded goods, such as services and commodities with high transport costs, must decline. The relative price shift means that it becomes more profitable to produce tradable goods, that is, to export more or to substitute imports. Hence the surplus of exports over imports will rise—the trade deficit will be smaller.

The second possible result of both restriction of the public deficit and a restriction of credit to the private sector occurs if the Law of One Price doesn't apply. Prices will then be determined by internal costs, and money demand will follow from equation 5. Set the increase in demand equal to the change in supply; by some accounting entelechy from equation 1, international reserves must rise. According to equation 2, with pre-specified capital inflows, the trade surplus will increase. We get the same result!

Financial programming boils down to the process of setting the elements in equations 1, 2, and 5 according to projections of their magnitudes on the part of Fund staff and economists within the country. Everybody knows that velocity can jump erratically, that the Law of One Price doesn't really apply (think of traders' margins, transport costs, and the dissimiliarity of national and imported products), that output is not strictly supply-determined, and so on. Nonetheless, these factors are not treated as variable for purposes of discussion about financial programming; the argument is about what values should be assigned to velocity, inflation, output growth, and the rest. When that is done, the equations give permissible levels of credit increases and the public sector deficit in light of projections of available capital inflows. Performance targets for monetary and fiscal policy come from dialogue between the Fund and the country around three simple accounting balances. The fact that equations 2 and 3 also apply in any functioning economy suggests that something is being left out of this formula.

Monetarist Stagflation

The missing links come from costs of production and demand. For example, looking at equation 3, if the fiscal deficit is reduced, there is an incipient excess of private saving over the uses of savings on the right-hand side of the equation. In effect, the economy starts to save more than there is need for saving, and aggregate demand goes down. The result is a reduction in economic activity, as the public sector spends less. In developing countries, as argued above, imports are largely used as inputs into the production process. With less production, fewer imports will be required and the trade deficit will decline. The improvement comes from recession, not from relative price shifts or accounting magic, as maintained by the Fund. One of the key monetarist assumptions—that output is set from supply considerations, independent of demand—is violated. In their country documents, IMF staff members almost routinely produce projected increases in output that are on the high side. Combining equations 1 and 5 and asserting that shifts in money supply will be reflected exclusively in changes in the average price level, not in output or velocity, is simply wrong.

A second link involves working capital, which may be a large component of costs when supply networks are fragile and inflation is high, as is often the case in developing countries. In order to both hold stocks of inputs in anticipation of production and meet wage bills, a firm has to borrow from banks (or forego deposits). An important consequence—stressed as often by conservative businessmen as by progressive economists—is that tight monetary policy drives up interest rates on loans for working capital, and thus increases one of the components of cost in equation 4. The normal business response would be to cut back on activity and attempt to pass higher interest on through higher prices. When working capital is important, restrictive monetary policy is counterproductive with respect to both output and inflation, but still manages to reduce intermediate imports through lower production. Such trade-balance improvement is the signature of the Fund.

Devaluation

Currency devaluation is supposed to reduce the trade deficit through the same "substitution" channel as monetary restraint. By definition, devaluation immediately increases the domestic currency prices of traded goods. (Whether prices of nontraded goods immediately catch up is another question.) It becomes more profitable to export or substitute for imports with domestic products, and the foreign accounts improve.

In practice, substitution responses are certainly slow and quite possibly weak, so the process is not as simple as the theory assumes. By altering relative prices, devaluation affects real incomes within the economy, and the responses of the gainers and losers can easily lead to economic contraction. Once again, the trade balance will improve through a reduction of intermediate imports, if it changes at all. The reason for the caveat is that "real" devaluation may not be feasible because the groups hurt may adjust the prices they control upward to offset the higher exchange rate and no price relations are changed. The only outcome is a spurt in inflation and increased class acrimony all around.

To detail this process, recall from equation 4 that imported inputs are an important component of cost. Devaluation drives their value up in terms of domestic currency, with the increase likely to be passed along through higher prices. If money-wage rates stay constant, then the purchasing power of labor income declines and the income distribution shifts toward profits. The saving rate from profit income is likely to exceed that from wages. Hence consumption demand declines and the familiar trade improvement by economic contraction follows. This result will not occur if workers can defend their income level by forcing up money wages in the wake of devaluation (for example, by a wage-indexing scheme). In that case, the real effects of devaluation will be largely nullified by inflation.

A second distributional shift takes place through the trade balance itself. Devaluation gives with one hand but takes with the other, increasing receipts of exporters but driving up import costs. Countries usually devalue from an initial trade deficit. The income loss from imports exceeds the gain from exports, and overall purchasing power declines. Contraction is the inevitable result.

Other linkages with similar effects can be described, but the message is clear: devaluation (like tight money) reduces the trade deficit in the short run by inducing economic contraction. Longer-term effects may include:

- A further output loss and import saving as investment demand falls off in response to lagging economic activity. The decrease in capital formation may be especially sharp if firms have borrowed heavily abroad, and the cost of their dollar-denominated debt is sharply increased by devaluation. The consequent reduction in the trade gap may be substantial, since imported capital goods make up a large share (up to fifty percent) of total investment in many countries.
- The real effects of devaluation are likely to erode over time as prices of nontraded goods (including labor) catch up to the sudden jump in traded-goods prices.
- As long as real depreciation persists, substitution responses, such as export promotion and import substitution, will grow in strength.

The long-term response depends on which of these forces is dominant. Computer-simulation studies suggest that devaluation may expand real output after ten quarters or so if wage indexing is weak. For a policymaker, that length of time constitutes a substantial wait.

Liberalization

To summarize the discussion so far, we have seen that standard IMF policies are based on an incomplete theoretical description of the economy which concentrates on monetary and external balances and ignores demand factors and important components of costs. When the latter are taken into account, both monetary contraction and devaluation are likely to be stagflationary, driving prices and interest rates up while reducing the level of output. The income distribution is likely to worsen, at least insofar as it is influenced by the real wage. On the other hand, the reduction in output will lead the trade balance to improve—the Fund's major goal.

These linkages are easy to trace and quantify in simple macro models based on the accounting identities set out here (see Taylor 1983). Detailed analysis of the effects of liberalization is more complex.

Some liberalization experiments, for example, simply fail. Argentina freed its capital market from restrictions in the 1970s while pursuing a relatively expansionary policy with a pre-fixed rate of devaluation over time. The rate of steady depreciation was set to a low figure in an attempt to reduce "inflationary expectations." One consequence was that the return on peso-denominated assets became very attractive (with return equal to the interest rate less the rate of depreciation). Argentine citizens switched from foreign-currency to peso assets, leading to an increase in bank reserves along the lines of equation 2. This was followed by a rise in lending and fairly rapid growth accompanied by increasing inflation. The real exchange rate lost value (appreciated sharply), causing exports to decline and imports to go up. The deterioration in the trade position led to fears of an impending maxi-devaluation, which in turn set off an enormous capital flight. The country ended up having a faster rate of inflation, being bereft of foreign reserves, and facing stagnation from the maxi-devaluation when it finally came. Capital-market restriction might better have been left alone in the first place.

Not all the results are so dramatic, but liberalizations can have unexpected and at times unpleasant effects. What gains are they supposed to create?

For over a hundred years, neoclassical economics has proposed two sorts of answers to this question. The first, based on the assumption that the economy is largely competitive, is that the benefits will be small in the aggregate. Removing a distortion—for instance, a tariff which keeps the internal price of an imported good above the world price (multiplied by a constant exchange rate)—will help the consumers of that good. The value of their benefit will be proportional to the price change multiplied by the extra amount that they buy because of the lower cost—in macroeconomic terms, a trivial change. Compared to U.S. GNP, the price differential between American and Japanese cars multiplied by the extra cars Americans would import from Japan if they were able does not amount to very much. The shift would be important for Detroit, but not to the economy as a whole (unless there were strong linkage effects, which is possible in this case).

The second answer is that removing distortions would permit greater efficiency gains and far more rapid economic growth. An economy with many distortions (tariffs, import licensing, food subsidies, income taxes, bureaucratic intervention, etc.) is inefficient by its very nature. This supply-side case is difficult to analyze except in historical terms because mere models cannot capture the forces involved. The conclusions are bound to be controversial because it is easy for partisans to point to specific features of successful (or unsuccessful) economies that support their case. Suffice it to say that many historically fast-growing economies did not follow liberal policies. For example, the United States was very protectionist until the 1930s and had massive state interventions, such as the subsidies given the railway companies through the nineteenth century. Japan typically followed a protectionist import policy and gave strong export incentives. South Korea and Brazil have authoritarian, *dirigiste* governments which meddle strongly in company decisions and do not allow internal price relationships to approximate international relative prices to any great degree. Both these countries have strongly resisted pressures from the IMF and other agencies such as the World Bank to liberalize their economic policies. Their growth record until the recent period of extreme external shocks suggests that they have been doing something right.

A final note, suggested by the Argentine example, is that liberalization may be difficult to implement in practice. Reduced import quotas, to take a common case, will have to be offset by a large, initially stagflationary devaluation. If the quotas serve as a form of wealth (say, as collaterals for loans), their abolition may lead to further contraction from asset liquidation as well. Attempts to take away input or food-consumer subsidies are likely to lead to great political unrest, as many governments (advised by the Fund) learned to their distress in recent years. Even if major efficiency gains were to result, such liberalization policies might well be offset by the short-run shocks to the economy that the process of eliminating "distortions" can bring.

Policy Malpractice

The track record of economists of all persuasions in passing out policy advice is not a wonder of the world. Do IMF economists perform any worse than their competitors? Unfortunately, there are two factors which suggest they might. The first stems from the incomplete nature of their model.

In the Mexican stabilization of 1982, for example, goals were set for inflation, balance-of-payments improvement, and output growth. It is of interest to trace how they interact. From equation 4, to reduce the rate of price inflation, some component of cost has to be cut. Of the four listed on the right-hand side of the equation, three were to be maintained in real terms as a policy choice: profits of large firms had to be supported to avoid bankruptcies, interest rates were held at high levels as part of a liberalization effort to stimulate saving and avoid capital flight, and import costs rose because of devaluation. Hence, wages and small proprietors' incomes had to be cut. Based on the shares in total costs of the four elements of equation 4, an easy calculation shows that reaching the inflation target would require that only about 65 percent of one year's price inflation be passed along in money-wage increases the next year. In the event, even the strong Mexican political system could not deal with such a shift in the income distribution, and the "pass-through coefficient" was higher—75 or 80 percent. The inflation target was missed, but real wages still fell very sharply.

What about output? The main components of demand are exports, consumption, government spending, and investment. In Mexico, investment declined because of entrepreneurs' doubts about future growth prospects, and government spending was held down by the Fund's fiscal targets. Consumption could not possible by buoyant because of the real wage loss. That left exports as the motor of demand. Presumably, sales abroad would respond to devaluation and unused productive capacity in many sectors. To an extent this occurred, but it was easy to see that reasonable export responsiveness would not be sufficient to sustain normal levels of production. Real GNP fell.

Finally, the balance-of-payments target was more than satisfied as imports plummeted. Perhaps what occurred was what the IMF had expected all along. If so, there was a degree of mendacity in the economic forecast that the Fund and the Mexican authorities agreed upon.

The events in Mexico were extreme, but understandable when one realizes how Fund staff members think. An incorrect view of a country's economic system is involved, but not pure incompetence. However, in some instances, Fund missions seem not to have performed up to the professional standards one can reasonably expect. This is the second reason why the IMF may commit malpractice.

Given the secretive nature of Fund missions, adequate documentation for poor performance is hard to provide. More or less on an anecdotal basis, we can mention the following:

- Errors are made in forecasting. Cases like Mexico's have been repeated endlessly, with the same biases in inflation, income distribution, trade account, and GNP projections. Examples by observers from a wide range of methodological positions are easy to come by.
- The basic model has simply not been manipulated correctly. In his original presentation, Polak scaled time units to set V equal to one in his version of equation 5. There are widely discussed cases in Africa—the area for which the Fund's regional economists are held to be the weakest—in which V was pegged at unity in financial programming. The error may seem trivial, but it makes all the difference for the numbers. The difficulties are compounded if, as sometimes seems to happen, staff members don't get their accounting balances quite right.
- Countries can evade monetary restrictions by transactions within the banking system. For example, the government in Chile recently borrowed heavily from banks that had previously been taken over by the state in a financial crisis. After due delay, the banks rediscounted the loans with the central bank. In effect, the government borrowed from the central bank, breaking conditionality. It took the IMF a year to catch up. Whether benign neglect or lack of understanding of Chile's financial system was involved is not clear, but there are similar examples elsewhere. Great acumen on the part of the Fund staff is not implied.
- Unique country developments may be misinterpreted. Over the years, Brazil gradually made its money supply subject to "financial correction" by paying interest approximately equal to the rate of inflation on outstanding government bonds which serve for transactions. The interest is covered by fiscal expenditure, and total payments are directly proportional to the rate of inflation. Hence, a substantial fraction of the Brazilian fiscal deficit is caused by inflation coupled with interest-bearing money. If one takes the deficit at face value, its expansionary effect on aggregate demand will be grossly overestimated—expenditures will be going to monetary correction and not to demand for goods. It took the Brazilians a few years to make the Fund see this fairly obvious fact.

Other examples could be presented, but these suffice to suggest that the Fund staff is not more competent than economists in the countries it advises, and may indeed be even less so (which would almost certainly be true in countries with sophisticated national economic professions, such as Brazil, Mexico, India, and Israel). Given the vast power the IMF holds, one might hope for better performance on its part.

What Is To Be Done?

The question not addressed in this paper is the IMF's role in the world economic system. To a large extent, its function is to make debtor countries bear the entire burden of balance-of-payments adjustment through recession. Such a mechanism may be fully in line with the desires of the industrialized powers (with the exception of the United States in the 1980s). If so, the goal of conditionality is simply economic contraction, and the Fund does what it was structured to do, not created to do—the founding fathers at Bretton Woods had different ideas, as Dell argues (Dell 1981).

The question then arises why countries with current-account deficits cannot find some other way to resolve their problems. Why must they liberalize, for example, instead of subsidizing exports or cutting imports by inwardly oriented, planned development strategies? Again, a purely functional explanation is possible. Dominant economies prefer open markets and free trade, especially on the part of their poorer competitors. The rationale offered to the poorer countries for opening up is the "gains from trade" (an argument presented in the section above on liberalization). Again, by pushing liberalization, the IMF—and the World Bank in the 1980s—acts in ways consistent with the interests of the industrialized countries of the world.

To a degree, these functionalist arguments no doubt apply. But they elude both the closed nature of the Fund and the true options for developing countries. With regard to the former, outside observers agree that the degree of control and socialization of staff members within the institution is extreme. Fund economists will not come up with alternative macroeconomic programs simply because they cannot. Especially after arriving at positions of authority within the organization, most are only able to think along strict-constructionist monetarist lines.

The intellectual burden thus falls upon those in the developing countries. Can their economies produce alternative stabilization schemes that avoid the more odious implications of conditionality as presently applied? There are reasons to think that they can, though they cannot be presented in detail here. The final problem is that such programs will never see the light of day unless the international community and the IMF as its agent are prepared to let poor countries try new approaches to their economic ails. Prospects for such open-mindedness in the mid-1980s are dim.

References

Dell, Sidney. 1981. "On Being Grandmotherly: The Evolution of IMF Conditionality," *Essays in International Finance, No. 144.* Princeton, NJ: Princeton University Press.

Polak, J.J. 1957. "Monetary Analysis of Income Formation and Payments Problems," *International Monetary Fund Staff Papers.* Washington, D.C.: IMF, 6:1–50.

Taylor, Lance. 1983. *Structuralist Macroeconomics.* New York: Basic Books.

4

IMF Conditionality and the International Economy: A U.S. Labor Perspective

Henry B. Schechter

This paper, respresenting a U.S. labor point of view, reviews the International Monetary Fund from both an operational and a moral perspective. The two are interrelated, since the operational mold of the IMF extrudes forms of morality, or immorality, which affect the success or failure of the IMF program and perhaps of the government in power in a country.

IMF spokesmen have included certain types of economic activities within the sphere of IMF operations and have omitted other activities. This selectivity circumscribes the economic policies that may be pursued as part of IMF economic adjustment programs and thus has an effect on how the burden of economic adjustment is distributed. Such selectivity in economic policies is not only a matter of moral consideration, it also concerns how effective adjustment programs are in fostering balanced, sustained economic growth both within the countries that find it necessary to adopt IMF adjustment and within the international economy.

It is doubtful that anybody could prescribe a combination of economic policies that would produce the optimum balance between progress toward sustained, balanced economic growth and economic equity. History provides warnings, however, against programs and policies that place undue emphasis upon rapid attainment of current-account surpluses to facilitate debt repayment at the expense of economic imbalances and inequities that stretch political tolerance toward and even up to the breaking point.

The current debt crisis brings to light some of the shortcomings of IMF programs. These will be explored here, with particular reference to Latin America. This paper will review the character of IMF adjustment programs, illustrate the effect of such programs in Latin America, and make suggestions for possible policy questions that should be included in IMF adjustment programs in the future.

IMF Purposes, Objectives, and Operations

During its four-decade history, the International Monetary Fund has evolved, as circumstances changed and new problems arose, to accept greater responsibilities, finding within its Articles of Agreement the power to change its operations. The IMF has helped the world financial system overcome unforeseen hurdles and continue to function. The increased tempo of economic change in the world in recent years, however, has created the need for policy changes that would both avoid greater inequities and give greater assurances of effective, albeit perhaps more long-term, solutions to international debt problems.

Looking back at the establishment of the Fund, one of the participants recently wrote:

> The Articles of Agreement of the Fund envisaged an international monetary system that would maintain orderly exchange arrangements and thus facilitate the expansion of world trade, the maintenance of high levels of output, and the development of the productive resources of its members. The exchange system established at Bretton Woods was based on fixed par values for the members' currencies. (Bernstein 1984, 6)

There were also provisions for adjustments to deal with current balance-of-payments difficulties, loans by the Fund, and quota subscriptions to the Fund by member countries.

The primary objectives of the financial purposes set forth in the first of the Articles of Agreement are described in later subsections of the Article. These objectives include "the promotion and maintenance of high levels of employment and real income and . . . the primary development of the productive resources of all members as primary objectives of economic policy." The Article also specifies that the correction of maladjustments in the balances of payments should be undertaken "without resorting to measures destructive of national or international prosperity" (Dell 1983, 17–18). The IMF record of recent years, which will be touched on here, indicates that operations to meet the financial purposes have received overwhelming priority. This course has led to neglect of and negative effects on employment, real income, and prosperity in some of the countries pursuing eeconomic adjustment programs negotiated with the IMF.

The system established in 1944 worked relatively well for about the first 25 years. After World War II, the U.S. aided the rebuilding and expansion of civilian production facilities in many countries through the Marshall Plan, the Economic Cooperation Administration, and other U.S. programs. Further aid was provided by the United Nations Relief and Rehabilitation Administration. Resource transfers under these programs, plus the convertibility of U.S. dollars into gold at a fixed price, supported and facilitated national and international economic growth.

However, in the late 1960s, the U.S. current-account balance became very small and there were some payment difficulties. The need to redeem dollars in gold began to drain U.S. gold reserves. The U.S. discontinued convertibility of the dollar into gold in 1971, and in 1973 it abandoned par value for the dollar in international exchange. In 1978, the Articles of Agreement were amended to permit IMF members to maintain a par value for their currencies in terms of IMF Special Drawing Rights (SDRs) or in other denominations, except gold. Although the member countries still had an obligation to cooperate with the Fund and other member countries "to assure orderly exchange arrangements and to promote a stable system of exchange rates," the amendment allowed floating exchange rates (Bernstein 1984, 6).

To fulfill its purposes of maintaining orderly international monetary exchanges and safeguarding national and international prosperity, the IMF helps member nations respond to payments deficits by making loans to them. IMF policies allow *limited* borrowing by member countries with little or no conditionality. However, countries that wish to borrow greater amounts relative to their quota (contributed share to the basic IMF fund) are subject to "high conditionality." That involves "the country's design of a specific set of measures to eliminate its deficit, Fund agreement that the program will be adequate for that purpose, and the country's commitment to implement that program" (Williamson 1983a, 607).

During the 1970s, it became evident that the IMF would have difficulty reaching agreement on adjustment programs with some of the less developed countries because of IMF emphasis upon demand management and restrictions on development. Such was the experience in Tanzania and Kenya (see Green on Tanzania, Killick on Kenya in Williamson 1983b).

A more recent dramatic event in a country under an IMF adjustment program was the forceful replacement of the existing government in Sudan, which followed union strikes and widespread unrest aroused by increases in food and gasoline prices. The price increases were reportedly made at IMF insistence, with $67 million in blocked American aid as an inducement ("The Sudan After the Fall" April 4, 1985). The IMF program did not succeed, and whether program conditions that were less harsh would have been more tolerable and economically viable cannot be determined.

The Debt Crisis

During the decade preceding the debt crisis of the early 1980s, the oil-producing developing countries benefited from the greatly increased oil prices and accumulated large surpluses of hard currencies, primarily dollars. This accumulation was greatly increased by the 1973 oil price hikes. The surplus funds were invested in securities, bank deposits, and real estate in the industrial countries. The leading banks of those countries then undertook to recycle the dollars by making loans to developing countries around the world. This lending, which included a significant amount to Latin American countries, continued through the second half of the 1970s, and has been described as follows:

> The financial permissiveness shown by the international private banking system in the second half of the 1970s and the intense and persistent efforts it made to loan its financial surpluses to Latin America encouraged a policy of external indebtedness on a scale without any precedent in the region in the last half-century. There were few countries in Latin America which did not follow this policy in order to finance domestic policies with widely varying aims, ranging from some which involved large investments that even overestimated the future expansion of domestic and international markets to others which promoted an exaggerated expansion of consumption—especially of imported goods—or a big increase in defense spending. In recent years, furthermore, a considerable and growing proportion of external financing was used to pay the servicing costs of the accumulated debt, so that this situation was accompanied in practice by a reduction in the real transfer of resources to Latin America. (Traverso and Iglesias 1983, 11–12)

After the second oil shock in 1979, problems of greater scope developed in Latin America. The second series of significent oil price boosts in 1979 greatly increased the borrowing needs of the non–oil producing developing countries. At the end of the 1970s and into the 1980s, under the influence of U.S. tight money policies, interest rates continued to be high in the leading Western industrial countries. What followed highlights the interdependence of different national economies in a world economy which has become much more integrated. Both industrialized and less industrialized countries which had been exporting a good deal to the United States faced drastic declines in their export trade.

The OPEC oil price shocks in 1973 and 1979 helped to set off inflationary pressures in industrial and in developing countries. Toward the end of the 1970s and in the early 1980s, the United States adopted tight money policies to fight inflation; these policies in turn generated high interest rates. In addition, in 1981 there was a reduction in U.S. budgetary expenditures for social programs which, combined with the high interest rates, reduced economic demand. The U.S. economy went into a deep recession in 1981 which continued through almost all of 1982 and spread to other industrialized countries.

As of April 1985, five of the eleven countries with the largest IMF loan programs were in Latin America—Brazil, Mexico, Argentina, Uruguay,

and Peru—and another four were African countries—Zambia, Ghana, Malawi, and Sudan. The other two were the Philippines and Yugoslavia (Farnsworth April 4, 1985, E3). The countries with the three largest IMF loan programs also had the largest overall debt, or combined private and public debt.

During the 1970s, there was an important change in the composition and terms of the Latin American debt. At the beginning of the decade, about 40 percent of the credit flows were private; by the end of the decade, 80 percent were private and the balance was owed to either foreign governments or multilateral organizations such as the World Bank. Maturities were shortened, and there was a shift from fixed to variable interest rates (Traverso and Iglesias 1983, 23). The variable interest rates rose during the 1980s, producing economic shocks for the debtor countries.

The economies of Latin American countries were hurt by a decline in the U.S. demand for agricultural, mineral, and manufactured products. Latin American countries' exports to the U.S. therefore decreased at the same time that their debt service requirements were increasing because of the rising adjustable interest rates. Consequently, Latin American international production was reduced and urban unemployment rose significantly.[1]

Increasing unemployment and a deficit trade balance led to the combined debt and economic crises in Latin America. Under the IMF-approved economic adjustment programs put into effect during the past few years, the Latin American countries with large debts have had to restrict imports and consumption to a degree which has caused a decline in their people's purchasing power and in total economic activity. Unemployment increased further, and there has been explosive social unrest, including the ransacking of food stores in Brazil and in the Dominican Republic which led to the deaths of dozens of people.

The economic declines in the U.S. and Latin America fed upon each other. The decrease in purchasing power in debtor countries has, in turn, adversely affected the demand for U.S. products, which was a factor in the growth of a huge U.S. negative balance of merchandise trade. Unemployment contracted the U.S. market, and it became difficult for the debtor countries to increase exports to the U.S. and to attain sustained economic growth.

The recession became long and deep and it is not over yet in some of the countries under IMF programs. As the recessions in the industrialized countries and in the developing countries fed upon each other, the workers bore the brunt of economic adjustment, whether or not this was the intention. Production capacity and purchasing power must be balanced in domestic economies and in the international economy as a whole for the national and international economies to have sustained recoveries and stable growth.

The IMF adjustment programs also seem to neglect alternative conditions which could lead to a slowdown of inflation and could encourage balanced growth by spreading the burden of austerity to other portions of the society, thereby reducing the austerity that people of limited income must bear. The IMF could gain more popular support for its programs if it included stricter enforcement of tax laws and if it changed tax laws to eliminate large loopholes, increase effective taxation of upper-income households and businesses, and improve tax collection, which is often lax in the countries being assisted.

Another serious problem is the flight of capital from the debtor countries. The IMF could use its good offices to encourage all countries to adopt and enforce the necessary rules to preclude capital flight when it is contrary to the laws of the country of origin, violates an agreed-upon adjustment program, or when it represents proceeds from illegal activities, including drug trafficking. Because of their interest in preventing default on the outstanding debt and in arriving at a viable debt restructuring plan, debtor countries should be called upon to help work out an international system to prevent capital flight from countries faced with serious debt problems.

In an article published in November 1984, entitled "Where the Latin American Loans Went," Larry A. Sjaastad concluded that wealthy individuals recycled about one-third of the borrowed funds into investments in the United States and Europe. Drawing on data from a Federal Reserve study, Sjaastad pointed out that as the borrowed funds were funneled into the economies of Latin American countries, residents of the borrowing countries, who were sensitive to the declining value of the local currency, converted such currency into U.S. dollars, which were used to buy foreign assets. He calculates that from 1973 to 1984 residents of four countries, Argentina, Mexico, Brazil, and Venezuela, acquired about $100 billion in foreign assets (Sjaastad November 26, 1984, 195).

More recently, there has been a spate of reports about "money laundering." The first was that the Bank of Boston failed to make required reports to the Internal Revenue Service on transactions to banks in Switzerland and elsewhere in Europe totalling $1.2 billion. The IRS requires reports of cash transactions of more than $10,000. The Bank of Boston had to pay a $500,000 fine ("Money Laundering" March 18, 1985, 74). Subsequently, other banks began to come forward, primarily those in New England but also some of the larger New York banks, to tell of unreported large cash transactions which generally ran to millions of dollars per bank. It is ironic that some of the banks which had been "laundering" millions of dollars, some of which may have originated in Latin American debtor countries, also happen to be large creditors of such countries—their intake of such funds would be counterproductive for debt repayment.

and Peru—and another four were African countries—Zambia, Ghana, Malawi, and Sudan. The other two were the Philippines and Yugoslavia (Farnsworth April 4, 1985, E3). The countries with the three largest IMF loan programs also had the largest overall debt, or combined private and public debt.

During the 1970s, there was an important change in the composition and terms of the Latin American debt. At the beginning of the decade, about 40 percent of the credit flows were private; by the end of the decade, 80 percent were private and the balance was owed to either foreign governments or multilateral organizations such as the World Bank. Maturities were shortened, and there was a shift from fixed to variable interest rates (Traverso and Iglesias 1983, 23). The variable interest rates rose during the 1980s, producing economic shocks for the debtor countries.

The economies of Latin American countries were hurt by a decline in the U.S. demand for agricultural, mineral, and manufactured products. Latin American countries' exports to the U.S. therefore decreased at the same time that their debt service requirements were increasing because of the rising adjustable interest rates. Consequently, Latin American international production was reduced and urban unemployment rose significantly.[1]

Increasing unemployment and a deficit trade balance led to the combined debt and economic crises in Latin America. Under the IMF-approved economic adjustment programs put into effect during the past few years, the Latin American countries with large debts have had to restrict imports and consumption to a degree which has caused a decline in their people's purchasing power and in total economic activity. Unemployment increased further, and there has been explosive social unrest, including the ransacking of food stores in Brazil and in the Dominican Republic which led to the deaths of dozens of people.

The economic declines in the U.S. and Latin America fed upon each other. The decrease in purchasing power in debtor countries has, in turn, adversely affected the demand for U.S. products, which was a factor in the growth of a huge U.S. negative balance of merchandise trade. Unemployment contracted the U.S. market, and it became difficult for the debtor countries to increase exports to the U.S. and to attain sustained economic growth.

The recession became long and deep and it is not over yet in some of the countries under IMF programs. As the recessions in the industrialized countries and in the developing countries fed upon each other, the workers bore the brunt of economic adjustment, whether or not this was the intention. Production capacity and purchasing power must be balanced in domestic economies and in the international economy as a whole for the national and international economies to have sustained recoveries and stable growth.

The IMF adjustment programs also seem to neglect alternative conditions which could lead to a slowdown of inflation and could encourage balanced growth by spreading the burden of austerity to other portions of the society, thereby reducing the austerity that people of limited income must bear. The IMF could gain more popular support for its programs if it included stricter enforcement of tax laws and if it changed tax laws to eliminate large loopholes, increase effective taxation of upper-income households and businesses, and improve tax collection, which is often lax in the countries being assisted.

Another serious problem is the flight of capital from the debtor countries. The IMF could use its good offices to encourage all countries to adopt and enforce the necessary rules to preclude capital flight when it is contrary to the laws of the country of origin, violates an agreed-upon adjustment program, or when it represents proceeds from illegal activities, including drug trafficking. Because of their interest in preventing default on the outstanding debt and in arriving at a viable debt restructuring plan, debtor countries should be called upon to help work out an international system to prevent capital flight from countries faced with serious debt problems.

In an article published in November 1984, entitled "Where the Latin American Loans Went," Larry A. Sjaastad concluded that wealthy individuals recycled about one-third of the borrowed funds into investments in the United States and Europe. Drawing on data from a Federal Reserve study, Sjaastad pointed out that as the borrowed funds were funneled into the economies of Latin American countries, residents of the borrowing countries, who were sensitive to the declining value of the local currency, converted such currency into U.S. dollars, which were used to buy foreign assets. He calculates that from 1973 to 1984 residents of four countries, Argentina, Mexico, Brazil, and Venezuela, acquired about $100 billion in foreign assets (Sjaastad November 26, 1984, 195).

More recently, there has been a spate of reports about "money laundering." The first was that the Bank of Boston failed to make required reports to the Internal Revenue Service on transactions to banks in Switzerland and elsewhere in Europe totalling $1.2 billion. The IRS requires reports of cash transactions of more than $10,000. The Bank of Boston had to pay a $500,000 fine ("Money Laundering" March 18, 1985, 74). Subsequently, other banks began to come forward, primarily those in New England but also some of the larger New York banks, to tell of unreported large cash transactions which generally ran to millions of dollars per bank. It is ironic that some of the banks which had been "laundering" millions of dollars, some of which may have originated in Latin American debtor countries, also happen to be large creditors of such countries—their intake of such funds would be counterproductive for debt repayment.

and Peru—and another four were African countries—Zambia, Ghana, Malawi, and Sudan. The other two were the Philippines and Yugoslavia (Farnsworth April 4, 1985, E3). The countries with the three largest IMF loan programs also had the largest overall debt, or combined private and public debt.

During the 1970s, there was an important change in the composition and terms of the Latin American debt. At the beginning of the decade, about 40 percent of the credit flows were private; by the end of the decade, 80 percent were private and the balance was owed to either foreign governments or multilateral organizations such as the World Bank. Maturities were shortened, and there was a shift from fixed to variable interest rates (Traverso and Iglesias 1983, 23). The variable interest rates rose during the 1980s, producing economic shocks for the debtor countries.

The economies of Latin American countries were hurt by a decline in the U.S. demand for agricultural, mineral, and manufactured products. Latin American countries' exports to the U.S. therefore decreased at the same time that their debt service requirements were increasing because of the rising adjustable interest rates. Consequently, Latin American international production was reduced and urban unemployment rose significantly.[1]

Increasing unemployment and a deficit trade balance led to the combined debt and economic crises in Latin America. Under the IMF-approved economic adjustment programs put into effect during the past few years, the Latin American countries with large debts have had to restrict imports and consumption to a degree which has caused a decline in their people's purchasing power and in total economic activity. Unemployment increased further, and there has been explosive social unrest, including the ransacking of food stores in Brazil and in the Dominican Republic which led to the deaths of dozens of people.

The economic declines in the U.S. and Latin America fed upon each other. The decrease in purchasing power in debtor countries has, in turn, adversely affected the demand for U.S. products, which was a factor in the growth of a huge U.S. negative balance of merchandise trade. Unemployment contracted the U.S. market, and it became difficult for the debtor countries to increase exports to the U.S. and to attain sustained economic growth.

The recession became long and deep and it is not over yet in some of the countries under IMF programs. As the recessions in the industrialized countries and in the developing countries fed upon each other, the workers bore the brunt of economic adjustment, whether or not this was the intention. Production capacity and purchasing power must be balanced in domestic economies and in the international economy as a whole for the national and international economies to have sustained recoveries and stable growth.

The effects of the economic crisis in Latin America were described as follows in 1983 by Richard Feinberg, a senior fellow at the Overseas Development Council and an authority on the region:

> Per capita income has actually been falling in most countries. Whiplashed by the global recession, governments are under tremendous pressures to cut back on social welfare programs. Already meager social provisions are being withdrawn at the very moment when real wages are falling and unemployment lines are lengthening. Beggars are reappearing in Latin capitals where they had become only a sad memory, infant malnutrition is rising, and typhoid, malaria, and other diseases are spreading where medicines are in short supply. In brief, the gains in social welfare accumulated in Latin America over a generation are being undone by a cruel international economy.
>
> Latin America today is littered with underutilized machines and men. This wasted capacity and the resulting lost output can never be recovered. (Feinberg June 23, 1983, 2, 3)

IMF Economic Adjustment Programs

When an IMF member country requests a loan, the IMF staff studies the country's economy and then negotiates with the government to establish an economic adjustment program. The IMF also provides "advice." Private banks, who are creditors of the government or of private borrowers in the country, are also involved. Private banks usually extend additional credit to the debtors so that they can make interest payments. In addition, the banks usually have to rewrite outstanding loans to allow longer maturities, and may allow a grace period on principal repayments. The bankers will generally not go into a proposed refinancing program until the country has agreed to an economic adjustment program which the IMF has approved.

IMF approval of a proposed adjustment program, therefore, has been of great importance to countries seeking additional financing or more favorable repayment terms in order to avoid either default or a cutoff from international credit. Most countries seeking loans from the IMF or private sources or seeking to restructure debt repayment schedules, therefore, are not in a strong negotiating position with regard to the type of economic adjustment program to be adopted. The IMF claims that it does not impose austerity on its members through economic adjustment programs. Although this is literally true, it hides the reality of the situation: In recent years, most debtor countries have had little choice but to accept in large part the type of adjustment program desired by the IMF.

The requirements placed on the debtor country as part of the program, generally referred to as IMF "conditionality," are designed to enable that country to meet a debt repayment schedule by achieving a positive balance of exports over imports and by retaining access to new borrowing. Some of the conditions often included are a devaluation of the national currency, which leads to higher domestic and import prices but to lower export prices; a reduction in budget deficits, which generally entails reducing social programs; and tighter monetary and credit policies, which keep interest rates high.

In addition, the agreed adjustment program may often contain a specific provision for a reduction in workers' real wages by reducing the established cost-of-living adjustments for inflation. Thus, the 1983 IMF-approved program for Brazil was subject to a revision of the Brazilian wage adjustment law before it could be adopted. Although the Brazilian congress objected, the military government then in power reduced the wage adjustment from 100 percent to 80 percent of the inflation rate. Resultant social pressures arising from the very stringent wage adjustment measure, in the face of continuing high inflation, led to rioting. In May 1984, sugarcane workers burned crops in one town (Guariba), and were eventually given an increase in their piece-work rates. At the Fiat plant in Betim, 12,000 workers staged a strike for higher pay. Government teachers and health workers also were involved in disputes (House 1984). Faced with the possibility of similar upheavals, the democratic government that took office in Argentina at the end of 1983 resisted the adoption of measures to lower real wages, and Argentina negotiated with the IMF for many months before reaching an agreement.

The IMF defends its economic adjustment programs by taking the position that countries cannot permanently live beyond their means and that it is counterproductive to seek to avoid or postpone needed adjustment. There can be little dispute over that assertion, but it does not mean that the IMF program is the only type of adjustment that will succeed. In fact, there is reason to doubt the efficacy of a program which focuses primarily upon achieving debt repayment as soon as possible, but which includes measures to reduce wages and imports that have the effect of reducing consumption inequitably and restricting economic growth for extended periods. Experience indicates that programs with such conditionality have not given adequate weight to the question of whether measures which cause great hardship for workers and other people of limited income will be tolerated politically or whether political opposition will engender a significant probability of failure. The previously mentioned difficulties in Brazil, the Dominican Republic, and Sudan are examples of intolerance and failure. In addition, in early 1985 there was an intense public outburst in Jamaica when fuel prices were raised to meet IMF conditions; as of mid–April 1985, Argentina and Brazil were on the IMF "noncompliance" list; Liberia and Zambia were seriously behind in payments of principal and interest; and Third World delegates to a Washington IMF meeting were reportedly warning of the likelihood of widespread defaults among borrowers (Farnsworth 1985).

The IMF adjustment programs also seem to neglect alternative conditions which could lead to a slowdown of inflation and could encourage balanced growth by spreading the burden of austerity to other portions of the society, thereby reducing the austerity that people of limited income must bear. The IMF could gain more popular support for its programs if it included stricter enforcement of tax laws and if it changed tax laws to eliminate large loopholes, increase effective taxation of upper-income households and businesses, and improve tax collection, which is often lax in the countries being assisted.

Another serious problem is the flight of capital from the debtor countries. The IMF could use its good offices to encourage all countries to adopt and enforce the necessary rules to preclude capital flight when it is contrary to the laws of the country of origin, violates an agreed-upon adjustment program, or when it represents proceeds from illegal activities, including drug trafficking. Because of their interest in preventing default on the outstanding debt and in arriving at a viable debt restructuring plan, debtor countries should be called upon to help work out an international system to prevent capital flight from countries faced with serious debt problems.

In an article published in November 1984, entitled "Where the Latin American Loans Went," Larry A. Sjaastad concluded that wealthy individuals recycled about one-third of the borrowed funds into investments in the United States and Europe. Drawing on data from a Federal Reserve study, Sjaastad pointed out that as the borrowed funds were funneled into the economies of Latin American countries, residents of the borrowing countries, who were sensitive to the declining value of the local currency, converted such currency into U.S. dollars, which were used to buy foreign assets. He calculates that from 1973 to 1984 residents of four countries, Argentina, Mexico, Brazil, and Venezuela, acquired about $100 billion in foreign assets (Sjaastad November 26, 1984, 195).

More recently, there has been a spate of reports about "money laundering." The first was that the Bank of Boston failed to make required reports to the Internal Revenue Service on transactions to banks in Switzerland and elsewhere in Europe totalling $1.2 billion. The IRS requires reports of cash transactions of more than $10,000. The Bank of Boston had to pay a $500,000 fine ("Money Laundering" March 18, 1985, 74). Subsequently, other banks began to come forward, primarily those in New England but also some of the larger New York banks, to tell of unreported large cash transactions which generally ran to millions of dollars per bank. It is ironic that some of the banks which had been "laundering" millions of dollars, some of which may have originated in Latin American debtor countries, also happen to be large creditors of such countries—their intake of such funds would be counterproductive for debt repayment.

The general thrust of IMF adjustment programs has been to achieve a surplus in international accounts as soon as possible. This requires increased exports and reduced imports. The reduced imports, by themselves, can begin to hamper economic growth because it becomes more difficult to import replacements and parts for various types of production machinery, and even more difficult to import new machinery which can enhance production. Increased exports are encouraged, largely on the assumption that economic growth in the industrialized countries will open up those markets for more imports from the debtor countries. As put succinctly in a report on the deliberations of one 1982–83 study group: "The choice has been made, in other words, to bet on recovery" (Gwin 1984, 24).

The optimistic assumption about growth in the industrial countries was supported by the facts in 1983 and 1984. Combined economic growth for the industrialized OECD countries rose from 0 percent in 1982, to 2.3 percent in 1983, and to over 4.5 percent in 1984. As this economic recovery progressed, the larger debtor countries were able to improve their external-account positions significantly. Argentina, Brazil, Mexico, and Venezuela, which had a combined current-account deficit of $25 billion in 1981, achieved a combined $5.5 billion surplus in 1984. This was due in part to a sharp reduction in imports. In 1984, it was also due to an increase in exports. In particular, Mexico and Brazil were able to show large increases in exports (Bergsten, Cline, and Williamson 1985, 8).

However, the outlook began to change somewhat in early 1985. The United States—the "locomotive" of the world economy—which had a 6.8 percent rate of economic growth in 1984, experienced a slowdown. In the first quarter of 1985, only a 1.3 percent annual rate of real GNP growth was reported. Some of the progress in Latin America also slowed down. Reduced worldwide oil prices adversely affected the export income of Venezuela and Mexico. Brazil, which had a $13.1 billion trade surplus and a 4.4 percent growth rate in 1984, saw its overseas sales begin to decline—in fact, Brazil's exports actually dropped. In both Brazil and Argentina, inflation was running at a higher level than the target set by the IMF adjustment program. The IMF has since cut off credits to these two countries, presumably temporarily, thus removing its seal of approval, an action which held up Brazil's and Argentina's reschedulings of long-term debt with private banks (Riding March 31, 1985, F8; Kristoff March 31, 1985, E5).

A recently published IMF staff study reported on the success of 30 IMF adjustment programs in Africa in terms of the projected macroeconomic goals. The authors found that in fourteen programs where most or all of the policy measures recommended by the IMF were observed, a majority of the program targets were achieved; two of these fourteen programs (in Mali and Somalia) were apparently quite successful. In nine programs where the recommended policy measures were not generally observed, the targets were not attained. The evidence was inconclusive for seven programs. Economic growth targets were achieved in about one-fifth of the programs, inflation targets in about one-half, and external sector targets in about two-fifths. The target ratio of budget deficits to GDP was exceeded in two-thirds of the countries. (A review of the study can be found in "Fund Study Examines the Causes of Success in Economic Adjustment Programs in Africa," April 15, 1985, 113, 125–27.)

However, such success may not continue, given the assumption for growth in the industrial countries which underlies IMF adjustment programs. Three senior members of the Institute for International Economics stated in April 1985 that the global economic outlook remained uncertain and predicted that either growth in the OECD countries would remain about two and one-half percent annually, or a new global recession would develop. One of these economists had, in 1984, assumed that a three percent annual growth rate for OECD countries was necessary in order for large debtor countries to meet their payments. Furthermore, they presented a number of alternative innovations for the developing countries in bank lending policies in the event that the scheduled debt repayments could not be met despite the IMF adjustment program ("Fund Study Examines" April 15, 1985, 113, 125–27). The economists were hedging on the bet on recovery, but still no shift in policy was recommended to deal with issues that affected equity. In fact, some of the defenders of IMF policies have recently backed the status quo by stating that the IMF has helped debtor countries, because they would otherwise be worse off (Farnsworth April 14, 1985).

The latter view was also reflected in a June 1984 pamphlet issued by the International Monetary Fund over the signature of the managing director, J. de Larosière, entitled "Does the Fund Impose Austerity?" (Larosière June 1984). This pamphlet did not discuss the policy measures that are regularly excluded from adjustment programs. Instead, it set forth a number of propositions which really avoid the basic issue, which is that the assortment of economic policies that now comprise IMF adjustment programs may need to be redefined to address the question of equity. The first point in the pamphlet was that economic adjustment is inescapable because no country can live permanently beyond its means. As mentioned earlier, nobody can quarrel with that.

Second, Larosière stated that adjustment, as perceived by the International Monetary Fund, is not synonymous with lower growth rates in Latin America or with economic retrogression. He pointed out that Latin American growth rates had begun to decline before the Fund intervened in the affected countries. He also explained that the programs are not aimed at avoiding recession, but rather at achieving a balance-of-payments equilibrium which would open the way for more vigorous and lasting growth. The IMF's good intentions are not in doubt, but the record of IMF adjustment programs does raise doubts as to whether more vigorous and lasting growth will actually be achieved and when. In addition, one may ask whether there has not in fact been economic retrogression in some cases. Bolivia, for example, has gone through the following series of events several times: IMF adjustment programs, rampant inflation, general strikes, and suspension of IMF program approval (the present status). Peru, which is $600 million in arrears on the interest payments on its $13.5 billion debt, has to devote 55 percent of the value of its exports to the interest payments. The president-elect has stated that following the orthodox IMF approach would prevent any reactivation of Peru's economy; he and his advisers are talking of fashioning their own austerity program with concessions from the bank creditors, thereby bypassing the IMF in seeking a debt-restructuring program (Riding April 22, 1985, D8).

The third point made by Larosière is that while the adjustment programs entail sacrifices, the austerity measures required must be compared to alternatives. The question is whether the countries in economic difficulty would be better off with the results of a nonadjustment program that would not be supported by the Fund's resources. This comparison with an unspecified straw man leads to the obvious conclusion that the consequences of "nonadjustment" would have been harsher than what actually happened in 1983. However, the issue is whether IMF programs could be restructured to include policies that have been ruled out (because they are defined as political and social) but that could lead to a more equitable distribution of sacrifices among various population groups and to more sustainable economic improvement that would enhance the debtor countries' ability to make foreign-debt service payments.

Reform of IMF Adjustment Programs

In examining the question of possible reform of the IMF, attention must be given to those policy issues that are now excluded from IMF consideration, but which may critically affect the success of any adjustment program. Some of these issues are currently ruled out because they are considered the proper concern not of the IMF, but of the government in question or of another international body.

One policy question currently excluded from IMF programs is the question of income distribution. As a matter of fact, the fourth point in the Larosière pamphlet cited above, made with regard to social costs, states that "the way these costs are divided within the society is not a matter for the Fund to design, but a question of political choices to be made by the governments themselves." Income redistribution is therefore ruled out as a subject of concern because by definition it is cast as being either political or social. Others have stated that income distribution is relevant to economic policy and should be added to the list of critical variables used in evaluating the state of a country's economy. In fact, it has been noted that the stabilization measures of IMF adjustment programs, through such measures as currency devaluation, wage restraints, and public utility rate increases, have a definite effect upon real income distribution among various segments of the population in debtor countries. The relative lack of attention now given to tax reform and to administrative reform in IMF programs serves to protect the existing income distribution (see Williamson 1983c; Lichentsztejn 1983; Killick et al. 1984).

IMF conditionality does then have an impact on income distribution. Nevertheless, in an article published in 1983, an IMF representative took particular exception to the idea that the Fund might appropriately promote the improvement of income distribution along with its other objectives (Finch 1983). Finch claimed that the Fund "has not been established to give guidance on social and economic priorities." He went on to explain that the "voting system of the Fund was not designed to give it the moral authority to oversee priorities of a noneconomic nature," and he argued that the authorities of a country are the sole judges of its social and political priorities (Finch 1983).

Yet income distribution is an important determinant of an economy's ability to grow. Two basic facts which have affected income distribution in the U.S. in large part explain U.S. growth over the past two centuries. Preceding the accelerated industrial growth of the country there had been widespread distribution of government land at nominal prices. Because of this, when industrial growth gathered momentum in the United States during the second half of the nineteenth century, there was a large base of small farm owners who, with the aid of government-sponsored research, free education, and credit programs, improved their productivity. With their earnings, they increased their own investment and also accumulated savings that provided some of the needed U.S. industrial investment capital. Incidentally, the rapid industrial growth experienced by South Korea and Taiwan in recent times was also preceded by widespread, low-priced land distribution which occurred in both countries shortly after the Second World War.

The second factor affecting income distribution and growth in the U.S. was that as industrial productivity in the United States improved, the increased income was widely distributed in the form of higher wages, a process helped by unionization as the country became increasingly industrialized. Distribution of income, therefore, was such that there was a balance between production and purchasing power which fostered balanced economic growth, although the balance has been temporarily interrupted periodically for business cycle adjustments. These two historical facts highlight the importance of equitable income distribution for economic growth.

Another issue currently excluded from the planning of IMF programs is the acceptability of the policies required under adjustment programs to the citizenry of the country in question. The IMF should increase its communication with nongovernmental groups in the debtor countries in order to assess the reactions of the various sectors in the society to the proposed programs. Ideally, the labor movement and other domestic organizations in each country should be able to exercise a degree of influence over the government so that the views of such groups are reflected to some degree in the policy instructions given to the country's IMF director. The governments of the debtor countries would also arrive at more workable programs and would enjoy broader-based support for such programs if they consulted with labor and other organizations and brought the views of these groups to their negotiations with the IMF.

The IMF tendency to avoid contact with nongovernmental organizations is apparently designed to avoid accusations that it undermines governmental authority. It would still seem to be desirable, however, that the IMF develop the means to judge the potential acceptability of various proposed conditions to the society as a whole and to influential groups within the society. Some channel, such as an ombudsman office or an organization-liaison office, might be established through which nongovernmental organizations could voice their views and which would then transmit these views to the IMF negotiators.

Channels of communication with such groups are not open in many countries where there is a totalitarian government, a military government, some form of benign dictatorship, or an entrenched ruling oligarchy. The IMF is at a handicap in attempting to negotiate an effective adjustment program with such governments, a fact the IMF may not recognize. If a program condition is established that will place unnecessarily harsh economic pressures upon workers or other low-income groups, the risks that the economic adjustment program will fail and that debt repayment schedules will not be met are increased. Therefore, for reasons of prudence and principle, the IMF should not lend to the nondemocratic governments. (It might be noted that two other international agencies, the United Nations and the International Labor Organisation, have adopted conventions which address this problem in calling for observance of human rights and freedom of association.)

In addition to addressing the questions of income distribution and communication with nongovernmental bodies, IMF programs should be reformed to deal with some of the macroeconomic policies of industrialized nations that give rise to and have an impact on IMF adjustment programs. The fiscal and monetary policies of the leading industrial countries, and the resultant interest rates, affect the exchange rates of less developed countries, the interest rates on loans these countries receive, and their trade positions. For example, the high interest rates which resulted from U.S. domestic monetary policy to bring down inflation caused European countries to adopt somewhat restrictive monetary policies and to keep interest rates at higher levels in order to counteract the outflow of capital attracted by high returns in the U.S. As a consequence, developing countries suffered from high interest rates on their loans. On the other hand, the resultant high value of the dollar has helped developing countries' exports compete with U.S. producers in the U.S. and elsewhere. At the same time, however, the U.S. is suffering from a massive, growing negative trade balance which contributes significantly to economic slowdown in the U.S., contracting the largest market for products from developing countries.

The whole quagmire of misaligned exchange rates and abnormal trade imbalances cries out for an international solution, and highlights the contrast between the significant progress that has been made in developing an international economy and the continuing lack of adequate international institutions to address the intertwined exchange rate and trade problems. While the IMF is charged with promotion of exchange stability and exercises "firm surveillance" over the exchange rate policies of its members, it does not provide a forum for the negotiation of an exchange rate alignment that will promote greater international trade and economic growth. The necessary international consultations and negotiations might be undertaken under expanded auspices of the IMF, the OECD, or in a special forum created for the purpose. In the absence of institutional innovations to address the international exchange problem, the central bank of each country will continue to give its paramount concern to domestic economic problems.

Furthermore, as has recently been suggested by some European officials, there is a need for international discussions on monetary policy which will parallel and be coordinated with discussions for modified trade agreements. Since the two types of policies necessarily interact, negotiations on the two policy matters must be coordinated. Some helpful trade-offs might even be negotiated; for example, country A might agree to follow a monetary policy to lower interest rates in return for lowering of tariffs or other barriers by country B.

Another macroeconomic factor that must be addressed is the wage gap between the developing and developed countries. Wages in some developing countries amount to only a small fraction of the wages paid for comparable work in the United States. The adoption of the foregoing monetary and exchange rate policy remedies would encourage more stable exchange rates and increased international trade. However, such measures would do little to close the serious competitive gap between prices of the products of the less developed industrializing countries and those of the U.S. and other advanced industrial countries, a price gap due to the huge wage gap. If U.S. producers sought to be price competitive, they would be required to pay wages that are so low they would cause a significant reduction in the standard of living and a contraction of the U.S. economy.

Allowing the low-wage products of many developing countries into the United States without any restriction would mean increased unemployment. There has been, over about the last fifteen years, a long-term upward trend in the U.S. unemployment rate. That unemployment rate has moved in a pattern generally inverse to the business cycle, and has been rising from one peak to the next and from one trough to the next. The resulting long and deep recessions have caused considerable slowdowns in economic growth, not when they occur but long afterwards as lost product income, savings, and capital formation continue to retard the economy. Incidentally, U.S. consumers get a relatively small part of the wage differential advantage, as the foreign producers, exporters, importers, and retailers each take advantage of higher prices in the U.S. market to increase their markup.

The worldwide recession during 1981 and 1982 illustrated the effect of a U.S. economic contraction on other developed and less developed countries. Against this background, and in the absence of multilateral measures to address the issue, the U.S. labor movement has advocated import quotas for various products which would permit a margin of growth for LDCs without overwhelming the U.S. economy. The advocates of pure free trade claim that workers who become unemployed because of imports should seek work elsewhere under the thesis that growth requires both labor and capital resources to be continually reallocated to their most efficient uses. (This thesis is even used as a rationale for curtailing unemployment compensation on the assumption that disincentives for people to move out of declining industries and areas into growing ones must be removed. In a more formal statement of the thesis, it has been said that benefits for the unemployed and unions do not allow labor "to clear the market.") In other words, labor should be treated as a commodity. That notion was outlawed in the United States when the Clayton Anti-Trust Act was enacted in 1914 with the declaration that "labor is not a commodity," exempting unions from legal characterization as a trust. The growth of unions in the U.S. during most of the intervening 70 years helped provide an income distribution that fostered balanced, long-term economic growth.

Multilateral measures should be pursued, perhaps through IMF programs, to address the international wage gap in order to foster long-term international economic growth.

Conclusion

In short, the international economy does not have an income distribution that fosters balanced economic growth, even to the less-than-satisfactory degree that is currently found in the United States. IMF adjustment programs tend to aggravate the inequitable distribution of income and economic imbalance which hampers growth in individual countries and in the international economy as a whole. It is essential that the economic adjustment programs of the IMF are modified to reduce both economic inequity and economic disequilibrium.

Note

1. Urban employment rose in Argentina from 2.0 percent in 1979 to 4.9 percent in 1983; in Brazil, over the same years, it rose from 6.4 percent to 6.8 percent; in Bolivia, from 6.2 percent to 12.6 percent; in Colombia, from 8.9 percent to 11.0 percent; in Chile, from 13.4 percent to 19.7 percent; in Mexico, from 5.7 percent to 12.5 percent; and in Peru, from 6.5 percent to 8.8 percent (see ECLA Information Service 1984, 11).

References

Bergsten, C. Fred, William R. Cline, and John Williamson. April 1985. *Bank Lending to Developing Countries: The Policy Alternatives.* Washington, D.C.: Institute for International Economics.

Bernstein, Edward M. September 1984. "Do We Need A New Bretton Woods?" *Finance and Development*. Washington, D.C.: IMF and the World Bank, p. 6.

Dell, Sidney. 1983. "Stabilization: The Political Economy of Overkill," in *IMF Conditionality*, edited by John Williamson. Washington, D.C.: Institute for International Economics.

ECLA Information Service. January 1984. "Preliminary Balance of the Latin American Economy in 1983." No. 387/388. Table 4, p. 11.

Farnsworth, Clyde. April 14, 1985. "The IMF's Help Can Sometimes Hurt," *New York Times*, p. E3.

Feinberg, Richard E. June 23, 1983. Prepared Statement before the Subcommittee on Western Hemisphere Affairs and International Economic Policy and Trade, Committee on Foreign Affairs, U.S. House of Representatives, Washington, D.C.

Finch, C. David. 1983. "Adjustment Policies and Conditionality," in *IMF Conditionality*, John Williamson, ed. Washington, D.C.: Institute for International Economics.

"Fund Study Examines the Causes of Success in Economic Adjustment Programs in Africa," *IMF Survey*, April 15, 1985, pp. 113, 125–27.

Gwin, Catherine. 1984. *Beyond Debt Crisis Management*, a report prepared for the Carnegie Foundation Study Group on International Financial Cooperation. Washington, D.C.: Carnegie Endowment for International Peace.

House, Richard. June 17, 1984. "Debts' Social Costs Plague Latin Nations," *Washington Post*.

Killick, Tony, Graham Bird, Jennifer Shipley, and Mary Sutton. 1984. "The IMF: Case for a Change in Emphasis," in *Adjustment Crisis in the Third World*, edited by Richard E. Feinberg and Valeriana Kallab. Washington, D.C.: Overseas Development Council.

Kristoff, Nicholas. March 31, 1985. "That International Debt Bomb Hasn't Stopped Ticking," *New York Times*, p. E5.

Larosière, J. de. June 1984. *Does the Fund Impose Austerity?* Washington, D.C.: International Monetary Fund.

Lichtensztejn, Samuel. 1983. "IMF Developing Countries: Conditionality and Strategy," in *IMF Conditionality*, John Williamson, ed. Washington, D.C.: Institute for International Economics.

"Money Laundering: How It Works and What Can be Done," *Business Week*, March 18, 1985, p. 74.

Riding, Alan F. March 31, 1985. "A Perilous Dip in Brazil's Exports," *New York Times*, p. F8.

Riding, Alan F. April 22, 1985. "Anxiety Growing over Peru's Debt," *New York Times*, p. D8.

Sjaastad, Larry A. November 26, 1984. "Where the Latin American Loans Went," *Fortune*, p. 195.

"The Sudan After the Fall," *New York Times*, April 4, 1985 (editorial).

Traverso, Carlos Alzamora, and Enrique V. Iglesias. May 16, 1983. "Bases for a Latin American Response to the International Economic Crisis," United Nations Economic and Social Council.

Williamson, John. 1983a. "The Lending Policies of the International Monetary Fund," in *IMF Conditionality*, edited by John Williamson. Washington, D.C.: Institute for International Economics, p. 607.

______, ed. 1983b. *IMF Conditionality.* Washington, D.C.: Institute for International Economics.

______. 1983c. "On Judging the Success of IMF Policy Advice," in *IMF Conditionality*, edited by John Williamson. Washington, D.C.: Institute for International Economics.

5

The IMF in Africa: A Case of Inappropriate Technology

Robert S. Browne

A cat should not be expected to bark.
—Anonymous

In this essay I will attempt to address a number of ethical considerations which attach themselves to the International Monetary Fund as it operates in Africa. The essay is not exhaustive nor is it limited solely to IMF activities. Instead, its scope encompasses the operation of the international monetary system, and while the IMF is the basic operating vehicle for this system, it is not, strictly speaking, coterminous with it.

Moral values are in large measure culturally determined, so the inventory of universally accepted moral absolutes is limited. Fortunately, however, there is some degree of consensus as to what constitutes ethical and unethical practice within defined areas of conduct. For the purposes of this paper, the explicit moral values which provide the norm (against which assessments are made) are: a strong aversion to inequity, an assurance of the dignity of the individual, and a commitment to providing a minimum standard of decency to all persons. It is readily admitted that this statement of values lacks precision, and that, furthermore, the world contains many inequities, both natural and manmade. As a minimum condition, however, human effort should not be expended to increase these inequities and any and all acts which have that result are by definition unethical. Of course, inequities often arise as a result of forces beyond human control, or as unintentional by-products of human action. Well-intended actions whose ultimate results are to spread inequity would not normally be considered unethical *ex post facto*, but once their inequitable character was detected they could hardly be continued without incurring moral censure. This, then, is the standard against which I will examine the IMF's operations in Africa.

The IMF's Evolving Relationship with Africa

The IMF recently celebrated its fortieth anniversary. Although it has been attracting some unflattering commentary in recent years, it has been held in high esteem by persons who were familiar with its work over most of its lifetime. Essentially, the IMF's charge has been to maintain monetary stability and to facilitate the growth of world trade. Although the original Articles of Agreement did not mention the term "international monetary system," there was a general belief that the Articles did in fact provide for the creation of such a system (Gold 1984, 24), popularly referred to as the Bretton Woods system.

Although much of the "system" was spelled out in the Articles of Agreement, either explicitly or implicitly, the system as we know it today is the result of four decades of development—shaping and reshaping made in an effort to meet the changing needs of the international economic community. Fund critics have sometimes charged that these changes have come too slowly and have been inadequate for the task. Others have argued that the basic foundation upon which the IMF structure rested was destroyed in 1971, when the link between gold and the dollar was broken, and that, at least for the sake of legitimacy, the IMF must be reformed.

The Fund has faced strong pressures to expand its role beyond the realm of maintaining monetary stability and facilitating trade. Its members, as a result, have extended its domain far beyond the making of short-term balance-of-payments loans and the occasional negotiation of exchange rate modifications, the activities which constituted the Fund's original agenda. The Fund's programs have changed because the world has changed.

Among the many changes which have affected the work of the IMF has been the political emergence of Africa, currently consisting of 52 independent nations and one colony. At the Fund's inception there were only three independent African nations, and, like most Third World nations, their role in the international monetary and financial scheme was virtually nonexistent. Even today, Africa's importance in international monetary affairs arises primarily from her international indebtedness. Absent this, it is doubtful that the IMF would find itself very preoccupied with Africa.

During its early years, the Fund concerned itself primarily with the industrialized nations. These were the countries which, by dint of their economic strength and the volume of their trade, constituted the principal participants in and beneficiaries of the international monetary system. This reality was reflected in the allocation of shareholder quotas in the Fund and in the distribution of Fund voting power. The U.S. was assigned (and retains) the largest quota and the largest vote, a reflection of its tremendous postwar economic strength compared with the war-devastated land of

Europe and Japan and with the colonies and near-colonies of Africa and Latin America. Rimmer de Vries, the well-known international financial expert at Morgan Guaranty Trust Company, wrote as follows (1980):

> Increased IMF lending to developing countries represents a significant departure from past lending practices of the Fund. The industrial countries traditionally have been the principal "users" of the IMF resources, accounting for about two-thirds of all drawings since 1947. It has not been until the past year or so that the developing countries have become the principal users of Fund resources.

The first IMF stand-by loan to sub-Saharan Africa was made in 1963, in the Fund's sixteenth year, and there were relatively few loans to Africa before the mid-1970s. This may not be surprising, given that most of Africa did not gain independence until about 1960, with several countries not lowering the colonial flag until the 1970s. There are, however, a number of other reasons which limited IMF activity in Africa, not least of which was the fact that the IMF was not conceived to deal with the financial problems most common in the Third World. The Fund was designed to provide short-term financing to enable countries to work their way out of payments deficits and thus avoid contractionary or restrictive measures which could destabilize the system and inhibit global trade. Weak African economies were not a likely focus for major IMF activity since they represented little threat to the system—although they certainly were provided with loans when they requested them. The reality was that they had little need for short-term, IMF-type loans.

By the late 1970s, however, much of Africa had become burdened with debt which it was unable to service. This automatically drew Africa into the domain of IMF concerns, which resulted in a massive increase in IMF lending in Africa. But the new relationship has not been without acrimony. A by-product of this massive IMF lending in Africa has been a wave of sentiment against the IMF. The Fund has been charged with having a number of faults and deficiencies, and the ethical nature of some IMF policies and actions has been questioned. In the following pages we will examine a number of these changes.

With the exception of some of the former Portuguese colonies, virtually all African nations have routinely joined the IMF upon independence. Why? Was IMF membership viewed as a necessary sign of national adulthood, like the ubiquitous national airline, for example? Or, were there real benefits to be derived from membership? A major incentive was undoubtedly access to World Bank resources, for which IMF membership is a prerequisite. The IMF itself had little to offer to Africa: Africa's financial needs were mainly for long-term development funds, and such financing was not in the IMF's tool kit. Prior to 1974, the IMF program of greatest interest to the Africans was the Compensatory Financing Facility (CFF), which met the need of the commodity-exporting LDCs to have access to low conditionality financing to meet their special problems. ("Conditionality" refers to the requirements the IMF imposes on borrowers as a part of the loan agreement.) In 1974, the oil facility subsidy account was established to help ease the balance-of-payments pressures created by the sharp increases in the price of petroleum, and in 1975, purchases from this facility accounted for 53 percent of the Fund's total gross flows to Africa. Easier access to IMF resources was also made available through creation of both the Trust Fund and the interest subsidy account, and it began to appear as if the IMF were making a genuine effort to accommodate the needs of its LDC members.

Despite this evidence of liberalization in the IMF's lending policy, the IMF, with its continuing emphasis on providing short-term liquidity, was hardly an appropriate institution to address the long-term structural (solvency) problems of most African countries. Yet, presumably in pursuit of its mandate to maintain international monetary stability, the IMF gradually assumed the leading role in addressing Africa's financial problems (by preventing widespread default on Africa's international loans). The IMF interposed itself between the borrowers and the lenders as a certifying agent without whose approval commercial lending, World Bank funding, and, increasingly, bilateral funding would not have been forthcoming.

Unfortunately, at the very moment of assuming these enlarged responsibilities, the Fund retreated from its liberalized posture, allowing its lower-conditionality facilities to expire, retracting its expanding access provisions, and channeling African loans increasingly toward the upper tranche, high-conditionality facilities. Whereas low-conditionality funds accounted for 80 percent of Africa's IMF loans in 1975 and 1976, by 1980 nearly 70 percent of IMF lending to Africa involved higher conditionality. Recently, some light has been shed on the reasons for this reactionary policy shift. In a remarkably candid article, the senior staff member of the National Security Council responsible for international affairs from 1981–83 explained a 1982 public shift by the U.S. from initial opposition to an IMF quota increase to ultimate support for it.

> Initial administration attitudes toward the International Monetary Fund (IMF) were thus understandably skeptical. This institution was perceived as drifting away from its primary role as lender of last resort and thereby weakening its leverage for economic adjustment by making more generous, longer-term loans earlier in the adjustment process. . . . The administration valued the IMF more for its policy than for its financing role. The administration concluded that until IMF policies shifted—again, at the margin—caution on new funding made sense. (Nau 1984–85, 24–25)

The Africans had no power to prevent a hardening of the IMF's terms just as they were moving to become major borrowers. Because the IMF assumed the roles of global debt collector and certifier of national creditworthiness, many African countries were left with no alternative but to become IMF clients, sometimes with dire consequences in terms of abruptly enhanced austerity, social unrest, and political upheaval. It is from this type of scenario that the IMF has received its most negative image, but the litany of complaints goes far beyond the issue of conditionality and indeed beyond the IMF itself. The international monetary system as now constituted is itself in flagrant violation of the ethical norm established here. The IMF, as the corporate embodiment of that system, should accept the charges leveled against it and transmit them to the member states that are responsible for shaping the offensive policies.

Evidence of Inequities: IMF Currency Reserves, SDRs, and Gold Stocks

Under the Bretton Woods system, a member country's currency is used as the international unit of account and reserve currency, and no yielding of sovereignty on the part of the currency-issuing country is required. Although a number of inequities surround such a curious arrangement, I am only interested in those consequences which represent unambiguous *extensions* of the area of inequity. One such inequity is the ability which this arrangement confers on the country issuing the reserve currency, in this case the U.S., to manipulate this international unit for its own benefit while ignoring the consequences this manipulation visits on others. Currently, for example, the U.S. monetary authorities elect to have very high interest rates. These rates contribute to a very high international value for the dollar and thereby impose unwarranted burdens on countries with large dollar-denominated debts and imports, such as African countries. To defend this practice by arguing, as some do, that the strong dollar attracts imports to the U.S. means little to Africa. Africa's sales to the U.S. are not so great in any case, and African exports are mainly commodities and minerals, items for which the demand is considerably less responsive to the strong dollar than is the demand for manufactured goods, which are widely produced in some other Third World countries.

A particularly controversial result of this system of employing the dollar as the international reserve currency and unit of account is that the U.S. has been able to run a virtually unlimited deficit in its domestic budget and to finance it largely by obliging foreigners to hold dollars. The objections to this privileged status for any currency have a long-hallowed tradition. We need cite only the fact that both of the architects of the Bretton Woods Agreement, Harry Dexter White and John Maynard Keynes, proposed that the postwar monetary system be based upon a new neutral international currency (which White called "unitas" and Keynes "bancor"). Apparently they recognized the strains created by the use of either a precious metal, whose supply would be unpredictable and problematic, or a national currency, which would be subjected to the domestic whims of the issuing country. The idea for a new international reserve currency was killed by the American government, which not surprisingly wished to retain the benefits which accrued to it from the unique and powerful role played by the dollar as the currency of international trade, investment, and banking. Perhaps the most prominent objector to this use of the dollar as the international reserve currency was President Charles de Gaulle of France, who complained bitterly about the ability of the U.S. to prosecute the war in Vietnam and oblige the rest of the world to pay for it. (Certainly, this practice violates our ethical norm with a vengeance.)

The restrictive consequences of the world's reliance on the supply of independently generated U.S. dollars for its liquidity is becoming intolerable, especially for the poor African countries whose access to dollars is extremely limited. The Group of 24 has repeatedly called for a substantial allocation of special drawing rights (SDRs), the international reserve currency which the IMF began to issue in 1969 as a first step toward "making the special drawing right the principal reserve asset in the international monetary system" (Article VII, Section 7; Article XXII). Indeed, from the tone of the plaintive communiqué which the Group of 24 issued the day preceding the Spring 1984 meeting of the Interim Committee, one suspects (as rumor strongly suggests) that it is the U.S. veto which prevents at least a modest expansion in SDRs at this time.

> Ministers deplored the fact that, in spite of a vast majority of Fund membership being in favor of an SDR allocation, no allocation had so far been made in the fourth basic period, thereby giving wrong signals to the international community regarding the commitment to make the SDR the principal reserve asset. They urged member countries that have not so far found it possible to agree to an allocation to urgently reconsider their position so that political consensus for a substantial SDR allocation would be developed in the Interim Committee. (Group of 24, 1984, 118)

The U.S. has stated publicly that it is opposed to a new issuance of SDRs. Whether its vote is solely responsible for preventing this broadening of the monetary stock is unknown. It is a fact that the U.S., with 19 percent of the votes on the IMF board, is uniquely able to veto virtually all important policy matters (such matters require an 85 percent majority for passage). This fact leads to wide suspicion that the U.S. is responsible, through the veto, for much of the IMF's illiberal policies toward Third World countries. This suspicion inevitably arises when a minority insists on retaining the covert power to deny the wishes of the majority. Although flagrant rejection of democratic practice does not qualify as unethical under my definition (because a respect for democratic values is not sufficiently universal to warrant its being considered a norm), it is clearly an unbecoming stance for any government and for the American government in particular. A privileged veto may have appeared to be a reasonable concession at the Fund's inception, when the U.S. was expected to provide the bulk of the resources to launch and maintain the institution. The veto has no justification whatsoever in today's world, and should be removed as part of a thoroughgoing restructuring of the IMF so as to make it more reflective of today's international relationships.

The matter of how to allocate SDRs raises interesting ethical questions. The LDCs have long argued that SDR allocations should be utilized as a fairly painless and efficient way to make an income transfer from the rich to the poor (the liquidity-aid link), an action which has been vigorously resisted by some of the wealthier countries who prefer to allocate SDRs on the basis of the existing quotas in the Fund. Because issuing SDRs is basically a costless act, the fairest method of allocating them would appear to be on an equal per capita basis (which would be neutral insofar as resource transfers are concerned). To allocate them according to existing quotas, as required by the present IMF Articles of Agreement, would seem to create an expansion of existing inequities and would thus violate our ethical norm. However, to skew SDR allocation toward the poorer nations would be an act of generosity well beyond the call of equity (although highly desirable in terms of alleviating the liquidity problems of the poorer countries and of shoring up the beleaguered international financial system).

In stark contrast with the SDR link, however, is the matter of allocating the increase in the value of gold which has occurred since the Bretton Woods Agreement was repudiated, especially of that gold held by the IMF. In 1976, the IMF, having decided that gold would play no further official role in the Fund, agreed to distribute one-third of its gold stock: 25 million ounces were sold to IMF members in proportion to their quotas at the price of $35 per ounce, while a further 25 million ounces were sold at public auction with the profits going to the Trust Fund for the benefit of the poorer developing countries. The justification for having allocated any of the enhanced value of the IMF's gold stock on the basis of quotas is dubious, and, as with the SDRs, a minimal ethical norm would call for the distribution to be on an equal per capita basis. The creation of the Trust Fund for the poorer countries was a commendable act of generosity, as well as a partial correction of the inequity arising from the chance distribution of gold reserves at the time of demonetization. (According to one article [Bradsky and Sampson 1981], the developed market economy countries enjoyed a net gain of $414 billion, or $521 per capita, on the revaluation of gold, using the admittedly high gold prices of 1979. The non-oil developing countries gained only $28 billion, or $15 per capita, while the least developed received $0.7 billion, or $3 per capita.)

The case for further disposition of IMF gold stocks is a strong one. Both the linked SDR and the gold seignorage Trust Fund concept offer relatively painless ways to ease the debt crisis of the poorest countries and to move them back toward the path of growth. The payments would promptly flow toward the creditor countries anyway, but in the process the banks would have their loans serviced and the LDCs would find that the pains associated with their adjustment efforts would be to some degree moderated and the adjustment itself perhaps rendered more achievable.

A case can also be made on the grounds of equity: the enhanced value of gold stock held in country reserves should also be shared with those other countries which, having chosen to accept the IMF's assurance that holding dollars was the equivalent of holding gold, consequently eschewed the holding of gold reserves. These are mainly poor countries, and to allow the windfall arising from the IMF's demonetization of gold to accrue mainly to the rich countries merely repeats the all-too-common phenomenon of the rich getting richer and the poor getting poorer.

To summarize this section, which focuses on the IMF as the embodiment of the international monetary system, we can say that the very manner in which the system is structured enhances global inequities and should therefore be characterized as unethical. The installation of a neutral international reserve currency (as called for in the IMF's Articles) and the removal of the U.S. veto over IMF policy constitute vital steps toward raising the moral stature of the IMF. A revision of IMF quotas to make them more reflective of today's relationships may also be in order. An immediate issuance of zero- or low-interest SDRs, allocated on a per capita basis rather than on a quota basis, and further disposition of IMF gold stocks along the lines of the Trust Fund model are rational ways to ease present inequities. These are also effective means for easing the debt crisis of the poor countries and getting them back on a growth path.

IMF Fails to Address Long-term African Development Needs

The foregoing complaints concern the overall operations of the global monetary system and only incidently deal with the specific actions of the IMF. There is another family of complaints which arise directly from the operational program of the Fund in Africa. They have to do with the manner in which the IMF imposes the adjustment process upon its clients.

A complaint generally put forth by both Fund supporters and detractors is that the Fund's ability to impose the burden of adjustment on various of its members is uneven. Members who are running a surplus in their balance of payments may be as disruptive to maintenance of international monetary stability as those who are encountering deficits; oftentimes it is precisely their domestic policies which are creating or exacerbating the deficits of the others. The Fund's leverage for imposing adjustment, however, derives primarily from its role as lender, and since the surplus countries have no need to borrow from the Fund, the Fund has little ability to influence their actions. This lack of symmetry in the Fund's ability to distribute the burden of adjustment constitutes a serious flaw in the operation of the Fund. Its inequity certainly raises ethical considerations. This is a flaw which has until now eluded remedial action despite broad general agreement that it should be corrected.

Although there are some differences among the conditionalities which the IMF imposes in each case of adjustment, the general pattern is predictable and entails a strong component of demand management, requiring reductions in government spending, restrictions on domestic and international credit creation, and enhanced revenue collection. Reductions in imports and currency devaluation are also likely to be mandated, and targets may be set for such variables as output growth, the money supply, and the permissible level of inflation. The purpose of such conditionalities is to permit the servicing and restructuring of the foreign debt while the balance of payments is brought into an equilibrium sufficient to restore the country's creditworthiness, attract new funds, and establish a basis for growth.

The effort to implement such programs as these has been the cause of much difficulty for the countries in question and has earned the IMF its negative image throughout much of the Third World. Adjustment programs mean austerity by their very nature, so it is perhaps not surprising that they arouse negative responses and in some cases lead to rioting and the overthrow of governments. A country, like an individual, can live beyond its means for only as long as its creditors permit it to do so, and when that limit is reached retrenchment is inevitable—an ideologically neutral reality which all governments presumably understand. In fact, among African leaders there seems to be little objection in principle to the concept of conditionality as such, or to the need for balanced budgets.

Instead, abstracting from the overarching Third World complaints about the inequities in the operation of the international monetary system (detailed above) and in the global trading system, the major conflict arises over how this balance is to be achieved, and within what time frame. There have been repeated instances in Africa where the performance targets agreed to by the borrower have proved to be unachievable and the loan has been suspended after release of only the first or second tranche. Indeed, this has almost been the pattern in Africa, as detailed in a recent study published by the IMF itself (Zulu and Nsouli 1985).

The IMF study lists three principal factors responsible for the unsuccessful implementation of its programs: unforeseen developments, insufficient political support by the government, and the appropriateness of the targets. Although the report offers little insight into what is meant by appropriateness of the targets, target achievement was measured within the time frame of one year, so speed was obviously an element in rating the success of efforts to meet the target results. This corroborates a classic complaint about IMF ajustment programs and provides the basis for the charge that the IMF, handicapped by limited resources and structurally geared toward short-term adjustment situations, is an inappropriate vehicle for addressing the African countries' economic crises, which are generally crises of solvency rather than liquidity.

But is there an ethical issue here? The question is whether the IMF merits being characterized as an unethical ogre because it demands that a government cut its spending abruptly, promptly devalue its currency by quite large amounts, and cut back even further the already sharply reduced level of imports—knowing that the result will visit severe hardships on the poorest elements of the society in the form of higher prices for staples, increased unemployment, possibly lower wages, and diminished social services. The answer is not an easy one, for budget cuts and austerity by definition mean that someone must bear a burden. The IMF defends itself by arguing that (a) the adjustment would have to be made eventually and the presence of the IMF actually eases the process; and (b) the borrower chooses what budget cuts it wishes to make, not the IMF (conceivably, military or other less socially wrenching expenditures could be cut rather than food subsidies or public employees). The Fund disclaims any responsibility for determining where these cuts are made on the grounds that to do so would be an unwarranted interference with the sovereignty of the borrowing country.

There is a genuine dilemma here, perhaps several. To be sure, the IMF is already infringing upon the borrower's sovereignty when it imposes any conditions at all. This is unavoidable, because all lenders impose conditions to help insure a loan's repayment. The issue, then, is at best one of the permissible degree of infringement which lender, borrower, and the larger society find acceptable. One possible way of dealing with the problem might be to include provisions for the least-favored segment of the society to be somehow insulated from the effects of the conditionalities. The implementation of such provisions may test the wisdom of Solomon, however, for the poor in every society are relatively ineffective in obtaining whatever rights and benefits the society may award them.

Not only are the poor penalized by the typical adjustment program, but frequently they are penalized disproportionately. Where the adjustment burden is inequitably shared there is clearly an ethical issue involved, and the obligation of the IMF to forestall such an expansion of inequity becomes considerably stronger. The dilemma which emerges here is that the IMF's general growth model calls for the attraction of investment capital to the borrowing country. Among the customary incentives for attracting such capital are low wages and the ability to repatriate profits, both of which conflict with the immediate interest of the poor and working classes while fitting neatly into most adjustment programs. Redirection of resources from labor to capital, from the poor to the rich, although unethical, may in fact be exactly what is desired by the IMF development scenario from the perspective of international competitive trading.

Relative to worker productivity, wages in Africa are generally considered to be much higher than in some other Third World regions, especially South Asia, so that this type of deliberately induced inequity may have sound theoretical justification. The reality, however, is that foreign private capital shows so little enthusiasm for investing in Africa, and the amount of African domestic private capital is believed to be so negligible that there would appear to be little justification for a policy of reverse income transfers for the purpose of attracting capital flows. The Africanization of the colonial bureaucracy may indeed have saddled the salaried sector of some African economies with too high a wage level, but the aggregate reduction of real wage levels throughout the economy is likely to inflict pain entirely out of proportion to any benefits achieved, not to speak of the fact that the spirit of such a reverse income transfer seriously violates the economic goals and social philosophy of most African countries. Africa probably needs another two decades of concessional aid flows to bring its human and physical infrastructure up to a level where it can become a magnet for private investment. The so-called economic miracles in Asia which are cited so often in the literature as "models"—South Korea and Taiwan—began to "take off" only after a certain infrastructural threshold had been reached, funded by massive aid flows. Africa will require an equivalent preparation, and the development climate is considerably less inviting now than it was when these Asian "miracles" were building.

Yet another dilemma with moral overtones arises from possible conflicts of interest on the part of African leadership elites, conflicts between their personal financial activities and the best interests of their countries. These situations can range from crude instances of mishandling of funds by financial systems lacking adequate accountability and controls to more sophisticated instances of capital flight. Third World elites are known to transfer and maintain vast sums of money abroad on a clandestine basis. Attraction of such funds back to the home countries could go far toward reversing the economic crisis, but there may be little that the IMF or anyone else can do to bring this about. IMF officials complain, however, that one means to retard future capital flight, devaluing generally overvalued African currencies to bring them more in line with their real value, is often vigorously resisted by borrower governments, ostensibly, of course, for other reasons. Here the charge of unethical practices rests on the borrower rather than on the IMF, so diplomatic sensitivites preclude its being a topic of open discussion.

The problem is further complicated by the fact that the intense attachment to devaluation on the part of the IMF and the World Bank is vigorously opposed by respected African intellectuals and economists who have no vested interest in hidden capital transfers but who genuinely feel that devaluation is not the appropriate instrument in many cases. One therefore cannot simply conclude that the arguments advanced against devaluation are always necessarily specious. (An interesting discussion of some often-overlooked aspects of devaluation in Africa may be found in Rwegasire 1984.)

Of the other frequent complaints against the IMF in Africa, three will claim our attention, although they do not necessarily have a moral content in the same sense as those already discussed. Two of them concern the validity or invalidity of the Fund's prescriptions.

The first complaint concerns the Fund's traditional policy of urging its clients to strive hard to cut their imports and to expand their exports as a means of ameliorating their balance-of-payments disequilibrium. But with so much of the Third World engaged in IMF adjustment programs, and with many of the industrialized economies suffering from slow growth, the IMF prescription is not only unworkable, it is actually deflationary. Rather than encouraging global trade, as the Fund was created to do, the Fund's programs discourage it. This prescription is especially poor as a long-term strategy for Africa, which exports a very limited range of commodities with long-term growth prospects that are particularly unpromising. Because Africa cannot, in the short or medium term, significantly alter its roster of exports, it admittedly has little alternative than to pursue this formula, but it would be foolish to expect it to produce much in the way of economic growth. The more likely result will be that each expansion of exports will trigger a further deterioration in Africa's terms of trade, leading to additional transfer of income from the poor to the rich, a blatantly unethical outcome. Although commodity prices are subject to world fluctuations of a short-term nature, there has clearly been a long-term decline in Africa's terms of trade. According to the World Bank, "between 1973 and 1981, low-income Africa lost as much as 23 percent in the purchasing power of its exports to buy manufactures" (World Bank 1984). In 1982, commodity prices reached a postwar low in terms of manufacturing prices.

The second major complaint, closely related to the first and especially ominous for Africa, has to do with the West's overall bias toward export-led development as the proper development strategy for Africa. The Fund claims that it does not have this bias. However, export-led development constitutes the "conventional wisdom" concerning African strategy. It provides the underlying assumptions for the World Bank's report, *Accelerated Development in Sub-Saharan Africa* (1983), which has become a bible of sorts for African development, and it fits neatly into the global structuring and national-security planning of the U.S. and probably of other major industrial powers.

The Africans have analyzed their problems and have concluded that export-led development is itself the problem. They feel that, in fact, it is their excessive dependence on the export of a few agricultural and mineral commodities as the basis for most of their economic activity that has placed them in the predicament they are in today. While recognizing the extreme difficulty of breaking out of this syndrome, Africans argue that it is a task which they must undertake for their survival. In the Lagos Plan of Action, they have offered some indication of how they would go about it, by pursuing a path of collective self-reliance. This is a Herculean undertaking and little imagination is required to enumerate a host of near-insuperable obstacles to its achievement. However, it is the Africans' own solution to their problem and, in the absence of a more promising one, it certainly merits more attention from the industrialized countries than it has yet received. This is particularly appropriate in view of the World Bank's own recent projections that the medium-term demand and price prospects for many of Africa's principal exports are gloomy indeed. The export-price index for the 1980s of eleven major export commodities of sub-Saharan Africa (excluding oil)—commodities which between 1976 and 1978 constituted over 50 percent of all African exports—is projected to be 15 to 20 percent below the prices prevailing in the 1960s or the level obtained in the second half of the 1970s (World Bank 1983, 3–4). Under such circumstances, it is highly insensitive for the IMF to fail to take this African analysis into consideration in designing its adjustment programs.

Some would argue that the IMF is justified in sidestepping the question of development strategy. In its 1983 report, the World Bank asserted that Africa's deterioration was primarily due to internal causes—to the faulty policies pursued by the African governments. African leadership challenged this view and argued that the principal causes were external, such as the oil and grain price shocks, the recession in the West, the drought, the deteriorating terms of trade, the high interest rates, and the strong dollar. The IMF's response was that the causes were irrelevant; the cure would be the same regardless of the cause. Is this really true? Superficially, of course, one can say that to eliminate a balance-of-payments deficit there is no alternative to carrying out some combination of a reduction of imports and an increase of exports. Given a sufficient time frame, however, there are a host of ways in which this can be done, depending on what one believes to be the principal source of the problem. (For an interesting discussion of this issue, see Bird 1981, 29–31.) As the response of a short-term lender, the flippant reply of the IMF may be correct, but is it really helpful in addressing Africa's problems? Is this not yet another example of the inappropriateness of applying short-term cures to long-term problems?

Finally, the IMF is subjected to a criticism which in a sense encompasses all the other criticisms, the complaint that the IMF, whether by design or inadvertently, has become the brain, the policeman, and the judge of the economic conduct of the Third World. Although the IMF's own resource base is fairly small, it controls the spigot through which virtually all other resource flows pass en route to the Third World. Commercial banks, private investors, and bilateral donors increasingly look for the IMF cachet as a precondition to committing their own funds. The World Bank is now collaborating with the IMF in Africa as never before. The IMF has thus gathered unto itself an unprecedented amount of power over the Third World nations, a power which varies inversely with the economic strength of the nation concerned. Africa, containing the bulk of the weakest economies, is particularly beholden to this powerful external entity which Africans complain is sapping their independence—and doing so not primarily in the interest of Africa's long-term growth, but for the purpose of insuring that Western lenders are paid.

This is a highly unstable situation and the Fund is advised to address it in a serious fashion before the desperation of the Africans drives them to take some action which may prove massively unsettling. As an institution, the Fund can neither bring about fundamental changes in the international monetary system nor change its own mandate and how this mandate is implemented. But the Fund can pull levers and ring bells to attract the attention of the industrial giants and to convince them of the necessity of providing some meaningful relief to Africa. If matters are allowed to deteriorate to the point where the Africans feel that confrontation is their only option, that they must pull those levers and ring those bells, then a great deal more could come tumbling down than the world can gracefully handle.

Conclusion: A New Multilateral Strategy for African Development

The IMF occupies a pivotal place in the international financial system. It provides the institutional support for the monetary system and monitors the capital flows toward many of the Third World countries, most especially the African ones. Unfortunately, the monetary system is itself seriously flawed and is in obvious need of reshaping to reflect current needs and realities. The volatility of exchange rates and the maldistribution of liquidity both attest to the instability and unsatisfactory nature of present arrangements. The overhanging Third World debt exacerbates matters.

Within Africa, the significance of the monetary and debt issues arises primarily from their impact on the development process. The IMF is concerned to insure that African countries retain creditworthiness and do not default on their loans. To achieve this, however, requires more than the provision of short-term liquidity; Africa requires long-term concessional capital inflow on a scale which the IMF cannot provide because it has neither the resources nor the mandate. The attempt to effect adjustment using injections of short-term capital accompanied by the imposition of demand management targets which are achievable only by the creation of intolerable levels of social unrest and political upheaval has given the IMF a poor image in Africa. The suitability of the IMF/World Bank development model for Africa is increasingly coming under question in view of both the medium- to long-term outlook for primary products and Africa's technological deficiencies in the area of industrial development. Export-led development does not appear to offer encouraging prospects for Africa or for large flows of private international capital.

Nearly one-eighth of the world's population lives in Africa. Many African countries are insolvent or are tottering on the brink of insolvency. Their development needs are enormous and they are attempting to grow in a global atmosphere quite different from that of the 1960s and 1970s. Institutions which hope to assist Africa must have the resources, the flexibility, and the creativity to be responsive to Africa's real needs. Both African leadership and the international community will need to free themselves from the orthodoxy and the rigidities which stifle the continent's effort to move from stagnation to growth.

The increasing convergence of the roles of the IMF and the World Bank creates unnecessary confusion. It is more appropriate to leave to the World Bank the problem of reconciling the legitimate social aspirations of the LDCs with the real availability of resources, and to allow the IMF to remain primarily a liquidity-providing institution. In addition, the SDR should be gradually installed as the international reserve currency and SDRs should be allocated more equitably than on the basis of quotas. IMF lending in Africa would be greatly reduced if it limited itself to liquidity shortages and referred insolvency crises to an ideologically uncommitted World Bank. By democratizing the IMF and erasing the polarization of members into borrowers and lenders, the IMF could move in the direction of becoming a global central bank. This is an achievement which requires universal respect and confidence, and the IMF is not likely to enjoy either if it continues to be used for tasks which it is ill-equipped to perform.

References

Bird, Graham. March 1981. "The IMF and the Developing Countries: Evolving Relations, Use of Resources and the Debate Over Conditionality," ODI Working Paper no. 2. London: Overseas Development Institute.

Bradsky, David, and Gary Sampson. 1981. "Implication of the Effective Revaluation of Reserve Asset Gold: The Case of a Gold Account for Development," *World Development*, vol. 9, no. 7.

Gold, Joseph. March 1984. "Some Impressions of the Early Fund," *Finance and Development*.

Group of 24. April 1984. "Group of 24 Communique," *IMF Survey*, p. 118.

Nau, Henry R. Winter 1984–85. "Where Reagonomics Works," *Foreign Policy*, no. 57.

Rwegasire, D.G. April 1984. "Exchange Rates and the Management of the External Sector in Sub-Saharan Africa," African Development Bank Economic Research Paper no. 3. Abidjan, Ivory Coast: African Development Bank.

de Vries, Rimmer. December 1980. "International Economic Issue and Priorities," paper presented to the Congressional Economic Conference in Washington, D.C., December 10, 1980. Reprinted in *World Financial Markets*.

World Bank. 1984. *World Development Report, 1984.* Washington, D.C.: World Bank.

______. 1983. *Sub-Saharan Africa: Progress Report on Development Prospects in Programmes*. Washington, D.C.: World Bank.

Zulu, Justin B., and Sahel M. Nsouli. 1985. *Adjustment Programs in Africa: The Recent Experience*, Occasional Paper no. 34. Washington, D.C.: IMF.

6

The IMF and the Debt Crisis

Pedro-Pablo Kuczynski

The International Monetary Fund is an important and often misunderstood organization. Along with the World Bank, its sister organization also launched at Bretton Woods as the Second World War was ending, it was mainly the brainchild of Lord John Maynard Keynes, who envisioned for it a much larger role than it was eventually given. Instead of becoming a world central bank, with the power to create an international currency and international reserves, it became instead a kind of international credit union, lending out the currencies of countries that are in surplus to those facing temporary, or at least hopefully temporary, international payments problems.

The first thesis of this paper is that the IMF has played a crucial and constructive role in the initial stages of the debt crisis. Since the debt crisis has been largely a Latin American affair, the IMF has focused its efforts there. Latin America was, in any case, the area where the Fund had traditionally been the most active. The role of the Fund since the crisis started has been threefold: to work out programs of austerity with the debtors, to support them with a modest inflow of resources, and, most important, to get the commercial banks to continue some lending instead of simply withdrawing completely, as the banks were tempted to do after the Mexican default of August 1982. It is fair to say that if the Fund had not played these roles, the debt crisis would have been a far more damaging and uncontrolled affair than it has been.

The other thesis of this paper is that the debt problem is part of a long-term development problem. The Fund was created to deal with short-term problems; by its very nature—by virtue of the fact that the funds in the credit union must revolve quickly and cannot therefore be lent out for long periods—it cannot provide long-term finance. However, for stabilization programs to succeed, there has to be a significant long-term inflow of external capital. The dearth of such an inflow has been one of the main reasons that several stabilization programs have failed. Unless this void is filled (a very difficult task indeed), the likelihood of a continuously successful role of the Fund in the debt problem is highly uncertain and, more important, the prospects for the debtor countries themselves are problematic.

When a family runs out of money, expenditure must go down while new resources of income and finance are found. This inescapable fact is as true for countries as for households. Nevertheless, a number of commentators about the financial problems of developing countries, especially about Latin America and Africa, seem to ignore this self-evident truth. The fact that the cupboard is bare, they seem to suggest, is the fault of the IMF. They imply that there is an alternative to cutting outlays and raising revenue. Indeed there is, but that alternative is not realistic today. It is to have a rich and generous uncle. In the 1980s, the rich uncle has virtually vanished as the United States has generally withdrawn its support of multilateral financial organizations. What support there has been has increasingly taken the form of bilateral U.S. aid to countries which are considered to have strategic value by the United States executive branch and Congress. For those countries, the rich uncle has been willing to provide arms and budget support. But for most countries that is not the case.

The only international agency that is designed to help countries overcome immediate financial problems is the Fund. The fact that it is by definition a bearer of bad tidings does not make it a popular institution. When the money runs out, countries have to take unpopular measures, with or without the Fund. More often than not, the Fund is a convenient prop for finance ministers and central bank governors who know full well that such measures must be taken, but who also know the measures do not have enough political support to be effectively enforced.

In order to understand the role of the Fund in the debt crisis, it may be useful to give a broad-brush view of its evolution. The Fund was originally conceived as an organization that would primarily help to correct disequilibria between the big players in world trade and currency movements, namely the industrialized countries. In the immediate postwar period, however, that role was played by the European Payments Union (EPU) and its predecessors, with large-scale support from the United States. The Fund was basically inactive in the industrialized countries and concentrated instead on its largest group of developing country members in Latin America. It provided considerable technical assistance to central banks in training and statistics, and, because commercial credit was limited, was actively involved in developing and implementing stand-by credits to support stabilization programs in Latin America and some other countries in Asia and eventually in Africa.

It was only in the 1960s that the Fund became active in industrialized countries. The activities of the EPU had been wound up and the Fund played a major role in organizing and providing stabilization credits to Britain, France, Italy, and even the United States, among others. In the 1970s, with the abandonment by the United States of the gold exchange standard and the shift to floating exchange rates instead of fixed rates, the Fund largely lost its role in the industrialized countries. Its role in Latin America was also diminished—with some exceptions such as Argentina, Peru, and Mexico in 1976, at the end of the Echeverria administration—because countries found it easy to borrow from commercial banks, and did not have to submit to the tough discipline of IMF stabilization programs.

Where the Fund was active, it did try to limit the growth of loans from commercial banks by setting limits to such borrowing and requiring minimum maturities which were usually beyond those available in the market. Unfortunately, these programs were too infrequent to cut back significantly the growth of the external debt of Latin American countries, which rose from $48 billion at the end of 1973 to $345 billion ten years later, or from 180 percent of annual merchandise export earnings to 390 percent. Loans from international commercial banks, at floating rates of interest and relatively short maturities, represented three-quarters of the increase in debt.

Over the years, the Fund has been closely associated with Latin America. The Fund conducts detailed annual reviews of the economies of member countries, which give its staff fairly continuous information. The fact that the Fund has emphasized the employment of nationals of the area has given the Fund the most consistent source of economic and financial information about Latin America among international organizations. However, the established employment pattern of the Fund, to keep its staff small with low turnover, has meant that the staff has been somewhat slow to experiment and innovate.

After August 1982, when Mexico was unable to continue to service its external debt, a pattern quickly developed to cope with the problems of the major debtor countries: austerity programs were negotiated with the IMF; a committee of lead banks was created to coordinate the refinancing of external debt with the hundreds of smaller and regional banks involved; some net new "involuntary" lending was made by banks to countries which complied with these IMF programs; and, in some cases, there was a refinancing of the supplier credits guaranteed by industrialized-country governments through the informal committee of government creditors known as the "Paris Club." Since the bulk of the Latin American debt was owed to commercial banks, the governments of the major industrialized countries scrupulously avoided being publicly involved in a bilateral affair between the debtors and their banks. Behind the scenes, however, the U.S. Federal Reserve and the other major central banks played a crucial role in supporting the IMF to induce recalcitrant banks—especially some of the smaller and regional banks, but also some of the European banks—to provide the new nonmarket lending, without which the refinancing agreements would have been completely unsustainable.

The Fund role in these events was by no means new. Since the 1950s, the major commercial banks as well as the U.S. Treasury and Federal Reserve looked upon the Fund as an impartial arbiter which was able to get countries to agree to stabilization programs and was then able to monitor or follow them with regularity. At the same time, the financial authorities in the debtor countries in most cases looked upon the Fund, on whose Board of Executive Directors they were represented, as a sufficiently impartial go-between that could get the lenders to come up with refinancings and some new funds. The trust placed in the Fund by developing countries reached its peak during the years when Pierre-Paul Schweitzer managed the IMF (1963–73). The support of the commercial banks for the Fund was enhanced by the episode in the mid-1970s when the experiment by major commercial banks to work out the financial crises in Peru and Zaire themselves, without the IMF, failed. The Fund role came back in full force during the Mexican financial crisis at the end of 1976.

The difference between the role of the Fund in the past and after 1982 was not only in the size of the problem but also in the fact that the Fund had to make an enormous effort, given the widespread crisis, to induce banks to avoid a complete stoppage of lending.

We should remind ourselves of the resources which the Fund has made available to the debtor countries since August 1982. The key element of this is the commercial bank loans which were made possible by the presence of the Fund: without the Fund's presence, many lenders would not have joined the additional nonmarket lending and a massive default on interest payments would have become a distinct probability. The debt crisis would then have spread to the far corners of the world banking system, putting the world economy at the risk of a financial panic that could have been followed by a slump, as occurred in the early 1930s.

Another difference between the role of the Fund before and after 1982, and one which has become more pronounced over the years, has been that Fund's lending role in relation to the balance of payments of debtor countries has lost importance while its role as a catalyst to stimulate lending by others has increased. This has been due in large part to the fact that Fund resources have lagged in growth in comparison with the growth of international finance and trade (purchases less repurchases by the IMF).

A key issue after the Mexican crisis of August 1982 was therefore whether and how much to increase Fund resources. At first, the U.S. government, especially at the annual meeting of the IMF and World Bank held in Toronto, downplayed the need to increase quotas, which had already

IMF and Commercial Bank Support of Major Debtors, 1983–1984 (in billions of U.S. dollars)

	Net IMF Disbursements[a]	Net Disbursements by Commercial Banks[b]
Argentina	1.4	0.6
Brazil	4.5	3.5
Mexico	2.5	8.0
Chile	1.0	1.1
Peru	0.4	—
Philippines	0.5	1.0
Total	10.3	14.2

[a] Purchases less repurchases by the IMF.
[b] To be revised. 1984 estimated by author.
Source: International Financial Statistics published by the IMF and Bank for International Settlements.

been on the agenda of the Fund for the previous year. When the Mexican crisis inevitably spread as bank lending stopped throughout Latin America, the U.S. Treasury reconsidered its position. A compromise quota increase was presented to Congress. A major battle ensued, however, in which Left and Right united in an isolationist position against the increase. In the tradition of American populism against banks which goes back to the Depression, the Fund was depicted as a tool of the large banks. The quota increase of the IMF would simply "bail out" imprudent borrowers and lenders alike. Some at the other end of the political spectrum argued that the IMF would not only bail out the banks but would do so at great social cost to the population of the debtor countries, helping to create even more political instability than already existed.

The criticisms hit home: they were indeed based on some elements of truth and they augmented the new isolationism bred both by the "America-First" sentiment which followed Vietnam and by the well-known federal budget constraints. The quota increase barely made it through the House of Representatives, with a large block of Republicans voting against it. Ever since, obtaining resources for the multilateral financial organization, indeed for all international organizations, has been a major uphill struggle.

A number of criticisms have been made about the role of the IMF in the debt crisis. Most revolve around the extent of "adjustment" or austerity required under IMF-sponsored stabilization programs. Perhaps the most important one is that adjustment has been too large and too sudden and has therefore had a substantial, and presumably avoidable, social cost.

There is little question about the extent of the actual adjustment. In 1981, the year before the crisis broke, the current-account deficit in the balance of payments for Latin America had been running at about $40 million, or five percent of GNP. This was an unsustainable level which could only be financed by massive recourse to short-term external borrowing, notorious in the case of Mexico. In Argentina, Brazil, and Mexico, the deficits were the result of very high public sector deficits, in the range of fourteen to eighteen percent of GNP. By 1983, the current-account deficit of the region had been cut to less than $10 billion as a result of a massive decline of imports, which fell to almost half their 1981 level. The budget deficits were sharply reduced everywhere, most of all in Mexico. In turn, there was a dramatic drop in incomes, on the order of twelve to fifteen percent measured by per capita income. Employment declines in major metropolitan areas were considerable. Hardest hit were urban lower- and middle-income groups. There was then a massive slump in the region. It is equally clear, however, that the IMF by itself had little to do with it: the main cause of the slump was the cut-off of external credit at a time of high U.S. dollar interest rates (80 percent of the debt of Latin American countries is, on average, denominated in U.S. dollars) and low commodity export prices.

Did the IMF make any difference? Countries would have had to take the medicine anyhow, because the money had run out. Some countries, such as Argentina and Peru at various times, had tried but proved unable to enforce continuous stabilization programs. Argentina had even managed to hold back the decline of per capita income for a while, and real wages increased massively in 1984, but the result was that there was even more hyperinflation than before, foreign exchange reserves collapsed, and even tougher austerity was needed in the future. One cannot deny that successful stabilization programs, such as that of Mexico in 1983–84, have been costly socially and politically, but the key point is that they would have been costly anyway, with or without the Fund.

The Fund made a crucial difference in two ways: first, by providing support for the actions which the financial authorities knew they had to take anyway; and second, by getting the cooperation of banks to continue some net lending, easing somewhat, but by no means eliminating, the pain of the transition. Both points are important. First, in societies with low incomes, relatively unsophisticated electorates, and large social disparities, financial discipline does not come easily. It may be the weak course to blame outside pressures, but often there is not much alternative. Second, in order to get second-tier banks to go along with some net new lending, confidence in an impartial arbiter was essential: stabilization programs monitored directly by the lenders, which were attempted ineffectively in the mid-1970s, are seen by the debtors as neo-colonialist and would have created strong political incentives to default.

Some critics, especially in the United States, have argued, rightly, that the banks got into the mess largely by themselves and, wrongly, that they should therefore get out of it by themselves. The point is that banks are fiduciaries of others' money: a bilateral confrontation between lenders and debtors, with no fresh money at all, would have greatly enhanced the chances of generalized default. The cost to the U.S. economy of having to avoid the panic which would surely follow such a default would undoubtedly have been far higher than the approximately $7 billion which the Congress approved over several years for the U.S. share of the 1983 IMF quota increase. The effect of such a default would have occurred largely through massive offsetting, inflationary, central bank lending to shore up shaky banks, as occurred on a smaller scale for Continental Illinois in the wake of the failure of one of its debtors, Penn Square. The multilateral approach indeed has strong rational arguments to commend it.

A second and more important set of criticisms concerns the content of IMF programs. The cases of Brazil and Venezuela illustrate different aspects of these criticisms. In Brazil, the bulk of inflationary pressure comes from a public sector deficit which, adjusted for the inflation-indexing of government domestic debt, has hovered around twelve to fifteen percent of GNP for several years. A gap of this size is obviously highly inflationary when no offsetting real resources are obtainable. Since virtually the whole deficit is due to indexing, to reduce it presents a complex problem. Under indexing, consumers transfer resources to savers (the latter in large part higher-income groups). The reversal of the process, de-indexation, would probably imply a large transfer of income to consumers, away from savers, and would be equally inflationary in the initial stages. That is, it would be inflationary unless consumers were taxed more heavily, in large part through indirect taxes and increases in public enterprise prices—yet by themselves, these measures are also inflationary. To simply squeeze more net revenue out of consumers causes inflation, while at the same time plunging the economy into recession. In a simplified way, that is what has happened in Brazil since 1981: more inflation, more recession.

In order to overcome this type of conundrum, solutions which are much more complex and gradual than a simple fiscal and credit squeeze may be required. The simplified money and credit model which the IMF has traditionally used in Latin America may be quite inadequate to cope with such a complex problem. This model is essentially a monetary balance-sheet approach under which the more the rate of growth in the resources of the banking system (such as deposits and capital) exceeds the rate of growth on the credit side, the more foreign reserves increase. (Conversely, foreign reserves decline if credit grows faster than resources.) Other approaches have been suggested (see Arida and Lara-Rezende 1985). Whether they will work is not yet proved. However, the present approach, under which Brazil has regularly missed the quarterly financial targets negotiated with the IMF and continues to have 200+ percent inflation, is certainly not successful. Greater experimentation may be in order.

In 1983 and subsequently, Venezuela refused to follow the IMF-suggested approach of a large-scale devaluation toward a unified exchange rate. Venezuela has not needed to get an IMF agreement, since its high level of reserves has allowed it to avoid the need for new lending from the banks. In a low-inflation economy which, like Venezuela, has a high propensity to import, a large-scale devaluation on the order of 300 percent, as suggested by the Fund staff in 1983, would be highly inflationary. The Venezuelan authorities went instead to a partial, albeit large, devaluation and a system of multiple exchange rates (anathema to IMF thinking), combined with tight domestic credit. The large existing inventory of imported goods, along with tight credit which held back consumer demand, restrained inflationary pressures (price controls were largely cosmetic), and Venezuela today has the lowest inflation rate of any of the major Latin American economies. Through these policies, and partly by also holding back foreign exchange for the service of private sector external debt (which the authorities suspected was backed by large private bank deposits abroad), Venezuela was able to build up a high level of international reserves. This greatly strengthened its hand in bargaining the refinancing with the banks.

The alternative strategy of a massive across-the-board devaluation would in all probability have been highly inflationary not only on the side of costs but also by creating pressures for looser domestic credit. The increase in revenues in Bolivares of the oil sector would have had the effect of generating more public expenditure and quite probably a loss of foreign exchange reserves, a phenomenon called the "Please effect" after Stanley Please, a former World Bank economist who demonstrated that additional revenue generally creates additional expenditure. In time, of course, Venezuela will need to move to a unified exchange rate or at least to a less-wide range of exchange rates.

The argument between gradualism and radicalism in exchange rate policy was also at the root of the landmark dispute between Colombia and the Fund in 1966. In the end, the system of Decree 444 installed by Colombia, along with gradually loosening exchange controls, served the country well.

Such cases do not argue against the need for stabilization or adjustment under IMF auspices, but they do suggest that the circumstances of individual countries may vary greatly and that because of this, a less generalized approach is needed. Simplified monetary models cannot cope with important variables such as expectations, inventory movements, and, most especially, outside forces beyond the control of individual countries, in particular the depressed commodity export prices and very high interest rates that detonated the debt crisis in the first place. It is obviously impossible and no doubt also undesirable to insulate economies from the outside, but neither the existing conceptual models used by the Fund nor its financing mechanisms themselves are sufficient to cope with the problems faced by its largest constituency, the highly indebted developing countries. For highly indebted commodity producers the question posed by Ragnar Nurkse (1945) forty years ago, of what is a temporary as opposed to a fundamental balance-of-payments disequilibrium, remains partially unresolved.

The Fund has played a crucial and positive role in easing the first steps of the debt crisis, yet although the "crisis" may be over, the problem certainly is not. No amount of projections and models about future growth of the world economy and of developing country exports can get away from the fact that in the case of the highly indebted countries of Latin America, plus a few others—the Philippines in particular—the debt is just too high. This means that for several years to come the burden of servicing the interest on the debt will use up a very high proportion of available foreign exchange. In 1984, almost 45 percent of the value of merchandable exports of Latin America was devoted to interest payments.

A major component of a permanent solution is for export earnings to grow faster than in the past and for international interest rates to be moderate. A scheme proposed by Anthony Solomon and further elaborated by John Williamson and others would enable countries to defer and capitalize interest payments when basic rates rose above agreed levels (see Bergsten, Cline, and Williamson 1985). The scheme would be a major palliative in times of rising rates, such as occurred in 1980–82, but obtaining financing for the scheme is not easy.

At the moment, interest rates are indeed coming down, but this is probably more a result of sluggishness in the U.S. economy, which will affect the prospects for world trade and for developing country exports. Increasing protectionism in products which have accounted for a major part of the rapid increase in Latin American manufactured products exports to the United States in the last two years, such as special metals, machinery, and more traditional items like shoes and textiles, makes the task difficult. At the same time, commodity prices remain low because of a mixture of long-term secular reasons, such as lower consumption of certain raw materials per unit of GNP in the industrialized countries, and shorter-term reasons, such as the relatively strong dollar.

The other component of a solution is the continuation of internal measures to cut budget deficits, redefine a narrower role for state enterprise, and pursue policies which make exports and the return of capital attractive. As the prospects for growth remain problematic, however, it becomes politically difficult to follow such policies. Already Argentina and Peru, two countries that have been unable or unwilling to follow IMF programs, are in financial collapse, with hyperinflation, rising unemployment, and defaults in external payments. It is therefore essential to stimulate growth as soon as possible. This is not a job which the Fund can tackle by itself, it requires a concerted package of various international measures.

In looking at possible measures, we must distinguish between those that can be effective in the near term, say the next two years or so, and those that can be effective in the longer term. For the immediate future, the greatest need is long-term capital inflows which will enable imports to recover and will allow a return to economic growth. These flows will most definitely not come from private direct investment, which fell drastically in the wake of the debt crisis and the 1981–82 international recession. In time, private investment flows will recover, especially if the conditions exist for the repatriation of some of the $60–70 million in liquid funds held abroad by Latin Americans themselves. The World Bank initiative for a Multilateral Investment Guarantee Authority (MIGA, or 'crumb' in Spanish!) may make a difference if the basic conditions in the countries are attractive and stable for investment. Nevertheless, we must look elsewhere for quick results.

Since 1982, an unspoken assumption has arisen in some circles that the highly indebted countries can somehow recover without major capital inflows. Capital can indeed be more efficient than it was in the go-go high-borrowing days of the late 1970s, but experience shows that capital inflows are essential to get the ball rolling, whether we look at the United States a century ago and today, or at countries as different as Korea and Australia. At present, the highly indebted countries have no major visible source of external capital. Therefore, they can survive and pay the interest on the debt only by maintaining large trade surpluses, which are the result of low imports and thus very low economic growth. The less external capital there is, the tighter the austerity programs have to be.

However, there is an opportunity to break out of this circle because some of the needed money is already there: World Bank and Inter-American Development Bank cash reserves are at an all-time high. The World Bank has complained that it cannot meet its lending targets because countries do not have the local resources to complement its loans. A coordinated approach between the multilateral development banks, the Fund, and the commercial banks is needed. The multilateral agencies could, for a temporary period, increase the percentage of disbursements on their existing loans, as long as:

- countries continue stabilization policies under IMF auspices;
- there is discussion of whether stabilization policies are to be pursued with full conditionality or partial monitoring, as in the recent case of Colombia; and
- commercial banks are willing to support such a program with additional parallel lending on a matching basis.

The resources which could be mobilized in this way could be very substantial, possibly on the order of $2.5 billion annually on the part of the two official agencies for a couple of years, plus a similar amount by commercial banks. A smaller amount might be organized under the Asian Development Bank for the Philippines. A promising beginning has already been made in the case of Africa with the special emergency fund recently organized by the World Bank, although the easing of the debt and management problems of most African economies is generally recognized to require drastic internal reforms as well as additional capital.

Any concrete plan to address the debt crisis will encounter objections. However, to simply continue as at present, waiting for the other shoe to drop, is likely in time to lead to serious strains. Many indebted nations have done their part to overcome their problems, as has the IMF. These countries are now looking for actions to help them reach renewed growth. The international community must respond, as long as debtor countries continue their own efforts. Lip service, of the type recently served at the economic summit meetings and at the Development Committee meeting, is not productive and may be negative, since it promotes expectations but little action. Until balanced and coordinated action is agreed internationally, the chances are that development in most of Latin America and Africa will be dead, quite dead.

References

Arida, Persio, and Andre Lara-Rezende. 1985. "Inertial Inflation and Monetary Reform: Brazil," *Inflation and Indexation: Argentina, Brazil and Israel*, edited by John Williamson. Washington, D.C.: Institute for International Economics, pp. 27–44.

Bergsten, C. Fred, William R. Cline, and John Williamson. April 1985. *Bank Lending to Developing Countries: The Policy Alternatives*. Policy Analyses in International Economics, No. 10. Washington, D.C.: Institute for International Economics and MIT Press.

7

The "Rashomon Effect": Ideological Proclivities and Political Dilemmas of the IMF

Irving Louis Horowitz

The title of my essay, invoking as it does the justifiably famous Japanese *cinema verité* production of *Rashomon*, might well strike a discordant note. However, my aim is not to confuse, but to clarify. The film describes a variety of eye-witnesses to a murder. Every individual, infused with different motives, "saw" a different event from other eye-witnesses. This is little more than a modern-day version of Walter Lippmann's observations on the ideological, interest-laden nature of the formation of public opinion in modern society, but it serves us well in introducing the topic of this essay.

What I am suggesting, and what I hope to demonstrate, is that with respect to the International Monetary Fund, we are in a paradox similar to that Lippmann pointed to in the sociology of knowledge. It is unrealistic to generate a policy called an IMF policy, or even a set of universally applicable guidelines as to which IMF loans should be approved at any given point, without clearing away the debris of ideology—or at least rationalizing that debris. My thesis is that the question of what type of conditions the IMF should attach to loans is actually a very political question. The IMF has come to stand for American society and American capitalism, despite the global character of IMF inputs and outlays. Whether this agency welcomes such a designation or not, and indeed in terms of its self-proclamation as banker of last resort it does not, the IMF is increasingly viewed as a fiscal vanguard of a heartless system. The IMF is said to display a series of symbols about American society. Viewed from such a perspective, the "soft" social scientist might be able to cast some light on the intractable dilemmas faced by the "hard" economic scientist.

The cycle of fashion in social analysis is such that political economy, a phrase which has been in a state of virtual disrepair since Adam Smith,

David Ricardo, and Karl Marx, has again taken a position front and center. The surging demand for IMF-approved loans has created a situation in which determining the appropriate resource base for the Fund raises a whole range of considerations which in the past could be either laundered by economic rhetoric or dismissed because of the relative equilibrium between donors and recipients. Such purely fiscal decision making has been made unthinkable by a supply factor of roughly $25 billion, and a demand factor of twice that amount. In such a non-equilibriated environment, noneconomic elements are invariably factored into the decision making process.

Prior to taking up the political economy of the IMF, it is important, in the light of general confusion, to make plain its organizational character. The IMF is essentially a consortium of international banks, pooling their resources to underwrite the fiscal needs of mostly Third World nations, including nonmarket economies. Big borrowers include such Communist regimes as Romania and Hungary—both in the top ten, and such strange nonaligned nations as Yugoslavia and South Africa. Big lenders are predictably the United States, the United Kingdom, and Japan, and somewhat less predictably, a Third World powerhouse, Saudi Arabia. One can already detect from this lineup of recipients and donors the sort of political issues to be encountered by borrowers as the price of doing business with the West.

At Bretton Woods in 1944, the United States and the United Kingdom came together to create a system for international economic development and stabilization of currencies to serve a shattered postwar period. The World Bank was established to make development loans, while the International Monetary Fund was conceived as a way to handle balance-of-payments problems that would inevitably arise as the world recovered from the effects of the war. The system was basically controlled by the United States, the nation which emerged fiscally intact from World War II, and worked to its benefit.

The IMF succeeded reasonably well in its mission until the early 1970s, when the United States was compelled to detach the dollar from gold in settling international payments and allow each currency to float freely. After the shock of the OPEC monopolization of oil prices in 1973, there was considerable destabilization and disarray in the international currency markets, often at the expense of non–oil producing Third World developing countries and sectors of the First World donor nations. Capital depletion and wealth transference became the norm. The problem of recycling excess OPEC funds was resolved through loans to the Third World group, either on a bilateral basis or through the IMF mechanism. However, as the OPEC money disappeared with the decline in petroleum prices over the next ten years (1973–83), the strain on the debt ridden Third World countries intensified. This led to discussions on increasing the capital available from IMF sources, and made the IMF increasingly a lender of first rather than last resort.

By the early 1980s, the original sponsor nations of the IMF were no longer able to control their creation. As the IMF became increasingly prominent, even in relation to the banking interests from many nations, it stimulated a steady erosion of the sovereignty national governments had over the money supply and a convergence of multinational banks into an integrated floating economy in exile. With this internationalization process came demands for a rationalization of the global economy as a whole. The Brandt report, issued in 1980, made a series of recommendations on revising IMF lending policies. The report urged the alteration of the international monetary system so that it would permit new exchange rates, a larger reserve system, and balance-of-payments adjustments, and it recommended an overhaul in the management of the system (Brandt 1980). The Brandt report further urged the creation and distribution of an international currency for clearing and settling outstanding balances among various national central banks, including an increase in special drawing rights (SDRs) to raise current fiscal quotas. Among the most serious points was that IMF loan conditions, which the Third World countries were presumably finding increasingly unbearable, should be improved, and that Third World countries should be encouraged to participate actively in the IMF decision-making process, which is currently monopolized by the leading industrial powers.

There is a considerable gap, however, between recommendations and policies. The policy recommendations of the Brandt Commission served to highlight the moral dilemmas of the IMF as presently constituted. The Brandt report urged a concentration on agricultural development, but for nations like Mexico and Nigeria such a recommendation could be (and was) interpreted as a call for sustained backwardness rather than for sustained growth. It urged austerity and the elimination of luxury imports, but to do so requires a powerful authoritarian sector, as do import-substitution policies. The report stated the advantages of barter between poor nations, although, it failed to actually stipulate such medievalization of the economy. It suggested reform of the tax system in Third World economies to reduce inequity of wealth and income, but when such reforms have been institutionalized, they have served to legitimate repressive statist measures; they have insured the repayment of loans (such as with Brazil), but at a cost to individual liberties (Horowitz 1980, 213–17).

Because the IMF is, after all, an international banking cartel, its fundamental requirement is for a financial community which is stable and capable of making repayments on loans—with interest. It puts together special loan packages to near-bankrupt nations, such as Mexico, Brazil, and Argentina, to prevent the loss of previously extended credit lines. But this in turn depends on the stable price of petroleum in an OPEC monopoly situation. Since Mexican loans, for example, are leveraged against future petroleum production, the incapacity of OPEC to determine prices may mean a serious inability by Mexico to meet its loan obligations. On the other hand, if the IMF were to lobby for stronger OPEC controls, it could weaken the prospects of recovery for oil-poor Latin American countries like Brazil. These stand a much better chance of growth in a world of lower, competitive petroleum prices (Bravo 1982a, 1982b). (More recently, Miguel de la Madrid has argued for restructuring and repayment, see "Restructuring of the Foreign Debt" 1984.) This suggests that even in an economic environment of maximum cooperation between the IMF and lender states, the number of uncontrolled free factors, such as an OPEC collapse or for that matter a revolutionary takeover leading to forfeiture, seriously jeopardizes the universality of IMF decision making.

It is at this point that considerations of a noneconomic sort, largely of a policy sort, enter into IMF considerations. Among its central calculations in estimating the creditworthiness of a borrower nation are global concerns of a paramount order. An itemized list would include the following:

- Should the IMF support a petroleum cartel like OPEC in order to support its loans to Mexico, if in so doing it undermines other petroleum-poor Third World nations and industrialized nations for whom high oil prices have been a central cause of sustained inflation?
- Should the position of the IMF with respect to oil-rich Third World nations who have to borrow heavily to invest in industrial development be based upon anticipated sustained high oil prices, or upon presently deflated prices? To adopt the latter stance invites the prospect of near-certain default on past loans—a consequence which would seriously disrupt the international monetary system. Although such loans would be of an exceedingly volatile sort, and might potentially result in an even more serious disruption at a future date, are there viable options to short-term aid?
- Should the IMF make loans to Communist satellites like Romania and Hungary in the hopes of moving them away from the Soviet orbit, only to further destabilize the Second World without the possibility of political support for their internal democratic forces (a situation which indeed has unfolded in post-Solidarity Poland)? Contrariwise, do such loans shore up the foundations of enemy states? Do economists even dare recognize such political categories?
- Should the IMF continue to underwrite loans to South Africa on the basis of that nation's essential creditworthiness, despite its continued reliance on a policy of apartheid and racial inequality, a policy widely con-

demned by Third World recipient nations and several donor nations as well?

- Should the IMF continue to increase its financial support to nations like Pakistan, which has displayed a demonstrated lack of creditworthiness but has a strong commitment to the Western alliance in the Asian–Middle East sector of the Third World, especially in aiding the Afghanistan liberation struggles?
- Should IMF high fiscal supports to nations such as Jamaica, Costa Rica, Honduras, and El Salvador, and its virtually nonexistent support for nations like Nicaragua, be determined exclusively by economic or also by political considerations? Indeed, what is the empirical mix between these concerns in granting or withholding funds?
- Should the IMF continue to hold to firmly established international "gentlemen's agreements," or should it develop special waivers, drawing rights, or other dispensations to further induce Second World, i.e., Soviet, participation? What would be the consequences in political and economic terms of such an opening to the East?

Genuine political concerns involve serious dilemmas posed by collectivities and individuals. These noneconomic issues tax simple minds and elude easy answers. Yet, how does an international banking system determine the place of politics in determining creditworthiness, or in less pretentious Lasswellian terms, how does it decide who gets what, when, and how much? The decision to loan money is a presupposition that involves a wide variety of considerations, including mineral wealth, political stability, rates of growth, and others. Also to be factored in are considerations of the dedication of the work force, the commitment, or lack thereof, of ruling elites to national survival, and the cultural character and social structure of the nation being aided and abetted. Far from the thin-lipped, bottom-line caricatures projected by and about the banking community, the far closer-to-truth imagery is of bankers having to choose and select among a host of factors—subjective as well as objective—in its decision making. They must also decide between autonomous modes of banking behavior and dependent roles of political behavior.

What I am proposing is a major effort to return economic doctrine to its roots in classical utilitarian theory, and, through the pragmatic filter of situational ethics, to come to a sharper and clearer understanding of the decision-making process of the IMF. We should not concentrate on *its minimal goals* of liberalizing trade, encouraging an increased use of private capital by multilateral institutions, or increasing the security of the world's food system, but rather on *its maximum goals* of supporting stability and democracy, a free-market ceiling, and a social-welfare floor. In this search, I would like to avoid the metaphysical language of contradictions and inevitabilities, preferring instead to examine problematic conditions and pragmatic solutions.

From its origins the IMF has been plagued by a dualism which also functions as its symbolism. Forty years ago, the United States and the United Kingdom were in fundamental disagreement. After World War II, the United States was a country with a large surplus, large gold reserves, and with its production facilities fully intact. Therefore, its impulses were directed toward limiting rather than accelerating transfers of resources abroad (unless some consideration was given in return for that kind of gratuity). From that point on, the United States exhibited a bias toward a gold-convertible dollar, which restricted drawing facilities—subject to economic policy conditions—with fixed exchange rates.

At that remote point in time, it was not Latin America, but the United Kingdom that took a dim view of tight IMF money policies. England's main representative to the original Bretton Woods conference, Lord John Maynard Keynes, argued a position that has now become familiar throughout the Third World; he advocated the creation of a new international liquidity and a reserve instrument linked only nominally to the gold standard. He urged the granting of substantial automatic credit lines, now called Special Drawing Rights (SDRs). Keynes also argued the case that the United Kingdom should have a large degree of autonomy in its domestic economic policy, and that it should emphasize deflationary policies to safeguard an external equilibrium under a system of fixed exchange rates that no longer seemed acceptable. What emerged was a fluid exchange rate.[1]

The advanced nations were urged to use the IMF's monetary advantage to massage the international economy, whatever its level of achievement or the terms of its structure. Thus, at the outset of Bretton Woods, the IMF unfolded with a set of contradictions which remain characteristic of its policies. Although the players are different, and the position of the United Kingdom then is quite different than the position of the Third World now, the argument remains essentially the same: creditworthiness at the donor level and easy credit terms at the recipient end.

Moving quickly into the modern time period we first witness a three-fold increase in the number of IMF member nations. There are now 151 member nations. But size has not changed structure. The same kind of arguments and trepidations are raised. Kari Levitt, a Canadian radical economist typifies the resurrection of the Keynesian nationalist argument in Marxian internationalist form. She is harsh in her judgments, but such emotionalism is worth mentioning, because it typifies a broad strata of recipient-nation opinion toward the IMF. She writes, "It is important to note that IMF programs are not designed to increase the welfare of the population. They are designed to bring the external-payments account into balance. . . . The IMF is the ultimate guardian of the interests of capitalists and bankers doing international business" (Levitt). In a slightly less strident form, a recent compendium notes of Brazil, that "major decisions are not made in Brasilia, but in New York, Detroit, Germany, and Canada" (Ritter and Pollock 1983, 284–85).

Such a point of view hardly goes unchallenged by donor-nation analysts. There are new players, Japanese in particular, who are not about to accept blanket condemnations. Roger A. Sedjo, currently a senior fellow at Resources for the Future in Washington, is typical. His views suggest that critics of the IMF speak nonsense. For Sedjo, "the world trade balance is a zero-sum game. For the Third World to have persistent trade surpluses requires that other countries accommodate this effort with comparable deficits" (Sedjo 1985). He adds that "as Japan and Western Europe are both running trade surpluses, the burden of running a trade deficit to absorb Third World net exports has fallen almost entirely upon the United States, and has significantly contributed to the higher United States deficit (Sedjo 1985). In addition, debt repayment considerations necessitate an extended period of debtor-nation surpluses; the fact that their deficits are expected to increase throughout the 1980s provides little relief.

There is another point of view, neither Marxian nor Friedmanian, that represents a cross between pro-capitalist economic interests and anti-Western political interests. Speaking for this unusual, special group—both a have and a have-not group, and both a Third World and non–Third World area—Fehmy Saddy, writing appropriately enough, in *The Banker's World*, argues that the IMF is at least part of the problem and not just a solution. "Power is held within these institutions by the major Western countries, particularly the United States. And it is reasonable to assume that any solution to the debt crisis designed by them must address primarily their own interests. U.S. protectionism and high interest rates, and, until very recently, recession *and* inflation are primarily responsible for the growth of the international debt crisis. The economic ills of the powerful in a world founded and operated on the basis of power politics are transferred to the less powerful" (Saddy 1985; Saddy 1982, esp. 1–8).

As a general overview then, economists are not exactly united by their discipline in a shared vision of the IMF. These reputable economists, not uncharacteristically, reflect positions, places, and nations of their choice. We are faced with a problem that the economists themselves are badly divided on what they consider to be the problem. Enter the Rashomon Effect.

Let us turn now for a moment to the situation with the fourth estate. This is not unimportant, since only one year ago in 1984, we were reading headlines in the world press saying that there was a crisis of absolute imminence. One year later, in 1985, one was able to read in the *Washington Post*, the *New York Times*, and elsewhere, that the permanent crisis had evaporated. The IMF is now optimistic about resolving world ills. Within one year, adjusted growth rates indicate Africa moving up, Latin America also moving up, the United States dipping but then levelling off, and Asia levelling off, but basically sustaining a rate of growth anywhere between three and five percent for the balance of the 1980s. That percentage, if maintained, is sufficiently high to offset inflationary bursts within either the United States or the Third World (see Rowe 1985; Reed 1985). The current consensus is that as the United States reduces its deficit pressures, Third World indebtedness will become less insurmountable in the near future. The IMF reports that for the first time in several years, the economies of each major region of the world, and each group of countries, are projected to grow at least as fast as their population. Estimates for the remainder of the century are that population growth will be overtaken by real economic growth in many Third World nations (Witcher 1985).

If the debt crisis is waning, what then remains of the IMF crisis? Here again, a variety of answers are forthcoming that indicate the existence of a moral worm eating away at the polished apple. Albert Fishlow argues, in point of fact, that this recovery is but a temporary hiatus and claims that there will again be a renewal of the debt crisis. The real problem of the moment, he says, is the shortfall of currency, i.e., the lack of money to finance imports (Fishlow and Diaz-Alejandro 1984). There is a medium-term debt problem that has not been addressed by long-term projections of stability. Professor Fishlow's argument is carefully rendered and is essentially that it would take a tremendous upward move in the gross national product, far beyond the current three percent norm, to get beyond a permanent repayment crisis by the Third World.

A similar cautionary note is struck by Rudiger Dornbusch. For him, the entire issue of an IMF crisis is a political question (Dornbusch and Simonsen 1983). Even by 1990, working-class standards of living in Latin America, for example, are not likely to return to 1980 levels. For him, IMF policies thus serve to accelerate class struggles. The IMF crisis is not over, in Dornbusch's view, it has merely been muted for a temporary period by virtue of the strengths of circumstances with respect to the reduction of the U.S. deficit. The lack of change in Third World economies and the lack of accountability of government to citizens postpones, but does not settle, the debt crisis.

In light of such proposed solutions, what is the problem? How does each side perceive the situation in terms of a particular kind of divisive issue such as Special Drawing Rights? Third World economists insist that they have a problem of liquidity. They argue the need to have increased Special Drawing Rights in order to improve their short-term cash requirements.[2] In this way, Third World nations can reach some kind of plateau in order to make long-term paybacks. But what do we hear in terms of the IMF economists from the most advanced nations? They assert that the problem is not Special Drawing Rights, but Third World general creditworthiness. From this perspective, the problem is that many underdeveloped countries have no creditworthiness; therefore, simply introducing Keynesian mechanisms to increase liquidity flows does nothing to address structural problems of industrialization (Kharas 1984).

The same kind of polarity of professional judgment found in the statement of issues can be seen in solutions. Economists are either talking past or through one another. While these are global issues, much of the debate over IMF policies on Third World borrowing remains an American debate, carried on primarily in the United States and in American terms. For example, one issue is the formulation of an appropriate overseas American ideology, and not just a lending strategy for the biggest donor nation in the IMF. What should the attitude of strict fiscal accountability be when it concerns political allies and potential upheavals?

The IMF crisis is in part a way of focusing upon the larger matrix of political concerns about what direction America and the West are headed economically. In the Latin American case, an area in which there are many economists of exceptional quality, the issue of exploitation versus creditworthiness is posed in sharp terms. Ramon Diaz, a major Latin economist, writes bluntly about Uruguay, saying that for a small country the size of Uruguay, economic reality means trade:

> Realism means opening up to trade and finance, accepting the consequent challenge, making the most of the upswings of the world economy, and adjusting promptly to the downswings. Uruguay had foolishly tried to ignore the law proclaiming that all successful small economies must be wide-open economies, like those of the Swiss and the Dutch, those of Hong Kong and Singapore, and the gods had delivered upon it a terrible nemesis. (Diaz 1984)

He concludes by saying that the oil shock was a blessing in disguise, moving Latin America (with the exceptions of Mexico and Ecuador) away from the pot-of-black-gold approach and forcing them to impose stringent policy measures that might otherwise not have been possible. Diaz poses the solution to the fiscal crisis in strict free-market terms.

At the same time, we hear other economic voices from Bolivia and Argentina speaking differently about the same problems. Gustavo Fernandez, the Bolivian foreign minister, says "This is not a question of paying the public debt with private banks, but of temporarily postponing payment while the debt is renegotiated" (Fernandez). He goes on to say that a formal declaration by a country does not mean that it will not meet its debt payments, although it does mean that the IMF cannot jeopardize long-term aid to a Third World country simply by virtue of short-term problems such a country may have. The IMF has to allow the government to proceed with emergency programs of debt rescheduling. Raul Alfonsín, president of Argentina, goes even further, and says that even debt postponement will not satisfy the working classes. The Labor Confederation, which represents every major labor group in Argentina, must be satisfied. Alfonsín ominously adds that "I do not want to provoke strikes. I would like if possible a national consensus" (Alfonsín). Speaking on his behalf, one of his treasury commission figures pointed out that Argentina is sitting astride a $47 billion foreign debt. Yet in its demand for a letter of intent, in the absence of debt restructuring, the IMF runs the risk of provoking a complete crisis, a complete systemic breakdown. Here again opinions seem neatly divided between the economists of advanced nations and those from developing nations.

John Loxley, writing from the Canadian Left point of view, offers a similar, if more muted, Third World analysis. Canadians are tremendously active and capable overseas; they are held both in awe and in animus; they have been more successful than Americans for a variety of reasons, often cultural (Loxley 1984, 29; see also Eisendrath 1983). Loxley writes that if the results of the government study can be taken as a reflection of IMF performance, as the managing director of the IMF seems to imply, then the findings should be equally valid as a record of IMF performance with regard to less developed countries. But that record is not impressive either in absolute or relative terms. The aid to less developed countries did not exhibit strong improvements on any of the measures employed for determining economic recovery. Further, in relative terms, performance of all indicators have not been significantly better for LLDC's (Least Less Developed Countries) receiving or not receiving IMF aid. He goes on to indicate that there is a vast difference between Latin American countries that have substantial developmental potential, i.e., Argentina, Brazil, and Mexico, and the virtually catastrophic condition Central African nations are in.

Why should this be? Again, we get a variety of economists talking past one another. One is the bottleneck theory proposed by Hugh Schwartz. He argues that the key to Latin American industrial development is not social structures but fiscal bottlenecks. Why should Latin America in particular and the Third World in general have been so inept if the funds given to them by the IMF are delivered for good intent and purposes? Schwartz answers that there are low levels of self-sufficiency and that there is a general deficiency in the rational distribution of available funds. From this perspective, the failure to undertake relatively aggressive marketing measures makes overseas sales stagnant. Then there is a shift in the distribution of income for an adequate level of demand for industrial products and in the composition of demand. Finally, there is a technical problem of the Third World not being aware of the shape of the demand curves beyond those of recent experience (Schwartz 1983, 23–24). This creates a series of bottlenecks which, according to the IMF, can be remedied through the correct use of investment.

The response to this bottleneck theory comes from those who cite "structural under-development," and claim that the bottleneck theory is simply a top-down banking conception of the world. Again, a Canadian, interestingly enough, R. Crawford Pratt, writing in a work called *Banking on Poverty*, critiques the entire IMF structure (Pratt 1983). He argues that there are three reasons for the debt crisis, none of which is related to those that Schwartz cites. Crisis began with the inability to repay foreign loans. It is not a new phenomenon for banks dealing with Third World countries. The problem is handled by negotiated agreements for rollover loans (Pratt 1983, 30–31). For whatever reason (Pratt does not say), banks grew anxious about being overextended in the Third World, and thus sought ways to cut their overseas commitment. The problem of economics starts with anxiety! Under such circumstances, the banks became more difficult in their loan portfolios. Mexico, Brazil, and Argentina were classic victims of a manufactured crisis. Advanced countries like the United States arrive at a point where they need holdings in order to rollover loans. The Third World needs more than funds to repay debts. They have to borrow simply in order to meet interest payments. When caught in the pattern of borrowing to meet interest payments, rather than to repay the principal loans, Third World borrowers are caught in a downward, demoralizing spiral.

Whether the problem is defined in terms of fiscal bottlenecks (chickens) or structural deformities (eggs), the need for resolution becomes apparent. However, here again, the economists are caught in the Rashomon Effect. They offer resolutions clearly reflective of the current state of political disputation in the field of economic theory. Arnold Harberger represents what might be called the Friedman School of economic thinking. He proposes as a basis for IMF lending policy a series of propositions, which in their broad outline indicate a faith in monetarist answers of a neoclassical sort. Harberger asserts the need for the following set of economic rules: Avoid false technicism in economic policymaking; keep budgets under adequate control; keep inflationary and deflationary pressures under reasonable control; take advantage of international trade, since some types and patterns of trade restrictions become excessive, and reducing them is politically impossible; mount an indirect attack on the program for increasing incentives for export; make the tax system simple and easy to administer; avoid excessive income tax rates; avoid excessive use of tax incentives to achieve particular objectives; use price and wage controls sparingly if at all; minimize quotas and licenses to arbitrarily regulate imports and exports; and make the borderline between public and private sector activity clear and well-defined (Harberger 1984; for the opposite viewpoint, see Maylor 1982). In short, Harberger's formulas for successful IMF–Third World relationships are unambiguously similar to the program of the Republican political leadership in the White House for successful national recovery.

Such recommendations sound fairly reasonable. In fact, they might be called the argument of the reasonable man. Why then do such policies fail in Third World contexts? Friedmanism writ large comes upon the political preconditions for economic equilibrium. Why has the free-market option become less widely accepted than hoped for? The answer tends to come not from the economists, but from the political scientists. Those who speak to this question take the position that the fiscal regimen being suggested by the IMF and by its advisers for Third World reform, while ostensibly non-political, has enormous political consequences to which most IMF officials remain oblivious.

Typical is David Pion-Berlin, who, in writing on political repression, argues that this free-market type of approach results in a political nightmare (Pion-Berlin 1983, 37–63). He says that it would not take a great leap of faith to assert that the use of coercion often parallels the implementation of orthodox stabilization measures like the IMF proposals. For instance, in Chile and in Uruguay, traditional bastions of democracy in the Western Hemisphere, the basis of violations of human rights at the hands of Chilean and Uruguayan security forces and secret police has been created since the adoption of IMF reforms. Unfortunately for Pion-Berlin, this argument does not explain why Uruguay has once more become democratic, whilst Chile remains under authoritarian-military rule. Blaming the IMF does little to explain the internal mechanisms of statecraft in each Latin American nation.

The strictly political point of view is typical and common to left-oriented Latin American positions. Such an ideology claims IMF-imposed structures create the basis of repression by making repayment schedules a class burden. Joan M. Nelson, writing on the political economy of stabilization, argues that the probability of violent outbreak is largely influenced by the general trust or the general distrust of government (1984). The degree to which public opinion is prepared, perhaps by earlier unsuccessful economic programs, for the failure of attempts to implement drastic measures is considered irrelevant. As she properly notes, the tradition of free enterprise really does not correlate well with IMF policies or with the lack of IMF policies.

Finally, there is the viewpoint of the free market in its holistic entirety. Lewis Engman argues that the problem is not that the IMF creates the foundations for tyranny, or right-wing military regimes, but the other way around: the absence of unfettered economic enterprise, the absence of IMF-sponsored programs, leads to state-run economies which are wholly incompatible with personal freedom and human dignity (1980, 1–40). Multinational companies can alleviate Third World poverty, whereas state-run economies are wholly incompatible with personal freedom and human dignity. In the long run, and for that reason, the free market system can also be the cause rather than the cure for political instability. The state which sets production priorities cannot permit its citizens to have what they want, or to keep what they earn. The state must fill the jobs available. The argument for free enterprise requires sacrifice, the argument for state enterprise requires only demagogic leadership, and worse, perpetual borrowing.

When this entire literature has been viewed and reviewed, one can see that the issue is not so much IMF policy toward a particular nation at a specific time as it is the possibility of capitalism surviving, or the prospects of communism taking its place. The technical arguments tend to be overwhelmed ultimately by this kind of larger reality or perhaps by a larger mythology—by the ideological parameters to which the IMF is captive as well as captor.

In the context of a permanent fiscal crisis, with inflationary pressures uncurbed by market forces, there is a rise of underground economies, a rise of parallel economies, and an emergence of the use of foreign hard currencies as a populist rebellion against inflation and weak national economies. From Argentina to Israel, the American dollar is used as a measure for determining real value and real wealth. People in developing areas go about their business with or without regard to IMF safeguards or retreats—and do so fairly well. This kind of pragmatic adjustment prevents political explosions from occurring on a regular basis. At a larger level, and more theoretically interesting, is the current round of debates over the status of the IMF, and between the IMF and the so-called debtor nations. The substance of the debates is less the kind of policy guidelines the IMF establishes than it is the weak status of an economic science itself still painfully linked to ideological proclivities. In nearly every case examined for this essay, national interest rather than universal science prevails as the measure of IMF decision making.

In an odd way, the argument of the IMF represents a new kind of economic world, not the economics of production but the economics of allocation. When one discusses the economics of allocation, one is talking essentially of politics: who is going to get what, why, and when. The policy issue is not a matter of what is produced, so much as it is a matter of what is allocated, or of how the political-administrative network disburses what has already been produced, bought, purchased, or borrowed. The infrastructure of the new global economy is made possible by this allocational emphasis. Whether it be Hungary or Romania, economic production systems are part of this IMF political-allocation network. In fact, the IMF is not just an instrument of capitalism. The IMF inhabits a world of allocation, of voluntary action for global stability. This IMF perspective threatens communism precisely because of its complete repudiation of issues that are based on class stratification and forms of production.

We are no longer in a universe of economic determinism. As a result, the IMF is operating at a level which has next to nothing to do with the deep structures of capitalism or socialism. The issue rather is the ability of some nations to get rich and the inability of others to break the debt barrier—whatever the name of the economic game. IMF decisions have to do with how rich nations are going to allocate their wealth, or better, how to make people who are wealthy a little less wealthy and a trifle more politically conscious (often against their will). At the other end, is the question of how the IMF can make people who are poor a trifle less concerned with their private needs and more concerned with their political responsibilities. For example, the working classes of Bolivia have to be propelled in some sense in the direction of austerity and abstinence by whoever is in charge of the state. The drive for a civic culture is the cutting edge of requests for global funding.

Austerity too is a political fact—equal to the fact that debtor countries must work hard for little reward in the name of sovereignty. The rich countries have the reverse problem; they have scant incentive for investing large amounts in less-than-profitable environments. Yet, sovereignty remains a bulwark against unfriendly political takeovers. What we have then is not some vague notion of politics, but rather a question of allocating resources—situated responses to immediate shortfalls. The wealthy have to allocate in such a way that they make less of a profit, the poor have to allocate in such a way that they suffer higher exploitation for austerity. These are political concerns with clear economic consequences.

I do not believe that there is an appropriate, purely scientific posture or an appropriate, correct policy. The IMF cannot magically resolve problems in the Third World by means of an Archimedian lever. It would be pleasant if this were the case, but I rather suspect that what we have in the IMF is typical of the way Americans generally deal with moral problems—they become filtered, if not resolved, through economic vehicles. The IMF is a moral force precisely because it establishes criteria for economic solvency, not because of any abstract commitments to good and evil. But these investment decisions involve a gamble on the future direction of nations.

The sooner this is realized by all concerned, donors and recipients, the task of allocating, evaluating, and measuring the worth and meaning of foreign-support loans can move ahead unencumbered by the myth of scientism which currently pervades much economic policymaking. Recognizing the Rashomon Effect of the IMF is one way of reaching broad, if short-term, understanding between nervously contending forces which still need each other.

In a longer run, the Rashomon Effect exists only as long as questions of debt and financing are considered structural prerequisites of national and international systems. When a perspective more modest and less concentrated on national interest is admitted, the Rashomon Effect of necessity dissolves into a series of strategic decisions, political policies, and political trade-offs. A bargaining model rather than a structural analysis helps to explain available options for donor and recipient nations alike. Indeed, it helps us to understand that an economic donor may in fact be a political recipient, and vice versa. For this sort of open-ended approach to be adopted, the same sort of flexibility demonstrated at Bretton Woods forty years ago, by bankers and politicians alike, will have to be demonstrated. Recent moves affecting Mexico, Brazil, Argentina, and other parts of the less developed world indicate that just such realism may indeed be taking root.

Notes

1. For an excellent European-oriented summary of the history and tradition of the International Monetary Fund, see Scharrer 1984; for a Latin American emphasis, see Powelson 1985.
2. The classic statements of this position were made by H.W. Singer (1950) and Paul Prebisch (1959). A more recent support for this position is contained in Brecher and Choudri (1982).

References

Alfonsín, Raul, cited in Peter T. Kilborn, "U.S. Gives Argentina More Time," *The New York Times*, June 1, 1984.

Brandt, Willy (with Anthony Sampson). 1980. *North-South: A Program for Survival*. Cambridge, MA: MIT Press.

Bravo, Francisco Carrada. 1982a. *Oil, Money, and the Mexican Economy*. Boulder, CO: Westview Publishers.

________. 1982b. *Mexico's Political Economy: Challenges at Home and Abroad*. Beverly Hills, CA: Sage Publishers.

Brecher, Richard A., and Ehsan U. Choudri. February 1982. "Immiserizing Investment from Abroad," *The Quarterly Journal of Economics*, vol. XCVII, no. 1, pp. 181–90.

Diaz, Ramon. 1984. "Uruguay's Erratic Growth," in *World Economic Growth: Case Studies of Developed and Developing Nations*, edited by Arnold C. Harberger. San Francisco: Institute for Contemporary Studies, pp. 377–401.

Dornbusch, Rudiger, and Mario H. Simonsen. 1983. *Inflation, Debt, and Indexation*. Cambridge, MA: MIT Press.

Eisendrath, John. February 1983. "How the IMF Makes the World Safe for Depression," *Washington Monthly*, vol. 14, pp. 14–20.

Engman, Lewis A. 1984. "How Multinational Companies Can Pull Back Third World Poverty," *Imprimis*, vol. 14, no. 3, pp. 1–40.

Fernandez, Gustavo, cited in Peter McFarren, "Bolivia Says It Has Suspended Debt Payments," *Wall Street Journal*, June 1, 1984, p. 29.

Fishlow, Albert, and C. Diaz-Alejandro. 1984. *Rich and Poor Nations in a World Economy*. New York: McGraw-Hill Publishers.

Harberger, Arnold C. 1984. "Economic Policy and Economic Growth," in *World Economic Growth: Case Studies of Developed and Developing Nations*, edited by Arnold C. Harberger. San Francisco: Institute for Contemporary Studies, pp. 428–35.

Horowitz, Irving Louis. Summer 1980. "When Worlds Collide," *The Washington Quarterly: A Review of Strategic and International Issues*, vol. 3, no. 3, pp. 213–17.

Kharas, Homi. August 1984. "The Long-Run Creditworthiness of Developing Countries: Theory and Practice," *The Quarterly Journal of Economics*, vol. XCIX, no. 3, pp. 415–39.

Levitt, Kari Polyani, cited in *Banking on Poverty: The Global Impact of the IMF and World Bank*. Toronto: Between the Lines Publishers, 1983, frontispiece.

Loxley, John. 1984. *The IMF and the Poorest Countries: The Performance of the Least Developed Countries under IMF Standby Arrangements*. Ottawa: North-South Institute.

Maylor, R.T. October 1982. "Reaganism and the Future of the International Payments System," *Third World Quarterly*, vol. 14, pp. 655–76.

Nelson, Joan M. 1984. "The Political Economy of Stabilization: Commitment, Capacity, and Public Response," *World Development*, vol. 12, no. 10, pp. 983–1006.

Pion-Berlin, David. April 1983. "Political Repression and Economic Doctrines," *Comparative Political Studies*, vol. 16, no. 1, pp. 37–63.

Powelson, John P. 1985. "Prospects for Economic Development in Latin America," *Latin American Research Review*, vol. XX, no. 3, pp. 228–34.

Pratt, R. Crawford. 1983. "International Bankers and the Crisis of Debt," in *Banking on Poverty: The Global Impact of the IMF and World Bank*, edited by Jill Torrie. Toronto: Between the Lines Publishers.

Prebisch, Raul. 1959. "Commercial Policy in the Underdeveloped Countries," *American Economic Review*, vol. XLIX (Papers and Proceedings), pp. 251–73.

Reed, Joseph V. October 16, 1985. Statement on the World Economy in the United States Mission to the United Nations. USUN 117-(85).

"Restructuring of the Foreign Debt." October 1984. *Mexico Today*, vol. 2., no. 10, pp. 1–12.

Ritter, Archibald R.M., and David H. Pollock. 1983. *Latin American Prospects for the 1980s*. New York: Praeger/CBS.

Rowe, James L. April 18, 1985. "IMF Optimistic on World Growth," *The Washington Post*.

Saddy, Fehmy. February 1985. "The Debt Crisis: An Arab–Latin American Approach," *The Banker*, pp. 14–16.

———, ed. 1983. *Arab–Latin American Relations*. New York: Transaction Books.

Scharrer, Hans-Eckart. July/August 1984. "The IMF: A Success Story?" *Intereconomics*, vol. 18, no. 4, pp. 162–67.

Schwartz, Hugh H. 1983. *Bottlenecks to Latin American Industrial Development*. Washington, D.C.: Inter-American Development Bank.

Sedjo, Roger A. January 15, 1985. "Third World Debts Create U.S. Trade Deficits," *Wall Street Journal*.

Singer, H.W. 1950. "The Distribution of Gains between Investing and Borrowing Countries," *American Economic Review*, vol. XL (Papers and Proceedings), pp. 473–85.

Witcher, S. Karene. March 26, 1985. "Debt Crisis is Waning in Developing Nations," *Wall Street Journal*.

8

The IMF as Market-Maker for Official Business between Nations

George M. von Furstenberg

As its principal task in the world economy, the International Monetary Fund is involved in adjustment, the business of re-orienting economic policies toward sustainable outcomes. Since many countries, developed and developing, have strayed from such outcomes, "adjustment" is on everyone's lips. A recent U.S. government publication uses the term in each of its three bullet segments, describing the role which the IMF plays between creditor and debtor as follows:

> IMF resources provided requisite financing while LDC debtor countries instituted adjustment programs designed to restore their creditworthiness;
>
> IMF support for adjustment programs furnished the recognized "seal of approval" needed for the restoration of creditor confidence that the adjusting country was pursuing reasonable and effective economic policies for dealing with its problems;
>
> and, the IMF has served as a coordinator in developing financing packages that provided the "critical mass" of resources required to assure the viability of adjustment programs. (National Advisory Council on International Monetary and Financial Policies 1985, 7)

Clearly, then, the IMF is in the business of promoting adjustment, but not all external observers agree that it should be, nor do they agree what is reasonable and effective in this regard. In fact, critics have a field day with the Fund and have little fear of refutation. The Fund, as an international institution with a distinct etiquette, does not respond directly to either friendly or hostile voices (though many of these voices shout into the wrong ear). Most critics, however valid their points might otherwise be, address themselves to the Fund as if the adjustment required in the practices and policies of international debtor countries is determined by the Fund according to its own lights, whichever it happens to switch on. After sampling some of these criticisms, this paper attempts to illustrate how differently the Fund and its adjustment programs may appear when the Fund is treated not as principal and self-empowered, but, more pertinently, as agent and market-maker intermediating between nations.

Potshots at Effigies

The Fund's adjustment programs are regularly criticized from both the Left and the Right—when they are not being pilloried simply for being inept. Critics from the Right commonly describe the Fund as facilitating only slow adjustment or no adjustment at all by continuing to provide balance-of-payments financing after others have backed off. Furthermore, they regard the conditions attached to Fund programs as paper-tiger soft in that they are too easily waived or circumvented. One prescription of those holding this view is that the IMF should be starved for resources so that it would have little choice but to ration its loan fund through more demanding conditions, which press for faster adjustment (see Bauer and Yamey 1981; DeGrauwe and Fratianni 1984; and Weintraub 1983).

Left-leaning critics do not disagree completely with this analysis, but draw different implications. While complaining about the harshness or inappropriateness of conditions, some critics from the Left seem nevertheless to agree with some on the Right who claim that these conditions can be circumvented or that they are, at times, neither imposed nor accepted in good faith. Thus Taylor (1985, 16) claims that "there was a degree of mendacity in the economic forecast that the Fund and the Mexican authorities agreed upon." Diaz-Alejandro (1984, 385) speculates that "the Brazilian military regime . . . seems almost to have relished signing unrealistic letters of intent; since December 1982 it has signed four of them." As a matter of fact, before President Sarney took over, this regime signed and violated three more.

In spite of ambiguity about the tiger's hold, most critics from the Left tend to regard its pounce as real. Writing from or for debtor countries, they often describe the Fund as clawing workers and poor people to extract a pound of flesh. The Fund is said to do this either quite blatantly for foreign financiers or to feed the spiteful conservatism allegedly bred into the institution. Dispassionate analyses of the tactics and incentives associated with the adoption and partial fulfillment of adjustment programs, such as those by Sachs (1985) and von Furstenberg (1985), are rare. Descriptions from the Fund's perspective of conditionality, and of the principles of adjustment that guide it, are contained in International Monetary Fund (September 1985, SF) and in Goode (1985).

Left-leaning criticisms of the Fund's austerity are legion, and some supply-siders have reinforced them from the Right. Comparatively mild volleys are that "stabilization programmes under the auspices of the IMF . . . in several Latin American countries have had devastating effects on economic activity, without setting a clear path for improvement . . ." (Dornbusch 1984, 159), and that the Fund errs on the side of overkill in macroeconomic policy (Diaz-Alejandro 1984, 384). It has also been claimed that "IMF adjustment programs tend to aggravate the inequitable distribution of income and economic imbalance which hampers growth in individual countries and in the international economy" (Schechter 1985, 22). More aggressive criticisms charge the Fund with economic "malpractice" and claim that, most likely, "the goal of conditionality simply is contraction" because this is what the industrial powers generally desire (Taylor 1985, 18). These desires are allegedly implemented by a staff which, through control and socialization in the organization, is said to have acquired a uniform "corporate" outlook, so that "most are only able to think along strict-constructionist monetarist lines" (Taylor 1985, 19). Some critics, occasionally including supply-siders, thus attempt to reflect on the Fund by explaining that they are pro-growth—never mind how growth is borrowed—and have no use for austerity as a means of adjustment.

Nationalists, to use another crude binary distinction, also attack the Fund from all directions, but internationalists are equally unhappy. Creditors tend to criticize the Fund for imposing excessive financing obligations on them while asking too little of debtors in the way of macroeconomic adjustment. Debtors, of course, tend to see the balance of violations of national sovereignty as tipping the other way. For nationalists, it is the impositions that count—not whether it is convenient to criticize them from the Right or the Left. From the debtor countries' perspective the "less on me" and "more on you" are well-illustrated, respectively, in Diaz-Alejandro (1983, 537) and Brandt (1980, 215).

Internationalists who appear to have held the pen in Brandt (1980) seek more imposition, most commonly on creditor countries, to implement their schemes of redistribution, restitution, and sharing. In the industrial democracies, none of these are rooted firmly in the agendas of governments or the mandates of their peoples. Judging by actions rather than words, nondemocratic donor countries tend to be even less sympathetic to the unconditional transfers which internationalists frequently favor. If internationalists get around to discussing requirements to be placed on borrowing countries at all, the standards suggested tend to have more to do with the ideological acceptability of the form of government in these countries than with the quality of economic management. Schechter (1985, 18), for instance, advises that the Fund should not lend to nondemocratic governments, a move that would disqualify most LDC members.

After all of this complaining about the Fund, one might wonder why most developing countries in external-payments difficulties choose to turn to the Fund. Why do they clamor the loudest for IMF quota increases to augment loan resources? (See International Monetary Fund, September 1985, G24.) If the Fund's conditions are so onerous and counterproductive, why would such countries ask for trouble by seeking to negotiate programs with it? Why do they not follow the former example of Brazil? Diaz-Alejandro describes this honorable aloofness, which contrasts sharply with threats to leave the Fund after having become heavily indebted to it, as follows:

> Unhappy experiences with the IMF during the late 1950s, plus special relationships with the U.S. government since 1964 and with international banks during the 1970s, led the Brazilian government to keep the IMF at arm's length until the last quarter of 1982. As late as mid-1982 suggestions (typically by foreigners) that Brazil either should or would go to the IMF were dismissed by most Brazilians, regardless of political views. Indeed, the 1981 austerity was partly sold to domestic audiences because it would make a trip to the IMF unnecessary. (1983, 534–35)

Questions of this kind will not be pursued here because the purpose of this paper is not to debate the critics or to question the logic of their views. Rather, it is to ask whether they are addressing the right object, while offering an understanding of the Fund's reason for being and knowing what it needs to function. There is reason to suspect misdirection on the part of the Fund because critics on all sides generally attribute a definite—and misguided—modus operandi to the Fund, but give no clear idea of why the Fund behaves in the way they envision. They take the Fund as an independent public body which it would be appropriate to berate in the hope of changing its basic attitude and purposes. By contrast, this paper attempts to explain why and how the Fund does what it does from the viewpoint that it is not an autonomous, self-styled entity but an agent. While it is interesting to analyze the circumstances under which agents succeed in intermediating in the business of nations, as will be done in the next section, agents are not normally promising objects for sermonizing; principals are the ones to address and talking at the agent may not be a good way of reaching them. The principals in this case are national governments whose representatives sit on the Executive Board of the IMF. If the Fund channels all the net benefits of its programs to creditor members, it will soon have no one to lend to. If it allocates all of these benefits to debtors, it will soon have nothing more to lend. It can thus move only within narrow margins of tolerance between creditors and debtors. Exhortations cannot give it more room.

International Brokerage and Its Limits

For an agent to arrange for an exchange of services by others or for conditional transfers between them, there must be a supply and a demand that can be matched better by him than by the principals on their own. In other words, there are efficiency gains to be had from using an intermediary. Furthermore, for the agent to remain in business, these gains must be recognized by both parties. Thus, both creditor and debtor members have to be fundamentally satisfied with the Fund if the Fund is to continue to function.

This basic agreement will rarely be evident since all members have an incentive to play down their overall satisfaction and to stress specific points of dissatisfaction with the Fund. They do so in hopes of moving the Fund toward outcomes more favorable to them and less favorable to others, while recognizing that the Fund cannot coerce those who view themselves as consistent net losers to go on playing. In practice, therefore, conflicts among the members of the Fund, to the extent they are aired confidentially in the Executive Board, are tempered by the requirement that all members should expect to gain by continued membership though not necessarily from every minor move. The consensual approach used to reach most major decisions in the Fund indicates such a basic understanding. Tacit consent may exist even when a country finds political advantage in railing and posturing publicly against the terms of any adjustment program proposed or adopted. This section attempts to explain the bounds within which a consensus can be reached given the objectives of the parties assembled in the Fund.

Some countries stand ready to supply credit to others at below-market rates in return not just for a promise to repay but for some other consideration that they find costly to settle on directly or bilaterally. They are prepared to use the Fund to get this other consideration out into the open and into contracts that can be monitored and enforced internationally without encumbering bilateral relations. The Fund is therefore cast in the role of intermediary through which creditor countries attempt to get debtor countries to do certain things which they are willing to do only at a price. Specifically, the Fund is charged with procuring adjustment services which are valued for a variety of reasons by its creditor members.

Creditors are averse to the political, economic, financial, business, and property risks associated with prolonged financial crises, particularly in developing countries. They want the Fund to help dissipate these crises as rapidly as feasible, more rapidly than a country would normally want to adjust unaided. Debtor countries are willing to oblige if a program can be arranged. They then agree to accelerate adjustment at a price that depends on their preferences, financial alternatives, and skills in negotiations. There are net gains from trade (organized exchange) to be distributed in situations of this kind, and there is no presumption that any deals struck—for example, adjustment programs adopted—systematically give more of the net gain to one side than the other.

With this introduction, let me briefly explain what is needed to identify the Fund-assisted product, accelerated adjustment, and how it is bought. A rigorous supporting treatment is available elsewhere (von Furstenberg 1985). To define what the Fund can do to accelerate adjustment, one needs first to find the path a country would choose unaided to work off any excess of external debt over debt capacity. The concept of external debt capacity is given operational meaning by defining it as the stock of (cumulative) net capital imports which optimizes the path of domestic consumption for given time-preference rates of discount and rates of population growth. The steady-state (long-run equilibrium) stocks of debt and capital are found under diminishing rates of return on productive capital and under the assumption of borrowing rates from private international banking sources, which rise at an increasing rate with the ratio of external debt to the domestic stock of capital.

A country that is initially in external-payments difficulties attempts to get its debt-to-capital ratio down to the long-run optimum. The question is how fast. By consulting the inter-temporal preference function, this debtor country can determine how large an initial cut in domestic absorption is justified to reduce the debt and its cost to a level compatible with financial stability later on. In most cases, the cut in living standards which a country in external-payments disequilibrium would choose unaided appears to be small, and the adjustment slow. Mathematical simulations with some plausible parameter values suggest that a developing country might try to spread the pain over decades if left to its own devices.

To creditor countries such lethargy would be little different from no adjustment at all. Programs involving unending commercial, financial, and political uncertainty and a high risk of interruption of debt-service payments sometime in the future do not deserve, or normally obtain, the support of creditor governments. If creditors are to make subsidized financing available (at least implicitly), they must ask something they value in return: accelerated adjustment. Because adjustment that is faster than the optimum determined by debtors in the absence of aid inevitably reduces their welfare, debtors will not agree to any such request unless they are compensated by creditor governments. Thus deals can be struck only when the Fund can match willingness to pay compensation with willingness to accelerate adjustment. Compensation essentially takes the form of industrial countries bankrolling risky foreign government adjustment programs through the Fund at interest rates at which they themselves can borrow in the domestic market.

The Fund can mediate this exchange within the limits set by the preferences of the two parties involved. It is precisely because creditor governments are meddlesome, or because they value faster adjustment by developing countries for any mixture of selfish and altruistic reasons, that debtor countries have something of value to sell. If creditor governments are not supposed or inclined to bother debtor governments, they will not bother to subsidize their adjustment efforts either. Conversely, if debtors would adjust just as rapidly from the start as creditor governments want them to, there is no need for a Fund program to realize any unused marginal opportunity for exchange because no such opportunity exists. In 1980 and 1981, Turkey was sometimes cited as an example of a country choosing to adjust at least as rapidly as the Fund required. In Argentina, the immediate effects of the fiscal and currency reforms of June 14, 1985 have also been at least as strong as those called for in the Fund program approved three days earlier. However, examples of overfulfillment tend to be both rare and episodic.

Creditors generally feel that tougher conditions and faster-acting programs than a country would choose raise the chance that the country will eventually attain complete adjustment. Creditors are not nearly as impressed with the risk of inciting political turmoil through demands of adjustment as debtor countries would like them to be. Fateful ideological shifts are rarely precipitated by austerity. Weintraub elaborates:

> Russian- and Cuban-sponsored revolutions have not been impelled by economic austerity programs in the past. And if the IMF's prescriptions turn out to be intolerably austere and threaten the survival of a nation's political authorities, the political authorities will scrap the IMF's conditions. . . . (1983, 40)

Many creditors are more impressed with the dangers, to them and others, of letting economic disequilibria fester fundamentally untreated than with the risk of provoking instant revolution. This difference in the (dis)taste for rapid adjustment among the parties is what makes exchange between them feasible. Negotiations determine how far, beyond debtors' optimum, adjustment should be carried with the support of creditors.

The assistance provided by the Fund with means obtained from its creditor members can take the form of financing more assured and less costly than that available from private international lenders. The institution's signaling and monitoring services, and the "seal of approval" attributed to programs and covenants concluded with the Fund, are valued by private lenders. Accordingly, these lenders may modify their terms and conditions on both rollovers and new loans in conjunction with Fund programs. Being unable to obtain Fund approval or losing that approval through program suspension can thus be costly to developing countries in ways that give the Fund some powers of enforcement. Within certain limits, the Fund, partly on account of its leverage over other lenders, is able to reward good results and to withdraw rewards for behavior disappointing to its creditor members.

With official creditors helping because they view it as in their interest to do so, and with debtors going out of their way in return for that help, both parties normally gain when they come to terms through the intermediation of the Fund. Neither can lose systematically since there is no warrant for forcing unwilling members to contract with the Fund. One would expect that the ebb and flow of altruism toward the non–oil producing developing world may have a little to do with how the benefits are split. The management of the Fund, supported by an international staff in bringing cases before the Executive Board and in exercising its judgment, can also affect the outcome to some degree. Like any good agent, the Fund can offer new products, facilities, or program techniques for use by its members. Now and then it might sniff the political winds and sound out member governments on whether broader initiatives are called for, including those that might involve the granting of new powers through amendment of its charter, the Articles of Agreement. In the end, however, the Fund can do no more than its creditors permit and provide for, or its actual or potential debtors are willing to take.

How Much Leeway for the Fund?

There is no insult or revelation in supposing that the Fund, *ceteris paribus*, might like to be able to afford more of a mind of its own. The organization would surely be lacking in spunk and healthy ambition if it never felt tempted to develop and execute policies with a greater degree of independence than it is given to enjoy. The reason why the Fund does not reach for this extra degree of independence is that it is not of independent means.

The Fund has made several attempts to become less subject to the resource constraints and appropriations of governments. Seeking authority for borrowing from private markets was one way of seeking to loosen the control exercised by member nations. Some elements in or around conservative governments deluded themselves into thinking that this might be a way of getting "the market" to discipline the Fund and to discourage it from taking "unwise" risks. Others knew that "the market" would not be nearly as restrictive as governments, particularly since the full faith and credit of member governments would stand behind the Fund's obligations. The case of the U.S. Federal National Mortgage Association (FNMA) shows that the market frequently does not question government guarantees, even if such guarantees are merely inferred to stand behind an institution or its debt obligations. This is shown in the discussions in the U.S. General Accounting Office of how FNMA has "traded" on the government's backing (1985). In the end, therefore, those who wanted to keep the Fund on a tight leash decided to keep the leash in their own hands and not to throw it into the private market where no one might pick it up.

The Fund has tried to reduce the need to vie for the support of members, particularly the least sympathetic among creditor members, in other ways. Since quotas are fixed in nominal terms, the Fund has to go begging merely to keep real resource constraints in place as inflation proceeds to reduce them. To keep up with real growth in the world economy, with world trade, or with the size of trade imbalances, even larger quota increases would be indicated. To reduce the trouble the Fund has to go through to get such increases approved by the required 85 percent majority of the total voting power, it has offered a menu of formulas for determining what the size of the Fund should be. It has offered these "rational" or "objective" guides, hoping perhaps that members would settle on one or the other formula for more or less automatic application in the future. However, all attempts to mechanize quota increases, or, for that matter, SDR allocations and changes in the size of borrowing from particular countries, have been resisted by members. They do not want agreed-upon formulas that bind them, but formulas they can choose from and tinker with to provide technical decorum and circumlocution for their political decisions and intent.

Members clearly wish to limit the Fund's discretion, not their own. This is reflected in the design and adaptation of some of the Fund's lending programs. Until a few years ago, for instance, there was a tendency to view access to the Compensatory Financing Facility as increasingly automatic. If a shortfall in export proceeds of primary commodities, calculated by a fixed formula, was sufficiently large in relation to surrounding years, and if it resulted essentially from circumstances beyond a member's control as more and more readily claimed and granted, then a country felt entitled to use the facility with no questions asked (for details see Goreux 1980). Members found out, however, that while reducing the possibility of Fund "interference," putting programs on automatic pilot in the Fund can take them for rides they do not want to take. When the Somoza dictatorship in Nicaragua (overthrown in July 1979)—and since then, South Africa—wanted to get something automatically, members did not like access to be so automatic at all.

These vignettes may show that the practices, guidelines, and doctrines surrounding the activities of the Fund change formally and informally as necessary to accommodate the wishes of the vast majority of member governments. Members do appreciate the Fund's taking a lead in developing concrete plans and applications in areas and directions they basically approve—however, they have no use for anyone other than their own domestic constituency telling them, by formula or otherwise, what they should basically approve.

Who, in the World, Needs the Fund?

Those who read from all of this that the Fund is the tool of industrial creditor countries usually would rather it oblige the developing debtor countries, as if tables needed to be turned. The president of Peru even said, after his country had borrowed about all it could from the Fund, that it might not be to its advantage to belong to an agency that serves the benefit of a single country, apparently referring to the United States (*New York Times,* September 24, 1985, p. 8). Since then Peru has failed, for at least two quarters, to make any payments to the IMF on its debt. Those who call for a new monetary order to meet redistribution objectives rarely put their desires plainly and unadorned, hiding instead behind moral precepts of justice or fairness between rich and poor, and between North and South. They may even remember to call for restitution by colonizers and imperial powers to their, presumptively exploited, erstwhile subjects.

My point is not to question these visions but merely to point out that the high road constructed with them will never see any traffic. The more an agent like the Fund is coerced into working for the interests of one party, and not also the other, the less business it will be able to arrange between creditor and debtor nations. Attempts have repeatedly been made by, or on behalf of, poor countries to tax the rich countries. Almost all such attempts to institutionalize unconditional unilateral transfers between nations (except arguably in the aftermath of war in the form of reparations), have failed. The protracted negotiations surrounding the "Law of the Sea," relating to the division of royalties from open ocean-bed mining, point up the difficulties (the polarization is evident from Akinsanya 1980; and Lowe and Churchill 1983). A succession of stillborn "link" proposals for SDR allocations (for example, allocating SDRs to developing countries by fiat and then having developed countries earn them from these countries to hold in international reserves) show that even modest proposals for institutionalizing favors of this kind tend to fail. Some form of the link, whose sterile history is explained in von Furstenberg (1983, 498–502), has always been advocated by the Intergovernmental Group of 24 on International Monetary Affairs, most recently at their August 1985 meeting in Washington, D.C. (International Monetary Fund, September 1985, G24). More extreme proposals of international tax-transfer schemes are identified in Bauer and Yamey (1981).

If membership in the Fund becomes onerous to creditor countries, they will cease to support it and shift their business elsewhere. In the external debt crises of recent years, the U.S. Federal Reserve, the Bank of England, the Bank for International Settlements, and others have participated in making bridge loans to Latin American countries and in coordinating a number of interests in much the same way as, and in cooperation with, the Fund (see Smith and Cuddington 1984; and Bergsten, Cline, and Williamson 1985). Membership in the Fund is undoubtedly still valuable to industrial creditor countries, but not so valuable or indispensable that the Fund could be forced to reduce their net benefits without risking the loss of their support and subscriptions. Some agencies or organizations of the United Nations—of which the Fund is not one—or, more accurately, the majority of their members, also thought they could make themselves ever more onerous to developed countries with impunity. The irony is that as some of the least masochistically inclined developed countries have walked away, these organizations have also become less interesting to developing countries because little useful business could continue. The high road is therefore not something developing countries can force developed countries to travel. It is useless for them to man the toll booths, draped in holy cloth, for there will be no traffic or sacrificial tribute. Only when the developed countries themselves build the high road, splendidly like in the Marshall Plan, or out of socialist or egalitarian zeal of the kind that sometimes appears to pay domestic political dividends in countries like Sweden and the Netherlands, may they agree to use it.

Let me offer a topical analogy in relating all this to the Fund. Expecting the Fund to act as the world's conscience is about as misdirected as expecting a broker to refuse to execute any lawful orders of his clients for South African gold stocks. Although I have never owned such stocks on account of small means, I would consider any such action by a broker impudent, while holding the broker as free as anyone to demonstrate his convictions with his own money. The member nations of the Fund certainly do own up, as some are more altruistic, and perhaps far-sighted, more than others. None of them wants to be forced into rigid, institutionalized, and henceforth automatic schemes of international redistribution.

It is not immoral for those who receive to offer something in return which the donor values so that both may benefit. What is immoral, at least by my lights, is to interdict mutual gain by destroying opportunities for exchanges of the kind the Fund helps realize. Moral zeal, when armed with petulance and self-righteousness, empties the house of nations. Some of the business that used to be conducted in that house will shift elsewhere, but some of it, and the collegiality and comity of the house, will not be easy to replace. Developing countries could well be the chief losers.

Conclusion

This paper tried to explain what the Fund can do well and what it should not be asked to do when its role as market-maker between nations is properly understood. The purpose of analyzing major activities of the Fund, particularly its adjustment programs, in this light was not to defend Fund programs against criticisms from Right and Left. Rather it was to point out that many of the critics take potshots at effigies, with little chance of ever hitting the real target.

It is essential to understand what an organization was designed for and what it needs to function before one can relevantly criticize its activities. The standards derived cannot simply be left to "critics' choice" without any reference to the Fund's official mandate. Matters are also not helped by pretending that this mandate can easily be changed. Amendments to the Articles of Agreement are time-consuming and difficult to negotiate. There is little demand for them except under exceptional circumstances or after developments in the world economy have made some of the Articles obsolete and have made new ones required to guide the Fund's day-to-day operations. At other times, critics might do well to respect the likelihood that the Fund's mandate is what the collectivity of its members wants it to be more than it is any other, including any that critics might conjure up.

The comparative advantage of the Fund, indeed its reason for being, lies in its ability to facilitate exchanges involving external-financing and economic-policy measures between creditor and debtor countries. These exchanges might otherwise be thwarted by nonexcludability problems attaching to bilateral agreements reached without the Fund. For instance, if country X keeps country Z afloat and on a path to complete adjustment, why should country Y contribute toward that same goal even if it values it? Moreover, bilateral arrangements may be impeded by political sensitivities to alleged infringements of national sovereignty on the part of particular countries, by conflicts among such agreements with different countries, by difficulties of enforcement, and much else. For these reasons, the Fund can generate benefits by acting as an intermediary enabling, or at least facilitating, exchanges. These mutually beneficial trades between nations might not otherwise have taken place at all, or might have taken place only at much higher transaction costs and with negative side-effects that are avoidable.

On the other hand, the Fund properly shuns the hopeless business of attempting to alienate international aid from donors without alienating the donors. It recognizes that charity, even international charity, begins at home and not in international institutions. Such institutions cannot hope to succeed by attempting to shame countries with applications of moral precepts not backed by their national constituencies. The Fund cannot even succeed by spurning those governments that respect no constituency and lack any semblance of legitimacy, let alone democracy. Such governments, whose practices Pol Pot, Idi Amin, and Anastasio Somoza Debayle (on a decreasing scale of abomination) would easily recognize, can be shunned only to the extent the majority of the Fund's members wishes. Members normally repress such wishes because they do not want to set undesirable precedents or encourage the Fund to become politicized in a way that is holier than they. Since all governments, even those that are fully representative, tend to have at best selective consciences in their bilateral dealings, there is no point of substance (as opposed to pretence and appearance) to be served in holding them to higher standards when they deal with each other in international institutions.

Postcript

Since the time this paper was first circulated in September 1985, a number of comments have been received from persons kind enough to communicate their insights in a private capacity, whether or not they are associated with the Fund. The summary that follows is based on letters from Charles S. Gardner, Sir Joseph Gold, J.J. Polak, and John Williamson. Several of these distinguished commentators judged the "market-maker" concept to be useful for explaining the business of the Fund and the constraints on its conduct. However, they would see a greater variety of products, other than just "accelerated adjustment," for which the Fund could intermediate an exchange of value to both creditor (or industrial) and debtor (or developing) nations.

There are two other possibilities, at least. There are cases where the creditors want accelerated adjustment and the debtors do also. This is the situation where the country wants a faster adjustment than is politically feasible, and it uses the Fund's "lightning rod" function to deflect the political tempest. Cast in this way, the Fund serves as a convenient buffer, subterfuge, and scapegoat, freeing creditors from appearing to impose their will on debtors and freeing debtors from appearing to succumb to the will of creditor nations. There are limits to the lightning-rod role because the Fund may also find it desirable to avoid the appearance of imposing its will too massively or too often. Another case can arise under "debt crisis," where the situation is desperate, and both debtors and creditors use the

Fund to slow down adjustment, thereby letting the debtor sidestep both default and the inability to import anything except what can be prepaid. In exchange for being enabled to slow adjustment by means of the resources provided by the Fund, the country would have to agree to adjust "along the lines of the Fund," i.e., predominantly on a market-oriented basis and with relatively little reliance on market restrictions.

Under both of these situations the interests of debtors and creditors are closer, and the Fund's leverage is greater, than in the case I dealt with. That case identified the Fund's adjustment activities as typically involving a rather narrowly constrained bargain between the industrial countries who wish to accelerate adjustment and the borrowing developing countries who would prefer slow adjustment. Several commentators stated or implied that there are other cases in which at least some elements in the government and in the central bank are reinforced in their own preferences by the Fund's position.

More such concordant bargains, designed to ease the pain of adjustment rather than to increase it in return for compensation, are implied also by an older, traditional view of the Fund as a credit union in which members alternate between being creditors and debtors. Members would then have an incentive to help countries ease the adjustment process in the expectation of receiving similar treatment as and when they find themselves in a comparable situation. However, it is difficult to think of industrial and developing countries as facing similar risks and probabilities of Fund assistance under the present exchange rate regime of managed floating among the major currencies. Altruism by donors and certain public-goods aspects of adjustment valued by all members may explain some part of the Fund's activities. On the other hand, the foresightful pursuit of self-interest advised by the golden rule, which is based on nothing more than mutuality, is not likely to be applicable between industrial and developing countries. It may only explain logrolling among many of the Fund's borrowing members in the Third World.

One commentator has pointed out that such logrolling may be successful under many circumstances even though the Fund's important decisions are taken with broad agreement. The fact that decisions on the use of the Fund's resources require only a majority of the votes cast exercises a strong influence on the tactics of borrowers and creditors. As the Fund has become an institution whose resources are used exclusively for developing members, creditors have tended to limit their exposure, for example by not letting the size of the Fund keep up with economic magnitudes and parameters of "need" related to its business. In short, this commentator felt that the Fund is valuable, but only up to a relatively modest point which can be lost unless great care is taken to remain of service to all sides.

References

Akinsanya, Adeoye A. 1980. *The Law of the Sea: Unilateralism or Multilateralism.* Lagos: University of Lagos Press.

Bauer, Peter, and Basil Yamey. October 1981. "The Political Economy of Foreign Aid," *Lloyds Bank Review*, no. 142, pp. 1–14.

Bergsten, C. Fred, William R. Cline, and John Williamson. April 1985. *Bank Lending to Developing Countries: The Policy Alternatives.* Policy Analyses in International Economics, no. 10. Washington, D.C.: Institute for International Economics and MIT Press.

Brandt, Willy. 1980. *North-South: A Program for Survival.* Cambridge, MA: MIT Press.

DeGrauwe, Paul, and Michele Fratianni. Spring/Summer 1984. "The Political Economy of International Lending," *Cato Journal,* vol. 4, no. 1, pp. 147–70.

Diaz-Alejandro, Carlos F. 1983. "Some Aspects of the 1982–83 Brazilian Payments Crisis," *Brookings Papers on Economic Activity*, no. 2. Washington, D.C.: The Brookings Institution.

________. 1984. "Latin American Debt: I Don't Think We Are in Kansas Anymore," *Brookings Papers on Economic Activity*, no. 2. Washington, D.C.: The Brookings Institution.

Dornbusch, Rudiger. June 1984. "On the Consequences of Muddling Through the Debt Crisis," *The World Economy*, vol. 7, no. 2, pp. 145–62.

Goode, Richard. 1985. *Economic Assistance to Developing Countries through the IMF.* Washington, D.C.: The Brookings Institution.

Goreux, Louis M. 1980. *Compensatory Financing Facility.* International Monetary Fund Pamphlet Series, no. 34. Washington, D.C.: IMF.

International Monetary Fund. September 1985. *IMF Survey.* Supplement on the Fund (SF). Washington, D.C.: IMF.

________. September 1985. *IMF Survey.* Supplement on the Group of 24 Deputies' Report (G-24). Washington, D.C.: IMF.

Lowe, A.V., and R.R. Churchill. 1983. *The Law of the Sea.* Manchester and Dover, N.H.: Manchester University Press.

National Advisory Council on International Monetary and Financial Policies. 1985. *International Finance, Annual Report to the President and to the Congress for Fiscal Year 1984.* Washington, D.C.: U.S.G.P.O.

New York Times. September 24, 1985.

Sachs, Jeffrey D. June 1985. "Some Thoughts on the Design of Adjustment Programs." paper presented at a conference retreat on Macroeconomic Adjustment and Growth of the World Bank's Economic Research Service.

Schechter, Henry B. May 1, 1985. "IMF Conditionality and the International Economy: A U.S. Labor Perspective." paper presented at a seminar sponsored by the Council on Religion and International Affairs, pp. 1–23.

Smith, Gordon W., and John T. Cuddington, eds. 1984. *International Debt and the Developing Countries.* Washington, D.C.: The World Bank.

Taylor, Lance. April 1985. "IMF Conditionality: Incomplete Theory, Policy Malpractice." paper presented to the Council on Religion and International Affairs, pp. 1–20.

U.S. General Accounting Office. July 17, 1985. *The Federal National Mortgage Association in a Changing Economic Environment*, Supplement to a Report by the Comptroller General of the United States. (GAO/RCED-85–102A) Washington, D.C.: U.S.G.P.O.

von Furstenberg, George M. June 1985. "Adjustment with IMF Lending," *Journal of International Money and Finance,* vol. 4, pp. 209–22.

________, ed. 1983. *International Money and Credit: The Policy Roles*. Washington, D.C.: IMF.

Weintraub, Robert E. April 1983. *International Debt: Crisis and Challenge*. Fairfax, VA.: Department of Economics, George Mason University.

9

IMF Conditionality and Agriculture in the Developing Countries

D. Gale Johnson

The IMF and its teams of visiting policy experts have now become excellent whipping boys for those who see in the policies espoused by the IMF the major cause of much of the political, social, and economic difficulties of many heavily indebted developing countries. To some degree, these attacks are like shooting the messenger who brings bad news: In all too many cases, the messenger is attacked and the underlying causes of the current unsatisfactory state of affairs are ignored. Unwillingness to accept responsibility for past and current policy mistakes seriously inhibits the prospects for the kinds of adjustments that will be required if the developing countries are to emerge from their current difficulties to follow a path of sustained economic growth.

I shall take a rather parochial view of IMF conditionality as it directly and specifically affects agriculture. In taking this view, I am supportive of efforts to remove the numerous distortions that have had and continue to have adverse effects upon agriculture in many developing countries—upon the welfare of farm people and upon the utilization of agricultural resources. I am supportive of removing such distortions whether the pressure for reducing the urban bias of food and export policies comes from the IMF or from some other quarter.

Most of the LDCs that currently have large debt problems have had food and agricultural policies that exhibit an enormous urban bias for two decades or more. These policies have been for the short-run benefit of the urban population at the expense of farm people. In spite of any lip service that may be given to achieving greater income equality or eliminating poverty, these policies work to transfer income from relatively poorer people to those who are relatively better off. With few exceptions, urban family incomes are substantially higher than farm family incomes. In Asia and Latin America, the ratio of urban to rural incomes is in the general range of 2:1 or 3:1, but in Africa, where some of the policies most exploitive of agriculture are to be found, the income disparities may be on the order of 4:1 or 9:1 (Lele 1981).

Agriculture is exploited in a variety of ways. One direct way is to heavily tax exports of farm products. Many developing countries have a limited range of farm products that are exported. Farmers are deprived of a large percentage of the international value of their product either through a monopsonistic marketing board or by taxes at the border. A second method is to maintain low food prices, generally only for urban consumers. These low prices are achieved either by the procurement of food from farmers at low prices or by the use of price subsidies. The price subsidies are almost always paid for, to some degree, by taxes paid by farm people, even though farm people very rarely have access to the subsidized food—Egypt seems to be the only significant exception to this rule.

A third way agriculture is exploited is through protection of the industrial sectors from international competition through tariffs or import quotas, which force farmers to pay unduly high prices for inputs such as fertilizer and machinery.

A fourth technique for exploiting farm people for the benefit of urban areas is an overvalued currency, which acts as a tax on exports and a subsidy for imports. Where agriculture is the major source of exports, the overvalued currency clearly discriminates against agriculture. Where the supply of foreign exchange earnings is adequate to more or less freely import food, imported food becomes available to the urban population at a low real price and gradually displaces domestically produced food. This has been the consequence of the great overvaluation of the Nigerian currency which has persisted for a decade and still persists and still does great harm.

It is relatively easy to make a strong case against the effectiveness of the IMF by showing that many of its clients, especially among the developing countries, are now no better off and are perhaps worse off than at the time of their first encounters with the IMF. If this is the basis for the evaluation, by reviewing the experience of African countries and a number of Latin American and Caribbean countries, one is likely to conclude that most bilateral and multilateral aid efforts have also failed to accomplish much, if anything. Yet it is not obvious that such a negative interpretation is justified. Excepting Africa, the majority of the developing countries—those with less than $1,500 per capita annual incomes—have had positive per capita income growth over the past two decades. Many of the growth rates, however, have been less than one would like to see and less than could have been achieved with different national policies. Nonetheless, as measured by economic growth rates and other measures of improvement in the quality of life, such as sharp reductions in infant mortality rates, marked increases in life expectancies, and the reduction of famines due to climatic factors, much of a positive nature has been accomplished during the past quarter century (Johnson 1985).

Furthermore, in evaluating the effects of IMF financing on the basis of economic growth during the period of the conditionality, it should be remembered that in the majority of the cases, the borrower has already suffered one or more serious reverses which induced it to apply to the IMF. In other words, the IMF deals primarily with sick cases when it applies significant conditions. Funds obtained from the Compensatory Financing Facility or the special Food Financing Facility are largely free of conditions, other than that evidence is required that the borrower is cooperating with the IMF in finding appropriate solutions for any balance-of-payments difficulties that are more structural in character. Yet, when conditionality is formally required, the country is usually in a situation which it cannot readily resolve by itself. Unfortunately, there appear to be some cases in which resolution is not possible even with the use of the resources that the IMF can and does make available.

IMF Conditionality and Domestic Demand

There is considerable confusion about particular IMF conditionality requirements and their effect upon the welfare of the population of the LDCs burdened with large external debts. Further, it appears that some hold that the proper roles of the IMF (and perhaps the World Bank) exclude conditionality terms, or very nearly so. In particular, the greatest disputes arise over what are considered to be IMF-imposed requirements to limit and reduce domestic demand as one of the important means to achieve a current-account surplus in trade and thus make servicing the external debt possible.

The reduction of domestic demand is, in most cases, associated with the reduction of the deficit in the government budget. Several of the LDCs have had what can be termed government deficits that are very large as a percentage both of all government revenue and of GDP or GNP. Some examples are: Argentina in 1975 and 1985, when the budget deficits were fifteen percent of GDP; Mexico in 1982, when the budget deficit was eighteen percent of GDP; and Morocco, where the budget deficit was at least eight percent of GDP every year from 1975 to 1983, reaching a peak of eighteen percent in 1976 (World Bank 1985). The government deficits have often been financed, in real terms, by foreign borrowing. Imports have exceeded exports and domestic consumption has exceeded domestic production. Consequently, it should be no surprise that when net foreign borrowing declines to zero or becomes negative in most of the heavily indebted LDCs, per capita real incomes fall. But the declines in real incomes are not primarily due to IMF conditionality; the declines are due primarily to the loss of access to foreign borrowing. IMF intervention may in fact cushion the decline in real incomes for some countries by permitting rescheduling and some new borrowing.

Imagine, if you will, what would occur if, in the absence of IMF support, foreign lenders simply refused to renew or rollover existing loans. Not only would there be no new inflow of capital, but the LDC would be faced either with having to restrict both domestic demand and income to provide the foreign exchange required to service the debts, or to default. In either case, domestic incomes and consumption must fall from the previous unsustainable levels. In the absence of IMF funds and intervention, incomes and consumption might well fall more rather than less.

The IMF prescriptions for adjustment include not only controlling domestic demand, in large part through controlling government deficits and expansion of the money supply, but also through requiring the abolition of policies and measures that adversely affect the productivity of the economy. Many of these measures, especially those involving price controls and subsidies, are related to the budget deficits. If food prices for urban consumers are heavily subsidized, these subsidies must be paid either from the government budget, or by exploiting farmers by paying them very low prices, or by some combination of the two. The case for abolishing food subsidies for urban consumers has absolutely nothing to do with the case for reducing the government deficit. If the urban food price subsidies are paid from the government budget and not by exploiting farmers, eliminating the food price subsidies obviously reduces the budget deficit. The same can be said about a wide variety of subsidies and income transfers—subsidies for energy, for urban transportation, for fertilizer, for interest costs of investment funds. Such subsidies clearly affect the level of budget expenditures. However, if tax receipts had equaled expenditures prior to IMF intervention, the subsidies would not have contributed to inflation or to a negative balance of foreign trade, although such subsidy policies generally would have had adverse effects upon the allocation of resources and the productivity of the economy (a point to which I will return later).

Currency Devaluation

An especially unpopular aspect of IMF conditionality has been the IMF's insistence upon the immediate devaluation of overvalued currencies. Such a policy prescription is often strongly criticized and resisted, apparently on the assumption that devaluation will cause a decline in domestic real income. This argument confuses cause and effect. Although overvaluation of a currency may result from a variety of factors, over a period of time the main cause of overvaluation is that the nominal exchange rate fails to reflect differences in rates of inflation between the country in question and its trading partners. With fixed exchange rates, changes in the terms of trade for export products can also result in currency overvaluation if the fall in export earnings is not offset by a similar reduction in imports, made possible by a reshuffling of domestic resources.

Why do governments resist currency devaluation when it is obvious that their currencies are significantly overvalued? And why do IMF critics tend to support the governments in their resistance? Not all of the reasons can be explored here, but a few are discussed below.

First, it is useful to look at some of the domestic implications of an overvalued currency. As noted above, overvaluation constitutes a tax on exports: an exporter receives less in domestic currency for his exports than the real value of the exports. Overvaluation is also a subsidy to all imports: anyone who gains access to foreign exchange at the official rate of exchange is receiving a subsidy when imports are actually made. The importer pays less than the real value of the imports, which is the cost of the imports in terms of the amount and value of the exports required to purchase them. Suppose the official rate of exchange is 1 peso per $1 (US), and the equilibrium or post-devaluation rate of exchange is 2 pesos per $1. A farmer exports 3,000 bushels of wheat and receives $10,000, which he must exchange at the official rate of exchange; he is thus credited with 10,000 pesos. At the equilibrium rate of exchange his 3,000 bushels of wheat would yield 20,000 pesos. An importer buys two cars worth $5,000 each, and pays for them with dollars purchased at the official rate of exchange. The dollars cost 10,000 pesos. The importer who has now just 10,000 pesos to spend would be able to purchase just one car at $5,000 (or 10,000 pesos) at the equilibrium rate of exchange. The overvaluation of the currency can be said to have cost the farmer half the value of his wheat and to have doubled the real value of imports that could be obtained with a given amount of domestic currency.

You may ask, why doesn't the farmer, given the overvalued currency, buy the two cars with his dollars, or one car and one $5,000 tractor? The reason is very simple—his government won't let him. When a country's currency is overvalued, there is simply not enough foreign exchange available to permit everyone to import as much as they would like, at least not for very long. An overvalued currency requires that the government control imports and thus decide who is permitted to import. A license to import at the official rate of exchange or the right to purchase foreign exchange at the official rate is a valuable asset, and apparently people are willing to pay, through bribes, to obtain the licenses and foreign exchange. A government may resist devaluation either because it is very corrupt, because it does not wish to reduce the degree of its intervention in the operation of the economy, or both. An overvalued currency helps to rationalize a wide range of subsidies and market interventions, and for a government that supports planning and an interventionist approach, these are positive benefits.

As noted earlier, an overvalued currency has a number of domestic distributional effects. For example, urban food prices are depressed. Perhaps equally important, an overvalued currency makes imported goods such as televisions, radios, automobiles, and other luxury items cheap to the middle class and to upper-level bureaucrats. Many critics argue against the IMF's emphasis upon devaluation because the devaluation causes the urban poor to pay more for food. Such critics ignore at least four consequences of currency overvaluation. One is that currency overvaluation is as likely, if not more likely, to transfer income from poor people to those who are better off than it is to make poor people better off. In most developing countries the average incomes of farm people are substantially lower than those of urban people. This is not to say that some of the urban poor are not worse off than some of the rural population, but it can be accepted that when the prices of staple food products are lowered by governmental action, the distribution of income is made more unequal. Devaluation, while raising costs for some urban poor, also raises the incomes of even larger numbers of rural poor.

A second consequence frequently overlooked is that an overvalued currency reduces the quantity of exports and thereby foreign exchange earnings. The adverse domestic terms of trade created by an overvalued currency discourages the production of export products. Because for most developing countries, the majority of export earnings come from agricultural products, an overvalued currency often serves as a tax on agriculture and results in transfers to the urban sector in the short run. However, in the long run, the benefit to the nonfarm sector may prove illusory—there is validity to the old adage about killing the goose that lays the golden egg.

A third effect of currency overvaluation is to dim prospects for increasing non-traditional agricultural exports and for creating new industrial ventures that are capable of competing in world markets. With an overvalued currency, new export possibilities are discouraged because imports become cheap. Even with imports rationed, as they must be after a time, investments in new export activities are more risky because the governmental controls over imports can be relaxed at any time.

Finally, an overvalued currency encourages capital outflows—an exporter will do many things to keep part of his export earnings abroad.

Much of the current debt of Mexico and Brazil is the result of two related economic policies of the late 1970s and early 1980s: overvalued currencies and governmental guarantees of private debts. These policies encouraged private foreign borrowing and, subsequently, the transfer of much of the foreign exchange abroad. It has been estimated that between 1979 and 1982 capital outflows from Venezuela exceeded capital inflows by $6 billion, or 37 percent; in Argentina, capital outflows were $19 billion, or 65 percent of the capital inflow; and in Mexico, capital outflow was $26 billion with a capital inflow of $55 billion (World Bank 1985, 64). Most of the foreign borrowing was guaranteed by the governments and even though the capital left the country, the governments remain responsible for its repayment.

Emphasis on Market-Oriented Policies

On a par with the opposition to the IMF's policy of devaluation is the opposition to the IMF's insistence that numerous policies of market intervention be eliminated. As noted earlier, the elimination of such policies is often associated with reducing the government budget deficit because many of the intervention policies involve large-scale subsidies. As I argued, while the two policy presumptions (reducing the budget deficit and eliminating subsidies) are related in the sense that subsidies cost money, the arguments for the two prescriptions are quite independent of each other. Reducing the budget deficit is a macro policy concerned with inflation and interest rates; the other policy—reducing subsidies and other market controls—is a micro policy concerned with how the nation's resources are allocated among alternative uses. Both policies, when implemented, affect the distribution of income, but these effects are clearly much more complex than the arguments for resisting the elimination of food price subsidies, for example, indicate.

However, I should not put too much emphasis on the independence of the deficit- and market-oriented policies. Cases exist in which the budgetary costs of subsidies become so large that there is no reasonable way to eliminate the budget deficit without reducing subsidies. For example, the cost of food and energy price subsidies in Egypt in 1984 was $7 billion out of a total government budget of $22 billion (*Washington Post* January 28, 1985, 16). In this instance, any effort to reduce the budget deficit would have had to at least consider these price subsidies, which made bread available at about 1 cent (US) per pound and gasoline available at 45 cents a gallon. I am sure that few people believe that low-priced gasoline transfers income, on balance, to the poor. In addition, the resource effects of the subsidies are significant. For example, it was cheaper to feed bread to livestock than grain, and cheaper for farm households to buy bread than to grind their wheat into flour and bake bread in the home.

A striking case of the negative impact of subsidies on resource use, foreign indebtedness, budget deficits, and inflation is that of Poland. To some considerable degree, the current state of affairs in Poland can be attributed to the impact of food price subsidies and low food prices on that economy. Food prices were held constant in nominal terms from late 1950 until 1970, even though during that period all consumer prices increased significantly. Efforts had been made to increase food prices in 1970 and 1976, but both attempts were abortive and were largely rescinded after rioting and other forms of unrest. In 1979, food prices in the cities were approximately the same as in 1960, although all consumer prices had doubled, and by 1981, meat price subsidies equaled the retail prices of meat.

What were the consequences of the meat price subsidies and other food subsidies? Throughout the 1970s, Polish agriculture was able to increase meat production at about the same pace as the growth in demand at the artificially low retail prices. The rapid growth of meat production, approximately 40 percent in a decade, was made possible by a large increase in grain and feed imports—between 1970 and 1979, imports of grain and feed increased threefold. As one Polish writer put it:

> A steadily increasing part of meat consumption is based upon imported fodders. It has been calculated that last year [1979] about 1.1 million tons of meat (including fat), i.e., about 27 kg. of meat and 3.5 kg. of fat per capita, was produced from imported raw materials. To simplify the argument, it may be said that every one of us bought 27 kg. of meat abroad. (Johnson 1981, 200)

In 1979, per capita meat consumption in Poland was 72 kilograms. Thus about one-third of Polish meat consumption was based on imported food, purchased with borrowed money. I estimate that approximately one-third of the nearly $20 billion increase in Poland's external debt between 1971 and 1979 was literally eaten and was not invested to improve the productivity of the economy. Part of the Polish economy's subsequent poor performance resulted from the failure to use these funds in a productive way.

Were there any benefits from the low meat prices and the enormous increase in the external hard-currency debt? Following are two evaluations of the effects made in mid-1980 by Poles (the second was made by the finance minister).

> Without risking to make an error, one may state that out of that 91.4 billion zl a lion's share were subsidies for the benefit of people in high income brackets because the more affluent buy more meat. . . . The meat subsidies system and the extensive pumping of money into the meat market creates a

> barrier to wage increases and necessitates the keeping of prices of products other than food at a relatively high level. Every wage increase, given the present price structure, increases the stresses on the market. (Johnson 1981, 201)
>
> I have already had occasion to tell the House the view that the problem of subsidies, despite their social motivation, arouses numerous controversies and reservations as regards their desirability as a form of social insurance. It is well known that they apply to all citizens, and thus the view that both those who earn more as well as those who earn less benefit from them, and perhaps those earning more benefit more, is correct. That is why we must not ignore the matter, but must search for methods which, while enabling us fully to guarantee incomes for lower and medium earners, will at the same time enable us to shape a more just distribution of goods among the nation. (Johnson 1981, 201)

I have emphasized the Polish price subsidies because their effects have been similar to those of such subsidies everywhere: resources are wasted if supply is expanded to equal demand, and most of the benefits go to the urban middle class. Whether the lower-income urban population gains a significant share of the total transfer depends on what products are subsidized. In general, the Egyptian price subsidies for bread have benefited low-income people more than would subsidies for other foods, like meat, which in low-income countries are consumed predominately by the urban, middle-income population and by high-income families.

IMF Conditionality and Agriculture

Some background on the price and other policies affecting agriculture in developing countries is useful to discussion of the effects of IMF conditionality on food and agriculture. In most developing countries, prices for most farm products are held at levels substantially lower than the international market prices. Even though officials and spokesmen for many developing countries criticize North-South trade relationships because LDC exports face unfavorable terms of trade, most developing countries hold domestic farm prices below those very international levels that are said to be too low.

Table 1 is based on studies of protection by Binswanger and Scandizzo at the World Bank (1983). The data is for developing countries only. Of the 57 estimates included in the table, only 5 represent cases of positive protection, or cases in which domestic prices exceed adjusted international market prices. Another 5 indicate negative protection of 10 percent or less. Thus in 47 out of the 57 examples, farmers received less than 90 percent of the international market price. In 8 cases, farmers received two-fifths or less of the international market price.

TABLE 1
Protection Coefficients for Low-Income Countries[a,b]

	Cocoa	Coffee	Cotton	Groundnuts	Maize	Rice	Wheat
Malawi	—	—	0.72	0.62	1.50	—	—
Mali	—	—	0.48	0.48	—	—	—
Senegal	—	—	0.65	0.57	—	0.70	—
Sudan	—	—	0.48	0.53	—	—	0.95
Zambia	—	—	—	0.58	0.62	—	—
Pakistan	—	—	0.61	—	0.90	0.68	0.76
Thailand	—	—	0.91	—	0.81	0.58	—
Togo	0.30	0.26	0.57	—	—	—	—
Ivory Coast	0.39	0.43	0.76	0.73	0.83	0.97	—
Egypt	—	—	0.44	—	0.67	0.34	0.76
India	—	—	—	—	0.80	0.65	0.80
Brazil	—	0.43	0.65	—	0.87	0.57	—
Kenya	—	0.74	0.85	—	0.91	1.30	1.13
Philippines	—	—	—	—	0.72	0.73	—
Cameroon	0.32	0.40	0.62	—	—	0.50	—
Ghana	0.05	—	—	—	—	0.06	—
Turkey	—	—	0.83	—	1.20	1.50	0.94

[a] The coefficients have been adjusted for the estimated overvaluation of the currency.
[b] A coefficient of less than unity means that protection is negative; farmers receive less than the international market price. A coefficient greater than one means protection is positive. A coefficient of 0.72 means that the farm price is 28 percent (1.00–0.72) less than it would be if farmers were permitted to export their product without governmental intervention. A coefficient of 1.30 means that the domestic farm price exceeds the international market price by 30 percent. The international market prices are adjusted to reflect potential farm gate prices by reflecting marketing and transportation costs and, where possible, quality differentials.
Source: Hans P. Binswanger and P.L. Scandizzo, *Patterns of Agricultural Protection* (Washington, D.C.: The World Bank, 1983), pp. 20–23.

These are some of the distortions that the IMF terms are designed to correct. Why is there such strong opposition to modifying policies that clearly exploit some of the poorest people in the developing countries? Those who oppose IMF efforts to make the elimination of such market interventions a condition for IMF loans either fail to understand how exploitive such policies are, or are willing to support the urban bias evident in such policies on grounds that the continuation of such policies is required for political and social stability *in the cities*.

Table 2 presents data on per capita food production in developing countries classified by major regions. It is immediately evident that Africa stands apart from the other three regions listed because it had a substantial

TABLE 2
Estimated Indexes of Food Production Per Capita for Developing Market Economies by Regions, 1966–84 (1961–65 = 100)

	Africa	Latin America	Near East[a]	Far East[b]
1966	96	101	101	94
1967	98	104	103	97
1968	100	103	103	101
1969	100	104	103	103
1970	100	106	103	105
1971	99	103	103	103
1972	95	101	107	97
1973	89	101	99	104
1974	93	103	105	99
1975	93	103	109	106
1976	94	108	111	105
1977	87	107	105	106
1978	88	110	110	113
1979	87	111	107	109
1980	87	112	107	110
1981	86	113	108	115
1982	86	113	108	112
1983	80	110	106	118
1984	81	110	106	118

[a] The Near East includes Northern Africa and the Middle East.
[b] The Far East includes South, Southeast, and East Asia.
Source: FAO, *FAO Production Yearbook,* various issues.

decline—nineteen percent—in per capita food production between 1970 and 1984. The Far East, by far the most populous of the regions, has had the best record. Latin America has had reasonable success in expanding per capita food production, although much more could have been achieved given the potential of the region.

The data in Tables 1 and 2 is not without some correspondence. The most egregious examples of the exploitation of farm people through high rates of negative protection are to be found in Africa, and it is no accident that Africa is the one region with declining per capita food production. Not only have farm prices been kept low in many developing countries, but in many of the same countries, there is other evidence of bias against agriculture in the allocation of investment funds, in the support of education, in the construction of roads, and in the supply of production inputs. Discrimination does not ordinarily occur in just one aspect of policies, it is usually found in many.

There are some examples, counter to those above, where measures have been implemented to offset the incentive and production effects of low farm prices. One example is the agricultural credit subsidies that were lavished upon the Brazilian agricultural sector between 1976 and 1981. Farmers were provided with low-cost credit, and the real interest rates were actually negative since the annual rate of inflation was greater than the annual rate of interest. Between 1976 and 1981, the subsidy component of the agricultural credit alone ranged between 13.1 percent and 19.6 percent of the gross domestic product of agriculture (Sayad and Zini March 1982). During these years, Brazil had an average annual inflation rate in excess of 60 percent and ran substantial budget deficits, with one of the uncontrolled items in the budget being the credit program, not only for agriculture but generally.

These figures may suggest that agriculture benefited substantially from the credit subsidies, and perhaps even enough to offset the relatively low output prices. However, it is hard to determine if this was the case—credit subsidies are very slippery and hard to trace. Putting aside the claim that much of the agricultural credit was the basis for the condominium boom in Rio de Janeiro in the late 1970s—which is almost certainly valid to some considerable degree—we do know that most of the agricultural credit subsidies went to a relatively few large borrowers. In 1976, 53 percent of the credit for crops went to 3 percent of the borrowers, and 47 percent of the livestock credit went to 4 percent of the borrowers. The borrowers in these groups received loans equal to 500 minimum-level salaries or more. On a comparable basis in the United States, this would have meant loans during a year of $1,000,000 or more—hardly the amount loaned to your ordinary family farm. The credit subsidy on a loan of $1,000,000 held for a full year would have been about $330,000 in 1980. In 1979 the largest 5 percent of all rural credit recipients received 46 percent of all funds loaned (Sayad and Zini 1982).

The Brazilian subsidy scheme was designed to benefit agriculture, at least to the extent of offsetting the effects of low prices. Instead, it imposed heavy budgetary costs, and while very few benefits were transferred to the farms of average size or smaller, very large subsidies went to a few large farmers. Thus it does not appear unreasonable that one requirement of IMF assistance to Brazil should be the elimination of such subsidies. A market-oriented set of policies, with both producer and consumer prices at world market levels, would be more effective in increasing production while releasing budget funds, some of which could be used to provide food subsidies for poor people. The current system of low food prices benefits all consumers, regardless of their income levels.

On Balance

Given the urban bias of governments in most countries with gross national product of less than $2,000 per capita, the IMF's emphasis upon eliminating subsidies and negative protection (exploitation) of farm producers can only work to improve the lot of most farm people. Clearly the emphasis upon "getting prices right," if carried out, will work to the benefit of farm people.

Other aspects of IMF conditionality may have adverse effects. For example, reducing domestic demand as a part of meeting inflation objectives, reducing imports, and increasing exports will reduce the demand *and* prices for some farm products. Most important in terms of potentially adverse effects may be limitations placed on imports of inputs important to agriculture—farm inputs, trucks, materials, and parts for processing and marketing. But if agreement can be reached between the IMF and the debtor country, on such policy issues, imports may well be as large or larger than they would without an agreement. In the absence of agreement with the IMF, most large debtor countries find it difficult to obtain new loan funds and are likely to be faced with failure to renew some part of the existing loan pool.

I don't want to imply that the IMF does almost everything right. Nor do I want to imply that the IMF and the World Bank have sufficient resources available to support the most appropriate transition from the current difficult situations; I simply do not know. If more resources are required, they will be available only if the major developed countries agree to make them available, and it is highly probable that they will do so only if there is evidence that the debtors have moved to eliminate the policies that were responsible, at least in part, for the existence of the current large international debts in the first place.

The IMF is criticized because its approach requires that all of the adjustments be made by the debtors and none, or almost none, by the creditor nations. This is a valid criticism, though not necessarily of the IMF. It is a criticism of the trade practices and domestic policies of all the industrial countries that affect the ability of the developing countries to expand their exports and thereby more easily service their debts. These policies include, for example, the incentives for the production of sugar and sugar substitutes in the U.S., the European Community (EC), and Japan; the unwillingness of Japan to import rice; the EC export subsidies for grain, beef, and dairy products; and the restrictions by most industrial countries on the import of labor-intensive manufactured products, such as textiles, clothing, shoes, and consumer electronics. Abolishing nontariff barriers to trade, such as the long-term textile agreement, would make it easier for the developing countries to make the adjustments they must make to once again become viable participants in international credit markets.

There are many difficult problems for which solutions must be found if the heavily indebted developing countries are to achieve significant growth while making it possible for their poorest populations to share in that growth. Although urban poverty is so easy to see, it should always be remembered that the majority of the world's poor people live in rural areas, not in the slums of the large cities. Consequently, we must hope that the policies agreed upon by the debtors, the international institutions, and private and public lending institutions in the industrial countries give appropriate emphasis to improving the incentives for farm people, not only to increase their incomes but to improve domestic food supplies and to contribute to a larger positive balance in the foreign trade account. If given the chance, farm people will respond; a broad range of experience indicates that there can be no doubt on this score. If the resolution of the current debt situation is the means by which the exploitation of farm people is eliminated or greatly reduced in many developing countries, a substantial benefit may be derived from the current difficulties.

References

Binswanger, Hans P., and P.L. Scandizzo. 1983. *Patterns of Agricultural Protection*. Washington, D.C.: The World Bank, pp. 20–23.

FAO (Food and Agricultural Organization of the United Nations). *FAO Production Yearbook*, various issues.

Johnson, D. Gale. 1981. "Food and Agriculture of the Centrally Planned Economies: Implications for the World Food System," in *Essays in Contemporary Economic Problems: Demand, Productivity, and Population*, edited by William Fellner. Washington, D.C.: The American Enterprise Institute, pp. 171–213.

________. September 17, 1985. "International Perspectives of Agricultural Development." Chicago: Office of Agricultural Economics Research, The University of Chicago, paper no. 85:10.

Lele, Uma. February 6, 1981. "Rural Africa: Modernization, Equity, and Long-Term Development." *Science*, vol. 211, pp. 547–53.

Sayad, Joao, and Alvaro Antonio Zini, Jr. March 1982. *Financiamento de Credit Rural No Brasil*, FIPE.

World Bank. 1985. *World Development Report 1985*. Washington, D.C.: The World Bank.

10

From Austerity to Growth: A New Role for the IMF

Alvin Rabushka

In the postwar period, many new nations, often referred to as developing countries, have faced the task of transforming their poor, traditional economies into modern industrial societies. To this end, most of these newly independent developing countries have actively sought foreign aid from abroad. Several have accumulated monumental external debts that jeopardize future prospects for growth in their own countries as well as the viability of the international financial system. Most of these new nations have disproportionately followed a strategy for economic development that is state-directed and state-led. The extent of government involvement in each country's economic development has ranged from that of a virtual command economy to one in which government does not try to manage all economic activity but does assume responsibility for all major capital investments and overall economic planning.

Socialist thinking has prevailed among many postwar development planners. Third World leaders have adopted policies which include high taxation in the interests of government-directed capital formation through steeply graduated personal income taxes and other excessive levies and to prevent an inequitable distribution of wealth and income that supposedly occurs as a country develops. Governments that attempt to lead and direct development typically impose on their economies foreign exchange controls, limitations on overseas investment or ownership, high tariffs, state control of businesses, and other restrictions on the free exchange of goods and services. In the past few years, the results of this developmental strategy have disappointed both its intellectual proponents and the inhabitants of the developing countries, vast numbers of whom are still mired in poverty with little hope for a better future.

Taking stock, in 1985, we can sift through a substantial body of evidence for the successes and failures of different economies among the postwar developing countries. For example, looking at such indicators as economic growth, real wages, productivity, per capita income, and even the distribution of national income, it is becoming increasingly clear that those countries which have emphasized free-market economic policies, and which have disproportionately relied upon their own resources, are faring best.

In Asia, such economies include those of Hong Kong, Singapore, Taiwan, Korea, and Malaysia. Since 1978, both Sri Lanka and India have undertaken liberal reforms, and their economies have shown accelerated growth. Under Rajiv Gandhi's leadership, India has cut the top marginal rate of tax in its individual income tax system from 97.75 percent in 1974, to 50 percent in 1985, precipitating a boom in the Bombay stock exchange. As a measure of the extent to which market-oriented strategies for economic development are coming into vogue, beginning in 1978, the People's Republic of China introduced a "rural responsibility" system in agriculture, under which peasant households lease land for private farming on fifteen-year contracts from collectives. After meeting assigned output quotas, these private households may keep, consume, or sell any surplus output in the free market without restriction or payment of taxes, an effective marginal tax rate of zero on above-quota output. China has also set up several duty-free export processing zones (mirroring those in Taiwan and South Korea), has authorized joint ownership with foreign business firms, and now offers other incentives to foreign and domestic business enterprises. In the past few years, more than a hundred "free-trade zones" or "export-processing zones" have been set up in dozens of countries around the world.

In Africa, the Ivory Coast, under the enlightened leadership of its only president, Felix Houphouet-Boigny, has defined the country as partial to a policy of liberalism and openness to foreign investors. The Ivory Coast is home to 50,000 expatriate French, 100,000 Lebanese and Syrians who supply service and middleman functions, and 2,000,000 immigrants from neighboring African countries attracted by the country's relatively greater economic opportunities: the government does not compulsorily procure agricultural output at below-market prices, does not penalize exporters by maintaining an overvalued currency, permits convertibility of the currency into French francs at a guaranteed rate, insures the free repatriation of profits and capital, does not set minimum wages at levels that damage the external competitiveness of the economy, does not try to redistribute income through the tax system, actively solicits foreign investment, downplays import substitution, and is gradually reducing the modestly distorting element of tariffs on internal prices.

Reliance on private enterprise in the market economy produced favorable results in Chile between 1973 and 1980, and fostered the strongest boom in Brazil's modern economic history from 1968 to 1974.

Free Markets and Economic Growth

The principal goal of economic policy is to insure that scarce resources are allocated as efficiently as possible, which has the effect of providing the highest possible standard of living for a country's people. It is generally recognized that the community's scarce resources can be efficiently allocated only by the price mechanism. For the pricing mechanism to work requires that neither the government nor a collusive private sector regulate prices or restrict entry for buyers or sellers. Free competition insures the lowest possible prices for consumers and insures least-cost production.

Of course, in every society the government plays a major economic role in providing such services as national defense, public safety, and public workers. It also provides the institutional framework within which economic exchanges take place. However, too often, government undertakes responsibilities it cannot afford and interferes in the economy by subsidizing or taxing different economic interests. The extent to which a government pursues sound policies has an important effect on overall economic efficiency.

The four Asian tigers—Hong Kong, Singapore, Taiwan, and Korea—are renown as the hyper-growth economies of the Pacific Rim. Sustained annual growth rates of nine percent over two decades have transformed these Third World developing countries into First World industrial nations. Translating sustained high growth into individual well-being means that residents who enjoyed per capita incomes ranging between $80 and $180 in 1950 now receive average per capita incomes between $2,000 and $7,000. This point is so important that it bears restating: millions of people poor a generation ago now enjoy middle-class living standards.

Since 1978, the leaders of Sri Lanka have imported what they term "the Singapore model," and the growth rates have doubled compared with the prior two decades. In the Ivory Coast and in Chile during the latter 1970s, the pursuit of free-market policies brought substantial economic progress. Taken together, these seven examples reflect differences in historical development, geography, climate, population, resource endowments, culture and tradition, and postwar political structures. Although no two have undergone the same exact experience, one can distill a core of policies that foster growth and uplift living standards.

Exchange Rate Policy

Most developing countries depend heavily on trade. The seven above are no exception. They export primary products, raw materials, and manufactured goods, and import, in turn, a wide variety of foodstuffs and finished products. The mechanism which links the internal costs and prices of a country's goods and services with overseas buyers and sellers is the exchange rate. A rate that is too high (an overvalued currency) harms the competitiveness of exports in world markets. Imports become artificially cheap. These circumstances invariably lead to a balance-of-payments problem, and motivate the government to impose a variety of tariff and nontariff restrictions on imports. Protection, imposed either to preserve scarce foreign exchange or to deliberately assist the growth of import substitutes, typically results in inefficient production, since producers are spared the test of market competition. Thus the price of domestic inputs into locally produced goods rises above least-cost levels. A correctly valued exchange rate is absolutely central in equating domestic and world prices. A correct exchange rate is one that would prevail under conditions of free trade, in other words, with no restrictions of any sort on imports and exports. Under free trade, buyers and sellers conduct their exchanges in domestic or world markets on a least-cost basis, and each country can exploit its comparative advantage in any good or service.

What stands in the way of maintaining a correctly valued currency, or, as is all too often the case, preventing an overvalued currency? Large public sector deficits frequently force the central bank to make inflationary purchases of public debt by issuing currency. The inflation tax becomes a primary vehicle by which a public sector deficit is financed. In the process, domestic prices rise above world levels. Unless the currency is correspondingly devalued, the exchange rate becomes overvalued. In addition, as public debt grows, debt-servicing payments rise, further straining the public finances. Those countries that have avoided public debt, domestic or foreign, and which have weaned themselves from dependence on foreign economic assistance (for example, Taiwan and Korea), have enjoyed the most rapid growth. Sound public finance goes hand in hand with free trade.

Regulations

Another serious obstacle to a correctly valued currency is government regulations, such as minimum wage standards, that push local costs above world levels, thus pricing local goods out of world markets. External free trade is the best way to insure internal free trade. It is desirable that domestic producers have access to all the factors of production—labor, raw materials, goods and services, and capital—on a least-cost basis. Policies that raise wages above market levels (as set by supply and demand), or distort the cost of borrowing through selective credit allocation, or unnecessarily increase the costs of any input above market levels mean a loss in efficiency. External free trade makes domestic regulations extremely costly and the effects readily visible, since any unwarranted increase in domestic costs damages external competitiveness.

Savings and Investment

Savings and investment policies also hinder or help long-run growth prospects. The most prudent strategy is to finance investment from domestic savings or foreign investment, rather than from borrowing. A burgeoning public debt drains resources away from investment into debt service and often implies higher future taxes to repay this debt, which in turn discourages new investment. A growing public debt also cramps fiscal flexibility. Hong Kong, Singapore, and Taiwan have relied on domestic savings and private foreign investment. Korea, the Ivory Coast, Chile, and Sri Lanka have borrowed heavily on both domestic and overseas financial markets and face a more unsettled economic future because of their heavy indebtedness.

Tax Policy

Another policy that encourages economic growth is the maintenance of a neutral, low-tax environment which does not destroy incentives to work, save, or invest. The overall burden of taxation rarely exceeds 20–25 percent, and the rates on any given tax are not punitive. Tax policy should aim at three goals:

- to remove as few resources from the economy as possible to pay for the legitimate activities of government (since resources in private hands are used more efficiently in producing goods and services than the same resources placed in public hands);
- to avoid distorting prices produced by the interaction of supply and demand, insuring neutrality between production and consumption, and among products and industries; and
- to minimize the costs of administration and collection. It is critical to avoid high rates of taxation lest they destroy incentives to work, save, and invest.

In the post–World War II period, a handful of countries have grown their way out of poverty to provide their people with sharply higher living standards. From their experiences we can collect an encyclopedia of possible reforms that can be assembled around the entries of taxation, expenditure, provision of public services, budgetary policy, trade, regulation, and monetary policy that, *in toto*, constitutes an overall developmental package. Each item represents a greater reliance on market forces that is likely to foster greater efficiency in that sector of the economy to which it is applicable, and thereby increase the supply of goods and services available in that society.

Taxation:	Establish a duty-free port without import duties or export taxes
	Maintain low direct rates of taxation
	Rely on consumption taxes to promote savings
	Grant tax holidays to encourage investment
	Permit accelerated depreciation
	Provide for loss carryover
	Grant reinvestment allowances
	Move toward greater tax neutrality
Expenditure:	Eliminate subsidies to business
	Reduce the overall size of the public sector
	Eliminate consumer subsidies
Budget:	Balance the budget
	Avoid deficits and borrowing
Public Enterprises:	Price products on commercial basis
	Rely on user fees where possible
	Contract out to private enterprise
	Make public enterprises independent and require them to be profitable
	Divest publicly-owned enterprises
	Allow private competition with public enterprises
	Abolish state marketing boards
Internal Regulation:	Install simple, inexpensive business requirements
	Maintain lenient labor regulations
	Eliminate government monopoly privileges for unions
	Eliminate protection for industry
	Eliminate rent controls
	Eliminate minimum-wage legislation
	Avoid excessive severance pay requirements
	Decentralize decision making
	Eliminate system of permits, licenses, and monopolies over private enterprises
	Allow agricultural prices to be set by the market
	Eliminate marketing board levies
External Regulation:	Allow free movement of capital
	Maintain duty-free port

Promote free trade
Remove quantitative restrictions on imports and exports
Attract private foreign investment
Minimize dependence on foreign aid
Establish export-processing zones
Provide free repatriation of capital, interest, and dividends
Provide guarantees against expropriation

Monetary Policy:
Maintain correctly valued exchange rate
Eliminate foreign exchange controls
Eliminate credit rationing
Allow the market to set interest rates
Maintain currency convertibility

U.S. Policy toward the Developing World

The vivid contrast between success and failure in the developing world, and its implications for U.S. policy, has not gone unnoticed. At the October 1985 IMF/World Bank meeting in Seoul, South Korea, U.S. Treasury Secretary James A. Baker III outlined a new U.S. approach to the question of improving the economies of the Less Developed Countries (LDCs). In essence, the plan calls for using these international institutions, the IMF and the World Bank, to achieve economic growth in the LDCs by encouraging the adoption of market-oriented policies. Those countries that adopt market-oriented, pro-growth policies would be rewarded by receiving additional loans and aid both from these international lending institutions and from private lenders.

Secretary Baker's approach to economic stagnation in LDCs grows from the Reagan administration's belief that many developing countries will remain ensnared in the poverty trap unless old state-directed and state-led interventionist policies give way to a pro-growth mix of new measures. Secretary Baker outlined the following three reforms which would be necessary to overcome economic stagnation in LDCs:

- Increased reliance on the private sector, and less reliance on government, to help increase employment, production, and efficiency.
- Supply-side actions to mobilize domestic savings and facilitate efficient investment, both domestic and foreign, by means of tax reform, labor-market reform, and development of financial markets.
- Market-opening measures to encourage direct foreign investment and capital inflows, as well as to liberalize trade, including the reduction of export subsidies.

The possibility of a new role for the International Monetary Fund in its relationships with the U.S., a major source of contributions, and with the developing world requires a brief review of postwar IMF activities.

The Origins and Transformation of the IMF

The IMF, along with the World Bank, was established in the latter years of World War II, and finalized in July 1944 at the famous Bretton Woods Conference. The U.S. based its currency on gold valued at $35 per ounce, and other countries pegged their currencies not directly to gold but to the U.S. dollar. The Fund's primary responsibility was the stability and integrity of the international monetary system. It was entrusted to reestablish and maintain free markets in currencies, eliminate multiple exchange rates and exchange controls, and foster stability in exchange rates. To attain exchange rate stability, it was required that countries gain IMF approval to change their exchange rates.

In its early years, the Fund focused on removing exchange and trade restrictions that had been introduced by the industrial countries during the depression and war years of the 1930s and 1940s. By the late 1950s, the industrial countries had largely restored convertible currencies at generally fixed rates of exchange. But neither the IMF nor domestic management of the economies of the industrial nations could preserve fixed exchange rates. The mismatch between British domestic interests and Great Britain's longer-run interests as the manager of the pound sterling area forced several devaluations of sterling in terms of other currencies. Later, chronic U.S. deficits incurred during the war in Vietnam and simultaneous pursuit of the Great Society at home forced President Richard Nixon to close the gold window on August 15, 1971, to quell a run on the dollar. The last anchor to the system of fixed exchange rates, the convertibility of dollars into gold at a guaranteed price, was abandoned, thus ending the era of fixed exchange rates. Since 1971, the world has been on a *fiat* monetary standard in which the price of one currency in terms of another depends on market forces of supply and demand.

With the passing of the Bretton Woods system, the primary function of the IMF disappeared. The IMF was created to help maintain stable exchange rates. A major original purpose of the IMF, trying to maintain convertible currencies at stable rates of exchange, has disappeared. Its publication, *International Financial Statistics, Supplement on Exchange Rates*, documents the stability of exchange rates among the industrial nations between 1952 and 1968. Since 1969, exchange rates have oscillated, sometimes sharply. The U.S. dollar, for example, was worth four French francs in 1980, and ten French francs in 1985. There was no longer any need for an international agency to lend money to keep pegged exchange rates from shifting and currencies from being devalued.

However, Robert Michels' "iron rule of oligarchy" applies to the IMF as well as to most other political organizations: "by a universally applicable social law, every organ of the collectivity, brought into existence through the need for the division of labor, creates for itself, as soon as it becomes consolidated, interests peculiar to itself." Maintenance and expansion of the organization soon become its prime purpose. The IMF has enjoyed an increase in its resources from $37 billion in 1979, to surpass $75 billion in 1984. The U.S. government, after much domestic political controversy, committed another $8.4 billion of its reserves with the Fund in 1983.

The IMF has remained in existence, seeking a new role and new applications of its old powers. One such function is the maintenance of international liquidity by creating Special Drawing Rights (SDRs), the international equivalent of bank credit. Another new role is to induce banks to lend money to LDC governments by giving banks an implicit guarantee that the Fund will bail out these countries if they find it impossible to pay or service their debts.

The arrival of the era of floating exchange rates among the industrial nations, coupled with the accumulation of vast external debts due to chronic balance-of-payments deficits among developing countries, has shifted the Fund's attention to the developing world. Overall, the IMF has 151 member countries. The original charter of the Fund assigned it not only the tasks of promoting international monetary cooperation and exchange rate stability, but fostering the expansion of international trade, and, when countries get into temporary difficulty due to a balance-of-payments problem, making the resources of the Fund available to members on a temporary basis to enable them to correct maladjustments in their balance of payments without resorting to measures destructive of national or international prosperity.

The Fund has increasingly become the provider of "temporary" balance-of-payments support for developing countries. But IMF support comes at the price of "austerity," or "conditionality," the adoption of a set of policies that IMF officials believe will permit the recipient nation to correct its balance-of-payments problem. Austerity means reducing imports and expanding exports to earn sufficient foreign exchange to meet interest payments on foreign debt and to repay foreign lenders.

How is this turnaround in the balance of payments to be accomplished? The usual strategy consists of attempting to dampen internal demand through the imposition of credit ceilings, reduction of government spending (especially on subsidy and social programs), and an increase in taxes. Greater fiscal discipline is required to curtail inflationary budget deficits.

Currency devaluation reduces imports by making them more costly in local prices, and promotes exports by making them less costly on world markets. Ideally, IMF support permits a nation to service its existing foreign debt while new policies restore economic solvency. The Fund's measures are intended to be short-term and not to represent a source of intermediate- or long-term development finance from one group of countries to another (which is the task of the World Bank or private lenders).

A debtor country goes to the Fund because it cannot finance its payments deficit in the private market. The IMF is thus able to impose conditions on its assistance. Critics of IMF assistance contend that austerity policies often have the effect of pouring gasoline on a fire. They argue that the IMF inflicts damage on both recipient and donor nations by focusing too narrowly on balancing current international trade accounts rather than on the fundamentals of economic growth. Policies that require raising taxes and reducing real incomes of poor people, thus prescribing reduced output, are a poor way to repay debt. Higher taxes erode individual incentives to work, save, and invest. Reducing imports contracts international trade. Slashing public spending on social programs fuels riots and political instability. The survival of governments allied with the United States is put in jeopardy (witness the riots in the Dominican Republic, Sudan, and other countries). Instead, policies are needed that encourage both foreign and domestic equity investment, less government intervention in the economy, less direct and indirect taxation, lower trade and investment barriers, and sound money.

The most damaging aspect of IMF conditionality is the common requirement to increase taxes. A fundamental cause of economic problems in the first place is the appropriation of funds from the private sector for public use. Higher taxes divert additional funds from the private sector, where they might be used for capital investments and private business expansion which increase productivity, to the public sector, where they are likely to be used to subsidize inefficient state-owned industries and overpaid state bureaucrats, to finance consumption, or to disappear in graft. Secretary Baker's remarks in Seoul reflect the concern that the IMF's austerity policies are detrimental to both U.S. foreign policy objectives and the requirements for pro-growth policies in recipient nations.

Critics argue that the IMF is partly to blame for structural balance-of-payments problems and the explosion in Third World debt, which rose from $97 billion in 1973, to $505 billion in 1982. Countries generate balance-of-payments problems by maintaining both overvalued exchange rates and protective devices to encourage import substitution which penalize exporters and subsidize importers, and by domestic fiscal policies which push aggregate expenditure above output. These policies quickly exhaust international reserves. A substantial portion of Latin American debt is due to the balance-of-payments bail-outs provided by international lenders, which frequently postpone realistic adjustments of the exchange rate.

Furthermore, much of the money borrowed from the IMF, the World Bank, the InterAmerican Development Bank, and other lenders has put governments in the business of power generation and distribution, telecommunications, shipping, railroads, and other ventures that charge monopoly prices and lose money. These ventures are not productive for their countries, and they also tax economically-productive enterprises to cover their losses. Thus international lending institutions stall economic progress by favoring government over private enterprise.

Critics who charge that IMF loans run counter to U.S. foreign policy objectives point to bail-outs of Communist countries, such as Yugoslavia, Romania, and Hungary, which shore up inefficient, repressive economic and political structures.

To the extent that IMF payments bail out bad loans made by private international bankers, why should U.S. taxpayers subsidize overseas economic mismanagement?

The IMF as a Moral Hazard

When the government provides flood insurance, individuals will forego the purchase of private coverage. When the government supplies full medical care, individuals may be less likely to take care of themselves. When the government supports poor people with financial and in-kind assistance, it runs the risk of creating a welfare dependency. When the government guarantees all deposits under $100,000 through its deposit insurance schemes—and, for all practical purposes, deposits exceeding $100,000 in large banks—it reduces the risk to depositers of imprudent lending by banks. If depositors stood to lose their funds as a result of bad loans, banks would either make more prudent loans or have to pay a higher premium to attract deposits.

In the same vein, critics of IMF lending practices charge the Fund with creating a global moral hazard. The Fund's own resources are insufficient to finance inflationary and other irresponsible economic policies adopted by developing countries, but are large enough to induce private banks to provide huge loans to the governments of developing countries by seeming to remove the risk of default. Many private bank loans have not been for particular projects or enterprises that might earn sufficient profits to repay interest and principal, but simply general loans to governments. The IMF promised implicitly that if debtor countries could not raise the hard currencies to pay back or service loans, the Fund would step in with needed funds. On this implicit guarantee, banks have lent hundreds of billions of dollars to developing countries, little of which found its way into productive, private-sector enterprises.

The debt crisis which began with the Mexican default in 1982 was in large part the result of the IMF's catalyst role. Since the IMF lacks sufficient resources to bail out such colossal debtor nations as Brazil, Mexico, and Argentina, its solution to the debt problem has been to solicit more funds from private banks to be poured into bankrupt LDCs, rather than to recommend that existing loans be written down or sold off to determine true market price (though perhaps the price of bank shares in the stock market takes into account the true value of bank assets including loans to LDCs).

Having abetted the cause of developing country indebtedness, the IMF then demands austerity, which in effect punishes the poor people in LDCs who must tighten their belts and reduce consumption in order for the nation to earn hard currency with which to repay foreign debts. By having encouraged private bank loans to LDC governments, the IMF has promoted the growth of public sectors at the expense of private sectors, irresponsible economic policies, and massive international debt. The United States is the major contributor to the IMF and therefore bears proportional responsibility for the global public debt, the mismanagement of LDC economies, the diminishing living standards of millions of people, and growing unrest and instability of allied governments who are forced to heel to IMF dictates.

Policies that produce high growth are important for raising the living standards of poor people. They are equally important for the evolution of democratic institutions and a concern for civil liberties in LDCs. I have assembled a variety of economic measures from the World Bank and the IMF on 104 developing countries, along with rankings on political rights and civil liberties which are published annually by Freedom House, in an extensive data file. Political rights range from the presence of a fully competitive electoral process, to a limited role for opposition parties within a predominantly one-party state, to the complete absence of free elections where despots rule unconstrained by public opinion or popular tradition. The range of civil liberties is from, on one hand, freedom of the press, court protection of the individual, free expression of personal opinion, and free choice in occupation, education, religion, residence, and so on, to the other extreme of pervasive fear, little independent expression (even in private), and swift imprisonment and execution by a police state. Tables 1 through 4 (appended) clearly display the relationship between rates of economic growth (annual average, 1960–82), levels of per capita income, and the presence or absence of political rights and civil liberties.

The data for more than 90 LDCs show that low-growth countries score poorly on political and civil rights; in short, leaders of stagnant economies grant their subjects few to no liberties. Conversely, the residents of nearly half of all high-growth countries enjoy considerable political and civil freedoms. Sustained high growth rates are the vehicle that turns poor countries into middle-income nations. Per capita income levels are directly related to the presence of democratic values. Of the 25 countries with per capita incomes below $400, 21 fare poorly on civil rights and 19 score low on political freedoms. Residents of countries with per capita incomes exceeding $700 typically enjoy a much larger measure of the political freedoms that are part and parcel of democratic societies and individual liberties that prevail under the rule of law.

Thus pro-growth economic policies are important not only to improve output, productivity, and living standards, but also to foster the evolution of democracy and instill respect for civil liberties. To the extent that IMF policies retard growth, they simultaneously suppress the growth of democracy and liberty.

A New Agenda for the IMF

The future activities of the IMF could include maintaining the status quo, increasing or decreasing the scope of its lending to developing nations, urging a return to a commodity-based monetary standard and stable exchange rates, changing the terms of conditionality in granting temporary balance-of-payments loans, or going out of business altogether. The latter prospect must surely frighten public and private sector members of the international financial community on the belief, correct or mistaken, that massive defaults would impair international trade, damage lenders, and cripple the access of LDCs to needed credit.

Dissolving the IMF

Closing up shop is attractive to the IMF's critics for two reasons. First, it would prevent the IMF from imposing its economy-contracting medicinal dose of higher taxes and reduced imports as part of an austerity package. Second, it would once and for all put international lending on a prudent basis: lenders could not look to any international agency to bail out their faltering assets. Borrowers in developing countries could only borrow for productive enterprises, since lenders would require assurance of repayment based on the merit of the loan, not the implicit or explicit guarantee of an international lending institution. In particular, general-purpose loans to LDC governments would cease.

In any case, however attractive the dissolution of the IMF might seem to many of its critics, the institution has been able to sustain its operations and even expand sharply in the face of the international debt problem. A major increase in contributions in 1983 committed the U.S. and other contributor nations to a prominent future role for the Fund. In the near future, the Fund is likely to remain an important player in international financial markets.

Changing the Terms of Conditionality

As the largest contributor, the United States is in a position to push for changes in IMF operating policies. Our primary objective should be the insistence that recipient nations adopt pro-growth policies. The IMF often correctly insists that recipient nations devalue their currencies in pursuit of external competitiveness. However, it typically insists on tax increases that are detrimental to growth. Neither does it forcibly require the dismantling and subsidization of state-owned enterprises, elimination of tariffs and other controls that impede external and internal free trade, abolition of state procurement and marketing monopolies, paring back of public sector employment, and the removal of other impediments to the efficient workings of markets. Secretary Baker's remarks in Korea should be followed by his stern warning that the failure to require pro-growth policies will force U.S. reduction in contributions to and ultimate withdrawal from the IMF.

An emphasis on pro-growth policies, in place of international welfare dependency, accomplishes several objectives: it produces higher living standards, fosters the growth of democracy and civil liberties, builds legitimacy for LDC governments, and injects free-market pressures into socialist and communist nations. Pro-growth policies also replace austerity for poor people with hope and rising living standards for all, and build support for free-market economic institutions and free trade on a global basis. In the absence of pro-growth policies, democracy will remain fragile in the developing world.

Restoration of the Gold Standard

Recall that the IMF was established to restore convertible currencies with stable exchange rates. The linchpin of the Bretton Woods system was a gold-backed U.S. dollar, with foreign currencies tied to the dollar. Proponents of a commodity-based monetary system argue that a return to gold, or some other commodity standard, would increase public confidence about future monetary policies. Public holders of dollars are less confident that the government can successfully follow a growth rule than a price rule in monetary policy. Uncertainty about future swings in the quantity of money among the currencies of industrial nations produces wide swings in exchange rates. Guaranteeing U.S. dollars in terms of gold, a price rule, should foster the stability of exchange rates among the major industrial

nations. U.S. monetary authorities would be able to sustain a fixed price for gold so long as the government avoided inflationary policies. A gold-standard currency would require changes in the practices of the Federal Reserve Board, but would go a long way to reducing budget deficits.

TABLE 1
Crosstabulation of
CODEG (Grouped Growth Rate)
by POLRTIDX (Political Rights Index)

	Count row PCT col PCT	POLRTIDX 1	2	3	4	5	6	7	Row Total
CODEG −2.0–0.0	1		1 8.3 5.6	2 16.7 20.0	1 8.3 12.5	3 25.0 17.6	2 16.7 13.3	3 25.0 18.8	12 12.9
0.1–1.0	2		4 30.8 22.2	1 7.7 10.0	1 7.7 12.5	1 7.7 5.9	3 23.1 20.0	3 23.1 18.8	13 14.0
1.1–2.0	3	1 6.3 11.1	4 25.0 22.2		1 6.3 12.5	3 18.8 17.6	2 12.5 13.3	5 31.3 31.3	16 17.2
2.1–3.0	4	1 5.9 11.1	2 11.8 11.1	2 11.8 20.0	2 11.8 25.0	2 11.8 11.8	5 29.4 33.3	3 17.6 18.8	17 18.3
3.1–4.0	5	3 20.0 33.3	4 26.7 22.2	2 13.3 20.0	2 13.3 25.0	2 13.3 11.8	1 6.7 6.7	1 6.7 6.3	15 16.1
4.1–5.0	6	2 18.2 22.2	1 9.1 5.6	3 27.3 30.0		3 27.3 17.6	2 18.2 13.3		11 11.8
5.1–6.0	7	2 66.7 22.2						1 33.3 6.3	3 3.2
6.1–7.0	8		1 25.0 5.6			3 75.0 17.6			4 4.3
7.0+	9		1 50.0 5.6		1 50.0 12.5				2 2.2
	Column	9	18	10	8	17	15	16	93
	Total	9.7	19.4	10.8	8.6	18.3	16.1	17.2	100.0

TABLE 4
Crosstabulation of
CODEPCG (Grouped PERCPGNP)
by CIVRTIDX (Civil Rights Index)

	Count row PCT col PCT	CIVRTIDX 1	2	3	4	5	6	7	Row Total
CODEPCG $0–200	1				1 14.3 10.0	1 14.3 3.8	1 14.3 5.6	4 57.1 40.0	7 7.4
$201–400	2			1 5.6 8.3	2 11.1 20.0	4 22.2 15.4	8 44.4 44.4	3 16.7 30.0	18 19.1
$401–700	3		1 6.3 6.3	3 18.8 25.0	2 12.5 20.0	6 37.5 23.1	4 25.0 22.2		16 17.0
$701–1000	4		3 21.4 18.8	2 14.3 16.7	2 14.3 20.0	5 35.7 19.2	1 7.1 5.6	1 7.1 10.0	14 14.9
$1001–1500	5	2 16.7 100.0	2 16.7 12.5	4 33.3 33.3		2 16.7 7.7	2 16.7 11.1		12 12.8
$1501–2000	6		1 16.7 6.3			4 66.7 15.4		1 16.7 10.0	6 6.4
$2001–4000	7		5 33.3 31.3	2 13.3 16.7	3 20.0 30.0	2 13.3 7.7	2 13.3 11.1	1 6.7 10.0	15 16.0
$4001–6000	8		3 75.0 18.8			1 25.0 3.8			4 4.3
$6000+	9		1 50.0 6.3			1 50.0 3.8			2 2.1
	Column	2	16	12	10	26	18	10	94
	Total	2.1	17.0	12.8	10.6	27.7	19.1	10.6	100.0

nations. U.S. monetary authorities would be able to sustain a fixed price for gold so long as the government avoided inflationary policies. A gold-standard currency would require changes in the practices of the Federal Reserve Board, but would go a long way to reducing budget deficits.

TABLE 1
Crosstabulation of
CODEG (Grouped Growth Rate)
by POLRTIDX (Political Rights Index)

	Count row PCT col PCT	POLRTIDX 1	2	3	4	5	6	7	Row Total
CODEG −2.0–0.0	1		1 8.3 5.6	2 16.7 20.0	1 8.3 12.5	3 25.0 17.6	2 16.7 13.3	3 25.0 18.8	12 12.9
0.1–1.0	2		4 30.8 22.2	1 7.7 10.0	1 7.7 12.5	1 7.7 5.9	3 23.1 20.0	3 23.1 18.8	13 14.0
1.1–2.0	3	1 6.3 11.1	4 25.0 22.2		1 6.3 12.5	3 18.8 17.6	2 12.5 13.3	5 31.3 31.3	16 17.2
2.1–3.0	4	1 5.9 11.1	2 11.8 11.1	2 11.8 20.0	2 11.8 25.0	2 11.8 11.8	5 29.4 33.3	3 17.6 18.8	17 18.3
3.1–4.0	5	3 20.0 33.3	4 26.7 22.2	2 13.3 20.0	2 13.3 25.0	2 13.3 11.8	1 6.7 6.7	1 6.7 6.3	15 16.1
4.1–5.0	6	2 18.2 22.2	1 9.1 5.6	3 27.3 30.0		3 27.3 17.6	2 18.2 13.3		11 11.8
5.1–6.0	7	2 66.7 22.2						1 33.3 6.3	3 3.2
6.1–7.0	8		1 25.0 5.6			3 75.0 17.6			4 4.3
7.0+	9		1 50.0 5.6		1 50.0 12.5				2 2.2
	Column	9	18	10	8	17	15	16	93
	Total	9.7	19.4	10.8	8.6	18.3	16.1	17.2	100.0

TABLE 4
Crosstabulation of
CODEPCG (Grouped PERCPGNP)
by CIVRTIDX (Civil Rights Index)

	Count row PCT col PCT	CIVRTIDX 1	2	3	4	5	6	7	Row Total
CODEPCG $0–200	1				1 14.3 10.0	1 14.3 3.8	1 14.3 5.6	4 57.1 40.0	7 7.4
$201–400	2			1 5.6 8.3	2 11.1 20.0	4 22.2 15.4	8 44.4 44.4	3 16.7 30.0	18 19.1
$401–700	3		1 6.3 6.3	3 18.8 25.0	2 12.5 20.0	6 37.5 23.1	4 25.0 22.2		16 17.0
$701–1000	4		3 21.4 18.8	2 14.3 16.7	2 14.3 20.0	5 35.7 19.2	1 7.1 5.6	1 7.1 10.0	14 14.9
$1001–1500	5	2 16.7 100.0	2 16.7 12.5	4 33.3 33.3		2 16.7 7.7	2 16.7 11.1		12 12.8
$1501–2000	6		1 16.7 6.3			4 66.7 15.4		1 16.7 10.0	6 6.4
$2001–4000	7		5 33.3 31.3	2 13.3 16.7	3 20.0 30.0	2 13.3 7.7	2 13.3 11.1	1 6.7 10.0	15 16.0
$4001–6000	8		3 75.0 18.8			1 25.0 3.8			4 4.3
$6000+	9		1 50.0 6.3			1 50.0 3.8			2 2.1
	Column	2	16	12	10	26	18	10	94
	Total	2.1	17.0	12.8	10.6	27.7	19.1	10.6	100.0

nations. U.S. monetary authorities would be able to sustain a fixed price for gold so long as the government avoided inflationary policies. A gold-standard currency would require changes in the practices of the Federal Reserve Board, but would go a long way to reducing budget deficits.

TABLE 1
Crosstabulation of
CODEG (Grouped Growth Rate)
by POLRTIDX (Political Rights Index)

	Count row PCT col PCT	POLRTIDX 1	2	3	4	5	6	7	Row Total
CODEG −2.0–0.0	1		1 8.3 5.6	2 16.7 20.0	1 8.3 12.5	3 25.0 17.6	2 16.7 13.3	3 25.0 18.8	12 12.9
0.1–1.0	2		4 30.8 22.2	1 7.7 10.0	1 7.7 12.5	1 7.7 5.9	3 23.1 20.0	3 23.1 18.8	13 14.0
1.1–2.0	3	1 6.3 11.1	4 25.0 22.2		1 6.3 12.5	3 18.8 17.6	2 12.5 13.3	5 31.3 31.3	16 17.2
2.1–3.0	4	1 5.9 11.1	2 11.8 11.1	2 11.8 20.0	2 11.8 25.0	2 11.8 11.8	5 29.4 33.3	3 17.6 18.8	17 18.3
3.1–4.0	5	3 20.0 33.3	4 26.7 22.2	2 13.3 20.0	2 13.3 25.0	2 13.3 11.8	1 6.7 6.7	1 6.7 6.3	15 16.1
4.1–5.0	6	2 18.2 22.2	1 9.1 5.6	3 27.3 30.0		3 27.3 17.6	2 18.2 13.3		11 11.8
5.1–6.0	7	2 66.7 22.2						1 33.3 6.3	3 3.2
6.1–7.0	8		1 25.0 5.6			3 75.0 17.6			4 4.3
7.0+	9		1 50.0 5.6		1 50.0 12.5				2 2.2
	Column	9	18	10	8	17	15	16	93
	Total	9.7	19.4	10.8	8.6	18.3	16.1	17.2	100.0

TABLE 4
Crosstabulation of
CODEPCG (Grouped PERCPGNP)
by CIVRTIDX (Civil Rights Index)

	Count row PCT col PCT	CIVRTIDX 1	2	3	4	5	6	7	Row Total
CODEPCG $0–200	1				1 14.3 10.0	1 14.3 3.8	1 14.3 5.6	4 57.1 40.0	7 7.4
$201–400	2			1 5.6 8.3	2 11.1 20.0	4 22.2 15.4	8 44.4 44.4	3 16.7 30.0	18 19.1
$401–700	3		1 6.3 6.3	3 18.8 25.0	2 12.5 20.0	6 37.5 23.1	4 25.0 22.2		16 17.0
$701–1000	4		3 21.4 18.8	2 14.3 16.7	2 14.3 20.0	5 35.7 19.2	1 7.1 5.6	1 7.1 10.0	14 14.9
$1001–1500	5	2 16.7 100.0	2 16.7 12.5	4 33.3 33.3		2 16.7 7.7	2 16.7 11.1		12 12.8
$1501–2000	6		1 16.7 6.3			4 66.7 15.4		1 16.7 10.0	6 6.4
$2001–4000	7		5 33.3 31.3	2 13.3 16.7	3 20.0 30.0	2 13.3 7.7	2 13.3 11.1	1 6.7 10.0	15 16.0
$4001–6000	8		3 75.0 18.8			1 25.0 3.8			4 4.3
$6000+	9		1 50.0 6.3			1 50.0 3.8			2 2.1
	Column	2	16	12	10	26	18	10	94
	Total	2.1	17.0	12.8	10.6	27.7	19.1	10.6	100.0

nations. U.S. monetary authorities would be able to sustain a fixed price for gold so long as the government avoided inflationary policies. A gold-standard currency would require changes in the practices of the Federal Reserve Board, but would go a long way to reducing budget deficits.

TABLE 1
Crosstabulation of
CODEG (Grouped Growth Rate)
by POLRTIDX (Political Rights Index)

	Count row PCT col PCT	POLRTIDX 1	2	3	4	5	6	7	Row Total
CODEG −2.0–0.0	1		1 8.3 5.6	2 16.7 20.0	1 8.3 12.5	3 25.0 17.6	2 16.7 13.3	3 25.0 18.8	12 12.9
0.1–1.0	2		4 30.8 22.2	1 7.7 10.0	1 7.7 12.5	1 7.7 5.9	3 23.1 20.0	3 23.1 18.8	13 14.0
1.1–2.0	3	1 6.3 11.1	4 25.0 22.2		1 6.3 12.5	3 18.8 17.6	2 12.5 13.3	5 31.3 31.3	16 17.2
2.1–3.0	4	1 5.9 11.1	2 11.8 11.1	2 11.8 20.0	2 11.8 25.0	2 11.8 11.8	5 29.4 33.3	3 17.6 18.8	17 18.3
3.1–4.0	5	3 20.0 33.3	4 26.7 22.2	2 13.3 20.0	2 13.3 25.0	2 13.3 11.8	1 6.7 6.7	1 6.7 6.3	15 16.1
4.1–5.0	6	2 18.2 22.2	1 9.1 5.6	3 27.3 30.0		3 27.3 17.6	2 18.2 13.3		11 11.8
5.1–6.0	7	2 66.7 22.2						1 33.3 6.3	3 3.2
6.1–7.0	8		1 25.0 5.6			3 75.0 17.6			4 4.3
7.0+	9		1 50.0 5.6		1 50.0 12.5				2 2.2
	Column	9	18	10	8	17	15	16	93
	Total	9.7	19.4	10.8	8.6	18.3	16.1	17.2	100.0

TABLE 4
Crosstabulation of
CODEPCG (Grouped PERCPGNP)
by CIVRTIDX (Civil Rights Index)

	Count row PCT col PCT	CIVRTIDX 1	2	3	4	5	6	7	Row Total
CODEPCG	1				1	1	1	4	7
$0–200					14.3	14.3	14.3	57.1	7.4
					10.0	3.8	5.6	40.0	
	2			1	2	4	8	3	18
$201–400				5.6	11.1	22.2	44.4	16.7	19.1
				8.3	20.0	15.4	44.4	30.0	
	3		1	3	2	6	4		16
$401–700			6.3	18.8	12.5	37.5	25.0		17.0
			6.3	25.0	20.0	23.1	22.2		
	4		3	2	2	5	1	1	14
$701–1000			21.4	14.3	14.3	35.7	7.1	7.1	14.9
			18.8	16.7	20.0	19.2	5.6	10.0	
	5	2	2	4		2	2		12
$1001–1500		16.7	16.7	33.3		16.7	16.7		12.8
		100.0	12.5	33.3		7.7	11.1		
	6		1			4		1	6
$1501–2000			16.7			66.7		16.7	6.4
			6.3			15.4		10.0	
	7		5	2	3	2	2	1	15
$2001–4000			33.3	13.3	20.0	13.3	13.3	6.7	16.0
			31.3	16.7	30.0	7.7	11.1	10.0	
	8		3			1			4
$4001–6000			75.0			25.0			4.3
			18.8			3.8			
	9		1			1			2
$6000+			50.0			50.0			2.1
			6.3			3.8			
	Column	2	16	12	10	26	18	10	94
	Total	2.1	17.0	12.8	10.6	27.7	19.1	10.6	100.0

nations. U.S. monetary authorities would be able to sustain a fixed price for gold so long as the government avoided inflationary policies. A gold-standard currency would require changes in the practices of the Federal Reserve Board, but would go a long way to reducing budget deficits.

TABLE 1
Crosstabulation of
CODEG (Grouped Growth Rate)
by POLRTIDX (Political Rights Index)

	Count row PCT col PCT	POLRTIDX 1	2	3	4	5	6	7	Row Total
CODEG −2.0–0.0	1		1 8.3 5.6	2 16.7 20.0	1 8.3 12.5	3 25.0 17.6	2 16.7 13.3	3 25.0 18.8	12 12.9
0.1–1.0	2		4 30.8 22.2	1 7.7 10.0	1 7.7 12.5	1 7.7 5.9	3 23.1 20.0	3 23.1 18.8	13 14.0
1.1–2.0	3	1 6.3 11.1	4 25.0 22.2		1 6.3 12.5	3 18.8 17.6	2 12.5 13.3	5 31.3 31.3	16 17.2
2.1–3.0	4	1 5.9 11.1	2 11.8 11.1	2 11.8 20.0	2 11.8 25.0	2 11.8 11.8	5 29.4 33.3	3 17.6 18.8	17 18.3
3.1–4.0	5	3 20.0 33.3	4 26.7 22.2	2 13.3 20.0	2 13.3 25.0	2 13.3 11.8	1 6.7 6.7	1 6.7 6.3	15 16.1
4.1–5.0	6	2 18.2 22.2	1 9.1 5.6	3 27.3 30.0		3 27.3 17.6	2 18.2 13.3		11 11.8
5.1–6.0	7	2 66.7 22.2						1 33.3 6.3	3 3.2
6.1–7.0	8		1 25.0 5.6			3 75.0 17.6			4 4.3
7.0+	9		1 50.0 5.6		1 50.0 12.5				2 2.2
	Column	9	18	10	8	17	15	16	93
	Total	9.7	19.4	10.8	8.6	18.3	16.1	17.2	100.0

TABLE 2
Crosstabulation of
CODEG (Grouped Growth Rate)
by CIVRTIDX (Civil Rights Index)

	Count row PCT col PCT	CIVRTIDX 1	2	3	4	5	6	7	Row Total
CODEG −2.0–0.0	1		2 16.7 12.5		2 16.7 20.0	2 16.7 8.0	3 25.0 16.7	3 25.0 30.0	12 12.9
0.1–1.0	2		1 7.7 6.3	3 23.1 25.0		6 46.2 24.0	2 15.4 11.1	1 7.7 10.0	13 14.0
1.1–2.0	3		2 12.5 12.5	4 25.0 33.3	1 6.3 10.0	2 12.5 8.0	5 31.3 27.8	2 12.5 20.0	16 17.2
2.1–3.0	4	1 5.9 50.0	2 11.8 12.5		3 17.6 30.0	4 23.5 16.0	5 29.4 27.8	2 11.8 20.0	17 18.3
3.1–4.0	5	1 6.7 50.0	4 26.7 25.0	3 20.0 25.0	2 13.3 20.0	4 26.7 16.0		1 6.7 10.0	15 16.1
4.1–5.0	6		3 27.3 18.8	1 9.1 8.3	1 9.1 10.0	3 27.3 12.0	3 27.3 16.7		11 11.8
5.1–6.0	7		2 66.7 12.5					1 33.3 10.0	3 3.2
6.1–7.0	8			1 25.0 8.3		3 75.0 12.0			4 4.3
7.0+	9				1 50.0 10.0	1 50.0 4.0			2 2.2
	Column	2	16	12	10	25	18	10	93
	Total	2.2	17.2	12.9	10.8	26.9	19.4	10.8	100.0

TABLE 3
Crosstabulation of
CODEPCG (Grouped PERCPGNP)
by POLRTIDX (Political Rights Index)

	Count row PCT col PCT	POLRTIDX 1	2	3	4	5	6	7	Row Total
CODEPCG $0–200	1			1 14.3 10.0			2 28.6 13.3	4 57.1 25.0	7 7.4
$201–400	2		1 5.6 5.6	2 11.1 20.0	2 11.1 25.0		5 27.8 33.3	8 44.4 50.0	18 19.1
$401–700	3		4 25.0 22.2	2 12.5 20.0	1 6.3 12.5	6 37.5 33.3	2 12.5 13.3	1 6.3 6.3	16 17.0
$701–1000	4	1 7.1 11.1	2 14.3 11.1	1 7.1 10.0	3 21.4 37.5	4 28.6 22.2	2 14.3 13.3	1 7.1 6.3	14 14.9
$1001–1500	5	2 16.7 22.2	6 50.0 33.3	1 8.3 10.0		2 16.7 11.1		1 8.3 6.3	12 12.8
$1501–2000	6		1 16.7 5.6	1 16.7 10.0		3 50.0 16.7	1 16.7 6.7		6 6.4
$2001–4000	7	3 20.0 33.3	3 20.0 16.7	2 13.3 20.0	1 6.7 12.5	2 13.3 11.1	3 20.0 20.0	1 6.7 6.3	15 16.0
$4001–6000	8	2 50.0 22.2	1 25.0 5.6		1 25.0 12.5				4 4.3
$6000+	9	1 50.0 11.1				1 50.0 5.6			2 2.1
	Column	9	18	10	8	18	15	16	94
	Total	9.6	19.1	10.6	8.5	19.1	16.0	17.0	100.0

TABLE 4
Crosstabulation of
CODEPCG (Grouped PERCPGNP)
by CIVRTIDX (Civil Rights Index)

	Count row PCT col PCT	CIVRTIDX 1	2	3	4	5	6	7	Row Total
CODEPCG $0–200	1				1 14.3 10.0	1 14.3 3.8	1 14.3 5.6	4 57.1 40.0	7 7.4
$201–400	2			1 5.6 8.3	2 11.1 20.0	4 22.2 15.4	8 44.4 44.4	3 16.7 30.0	18 19.1
$401–700	3		1 6.3 6.3	3 18.8 25.0	2 12.5 20.0	6 37.5 23.1	4 25.0 22.2		16 17.0
$701–1000	4		3 21.4 18.8	2 14.3 16.7	2 14.3 20.0	5 35.7 19.2	1 7.1 5.6	1 7.1 10.0	14 14.9
$1001–1500	5	2 16.7 100.0	2 16.7 12.5	4 33.3 33.3		2 16.7 7.7	2 16.7 11.1		12 12.8
$1501–2000	6		1 16.7 6.3			4 66.7 15.4		1 16.7 10.0	6 6.4
$2001–4000	7		5 33.3 31.3	2 13.3 16.7	3 20.0 30.0	2 13.3 7.7	2 13.3 11.1	1 6.7 10.0	15 16.0
$4001–6000	8		3 75.0 18.8			1 25.0 3.8			4 4.3
$6000+	9		1 50.0 6.3			1 50.0 3.8			2 2.1
	Column	2	16	12	10	26	18	10	94
	Total	2.1	17.0	12.8	10.6	27.7	19.1	10.6	100.0

11

Prospects for Cooperation between Commercial Banks and Multilateral Financial Institutions: The Future of the Baker Plan

Lawrence J. Brainard and Sally Shelton-Colby

The international debt problem has recently leaped from the back burner, where it has been since it first erupted in August 1982, to the forefront of U.S. relations with most of the Third World. This is especially true with regard to Latin America, which accounts for roughly one-half of total Third World debt. The debt issue has surged to the top of the U.S.–Latin America agenda as a result of the Reagan administration's conclusion that fundamental U.S. interests in the region were being jeopardized by continuing economic stagnation in most countries in the area.

Out of this perception was born the Baker Plan (more formally, the Program for Sustained Growth), announced last October at the joint annual meeting of the IMF and the World Bank in Seoul. At the heart of the Baker Plan, itself the centerpiece of a new strategy for managing Third World debt, is a requirement for substantial new lending commitments by the international financial community as well as substantial new adjustment efforts by the debtor countries. We will briefly explore the conditions which gave rise to this new initiative, assess how much or how little progress has been made to date, and review possible future avenues of cooperation among the key actors involved.

Recent Economic and Political Trends in Latin America

The economic scene in Latin America has improved in some respects since August 1982. The external deficits of debtor countries have been reduced, export growth has expanded as a result of OECD recovery, reserves have been strengthened, and some degree of economic recovery has been achieved. In 1984, Latin America's GDP increased by two percent, after having fallen by one percent in 1982, and by over three percent in 1983. Latin America also achieved an unusually large trade surplus in 1984 (four times higher than that recorded in 1982, according to the Economic Commission for Latin America). This trade surplus was due not just to a reduction of imports, but more to a substantial expansion of exports caused by various currency devaluations and by recovery in the industrialized countries. The trade surplus helped bring about a reduction in the deficit on current account, and a surplus in the balance of payments was even achieved. Reserve positions thereby improved and the external debt, while still growing, grew at a slower pace than in previous years. In fact, the rate of increase of external debt was slower than that of exports, so the debt-to-exports ratio, while still high, fell for the first time in years. Moreover, the terms on which several Latin American countries renegotiated their debt improved as fees and spreads were reduced and repayment periods were extended.

In spite of this progress, there are still serious problems. Attention to the general improvements tends to mask continuing economic stagnation, or even reversal, in individual countries of the region. Population growth rates continue to be very high, slowing the rise in per capita product to only 0.2 percent in the region as a whole, and actually causing it to diminish in twelve of the region's nineteen countries. This makes Latin America's per capita output nine percent lower than it was in 1980, and roughly analogous to that attained a decade ago (except in Peru where it is equivalent to that of two decades ago!). Unemployment, now at alarming levels, continues to rise. Inflation has soared to an all-time high of 17.5 percent regionwide. The rate of increase in the debt, while slower than in previous years as noted, nevertheless grew at a rate of 5.5 percent. The debts-to-exports ratio, while lower, is still very high; the previously projected decline has not materialized. The ratio of interest payments to exports continued to be high, despite a sharp drop in dollar interest rates, and the terms of trade (apart from oil) have not improved. Anticipated export earnings for 1985 will only just cover interest payments on the region's foreign debt, leaving little for growth.

The social consequences of this economic reality have been severe. Unemployment and underemployment have risen sharply in an area that has only a limited social security safety net. Real wages have dropped to levels of roughly a decade ago. Health and nutritional conditions have deteriorated. The social investments that need to be made in order to cope with the anticipated doubling of Latin America's population in coming decades have been sacrificed to economic adjustment. The private sector has borne much of the burden of the recent adjustment. Business confidence has eroded, new investment is down, idle capacity is up, and capital flight continues.

Politically, Latin America is experiencing serious new pressures for debt relief. Young, relatively inexperienced democratic governments are being subjected to intense demands for social and economic recovery. Pressure comes from political parties, labor unions, business organizations, intellectuals, and now even from the military. The accumulated savings of the 1960s, which cushioned the impact of debt until now, are being depleted, and the extended family network can function for only so long in the absence of economic recovery. Latin American heads of government are becoming increasingly insistent on the need for creditor governments to play a more positive role. While most Latin American heads of state and political leaders acknowledge the need for the structural adjustments which the IMF and the commercial banks insist on, they also argue the need for more time in which to realize them and the need for growth to make those adjustments palatable.

Realizing the potential threat continuing economic stagnation poses for political stability, U.S. export performance, and other U.S. interests in Latin America, the Baker-Volcker team developed a plan for helping eligible Third World countries pursue a resumption of growth. The plan envisions a dominant role for the multilateral development institutions and the commercial banks; the role of the U.S. government has not yet fully evolved. How does the Baker Plan envision the management of the next phase of the debt crisis?

Key Elements of the Baker Plan

The approach taken to deal with the debt crisis when it first emerged in later 1982 was based on IMF austerity programs and on new money packages from banks. The second approach relied on multi-year rescheduling agreements (MYRA), introduced initially in Mexico in mid-1984, and later in Ecuador, Yugoslavia, Venezuela, and Uruguay. This approach was "sold" to the banks and debtor countries as a means to reward those countries which had been successful in their adjustment efforts. It was seen as a way of moving away from "crisis management" on a year-to-year basis toward a more normalized process, one which would lead to voluntary new lending by banks.

The Phase Two strategy, or MYRA approach, was successful in helping to preserve both earlier commitments to economic adjustment and the process of negotiation among the various creditors and debtors. Several weaknesses have since become evident in this approach, however. The strategy is silent, for example, on how the short-term gains from IMF-inspired adjustment programs are to be translated into self-sustained economic growth over the medium term. Although the IMF was given greater Article IV monitoring responsibilities ("enhanced surveillance"), it was not given an active role in developing such programs. In large part, this was due to a political backlash against the Fund in most of the debtor countries which resulted from the heavy social costs of the IMF programs adopted during the early period of the debt crisis. This and the absence of a specific role for institutions that are best qualified to develop and finance medium-term adjustment programs, such as the World Bank, left a void. The debtor countries have been left without support and guidance in their efforts to resume economic growth, while the creditors pretended the problem was solved. The Fund, in fact, has described enhanced surveillance as being best suited for countries "that already have achieved a substantial part of the required external adjustment." Such a perspective reflects a static, unrealistic view of the obstacles to successful medium-term economic adjustment in the debtor countries.

Another shortcoming of the MYRA approach is that it does not spell out the responsibilities that each of the participants—the banks, the debtor countries, and the industrial governments—must shoulder. Nor does it create a structure to bring them together to discuss the key issues at the heart of the current crisis. Indeed, one of the frequent complaints of Latin American governments is that the United States has refused to enter into a dialogue concerning the debt crisis. The countries were left to design recovery policies themselves, without the benefit of external support for dealing with unforeseen contingencies. Provided events will continue to move in the desired directions, this arrangement may be appropriate. If, however, it becomes necessary to modify the agreement, either because of policy failures or adverse external conditions, no structure exists to facilitate such a move. This shortcoming has been highlighted by recent problems in Mexico, which were due to both policy failures and adverse external developments.

The Program for Sustained Growth outlined by Treasury Secretary Baker reflected an effort to remedy some of the weaknesses of the MYRA approach. The Baker Plan underscores the fact that a revival of economic growth in the debtor countries is an essential component of a viable debt-management strategy, and it also spells out specific roles for commercial banks, debtor countries, and international institutions. The three essential elements in the Baker program are:

- the adoption of comprehensive changes in macroeconomic and structural policy by debtor countries to promote growth and balance-of-payments adjustment;

- enhancement of the effectiveness of the international financial institutions, in particular, increased financing by multilateral development banks which is tied to such market-oriented policies for growth and adjustment; and
- increased lending by private banks in support of debtors' comprehensive economic adjustment programs.

The willingness of the banks to fulfill their assigned role in the program by increasing their lending to these countries will depend in large part on whether the first two parts of the program can be implemented satisfactorily. The following two sections explore banks' views on these issues.

Performance Criteria for Sovereign Reschedulings

As a practical matter, banks are dependent on international institutions such as the IMF or on their own governments for setting and enforcing performance criteria—or, conditionality—in sovereign reschedulings. In the case of a loan restructuring with a private borrower, banks have considerable leeway to define such matters as the terms of payment deferral and ongoing financial controls on the company's management. In sovereign reschedulings, however, banks have little leverage over matters related to economic policy and performance. Here, the banks have looked primarily to the IMF to set the conditions for disciplining debtor countries.

Why have the banks been willing to promote a process that does not give them a direct role in influencing the policy changes in debtor countries that are essential to the servicing of their debt over the long term? Many banks believe that an active role in policy advice is inappropriate for them, reflecting a perception that past efforts at bank monitoring have failed—the Peruvian experience in 1977–78 is often cited as evidence. Thus, on concluding each of the MYRAs, for example, the banks disbanded the various advisory committees and economic subcommittees which were originally set up to monitor ongoing developments in debtor countries. Banks were willing to pay the price of reduced spreads and no fees in order to leave the monitoring and policy advice responsibility with others.

A second important consideration underlying banks' move to relinquish a direct role was that no new money was required from them. Many of the banks felt they should play no role beyond rescheduling existing debt and maintaining trade-financing lines. The Baker Plan, however, assumes a continuing role for the banks in helping develop and monitor the performance criteria of medium-term programs that are implied by the plan. Since no details of implementation were offered, the prospective role of banks under the Baker Plan remains an open issue at this time.

Although traditional views of the respective roles of the Fund and the banks are likely to receive continuing support, the success of the Baker Plan may very well hinge on success in creating an active role for the commercial banks in helping develop and implement the needed medium-term programs in debtor countries. The banks' monitoring efforts in Peru in the 1977–78 period failed because the banks were trying to substitute for the Fund. The current attempts at monitoring within the framework of MYRAs have failed because the approach itself contains fundamental flaws. What is required is the creation of a new institutional framework in which a medium-term program for economic adjustment and resumption of growth can be elaborated cooperatively by the country concerned, the various multilateral financial and development institutions, and the private bank creditors. Within this framework, the participants would seek to define appropriate "terms of reference," that is, the ability and willingness of a country to undertake meaningful policy changes and the scope of financial support forthcoming from international agencies and the banks. Where the process goes from there should depend on the specific circumstances of each country. For this reason, the framework should be ad hoc in nature.

A New Role for the Multilateral Development Banks

When the international debt crisis emerged fully at the end of 1982, the international community demonstrated an impressive degree of skill and cooperation in dealing with the problem. During Phase Two, attention was shifted to focus on the solution promised by MYRAs rather than on the continuing problems and challenges. The Baker Plan provides a framework in which these continuing problems and challenges can be reassessed in a realistic way.

The key challenge facing the international community today is to find ways to implement medium-term structural changes essential to increasing a country's productive use of resources over time, while maintaining an acceptable minimum rate of economic growth. Programs of structural adjustment take both time and money to implement, and it is unlikely that a given model can be replicated in other countries. A necessary first step has been taken in recognizing the problem and in highlighting the potential contribution to be made by the World Bank. Now comes the hard part: developing and implementing the needed programs.

For reasons covered in the previous section, a new institutional framework would aid in crafting the programs. The U.S. government, acting through the Treasury Department and the Federal Reserve, must also undertake a new leadership role in supporting this initiative. Active leadership is essential because neither the IMF nor the World Bank is able to create such a framework on its own. Each lacks sufficient political "clout," and their historical roles have created a climate unfavorable to either assuming such a role; in debtor countries this is due to IMF short-term conditionality, and in the creditor countries this is due to past lax conditionality of the World Bank. Furthermore, many of the developed countries would not welcome wholesale changes in the functions of these institutions because such reforms would then have to be applied across the board, even in countries where they are not really needed. The IMF and the World Bank each have essential roles to play. Rather than changing the charter of these institutions, their roles can be most quickly and effectively elaborated within an ad hoc framework under the leadership of the United States and other developed countries.

Commercial banks clearly welcome an enhanced role for the World Bank. Most banks support the concept of growth-oriented structural change, although many banks probably remain skeptical that World Bank conditionality will really be effective. Banks would also like to see an even greater financing role for the World Bank through expanded guarantees on private bank credits. In his speech in Seoul, Treasury Secretary Baker was careful to tie quicker and increased disbursements from the World Bank to sound economic programs. Subsequent statements from the Treasury Department have discouraged the banks' hopes that a substantial expansion of guarantees is contemplated.

The projected role of the IMF under the Baker Plan is not clearly spelled out. While the Seoul speech emphasized that the IMF was to play a critical role, the Fund's contribution to filling the projected resource gap in the fifteen countries was not adddressed. Currently, a substantial portion of the $17 billion owed to the Fund by these countries is scheduled to be repaid during the next three years. To the extent that new stand-by programs are negotiated during this period, new funds will be made available. In contrast to the targets suggested for new lending by the MDBs (multilateral development banks) and the commercial banks, the Baker Plan is silent on projected net lending by the Fund. There is, therefore, a concern on the part of some bankers that the IMF will receive a net repayment from these countries. Whether this uncertainty is serious enough to discourage participation in the Baker Plan by some banks remains to be seen.

The role of the Fund must continue to be a central one. Absent such a role, Latin America's commitment to structural adjustment will be less strong. Modifications in the Fund's activities can certainly be envisioned, but it is critical to the recovery process that the Fund remain centrally involved in supporting the adjustment process.

Several policy ingredients, in addition to the Baker Plan, should be included in the new institutional framework we have suggested for managing the next phase of the debt crisis. One such component is a significantly more active role for the U.S. government. Sound U.S. macroeconomic policy is clearly a prerequisite to the resumption of growth in our major trading partners. Reducing the U.S. federal deficit while maintaining adequate levels of growth is a difficult but not impossible task, and this is essential to bringing down real interest rates. Maintaining a U.S. commitment to fight protectionist pressures and continuing to press ahead on efforts to bring down the overvalued dollar will help stimulate world growth and Third World exports.

Under the new institutional framework we propose, resistance to Export-Import Bank financing should be set aside and a new emphasis should be placed on official sources of trade financing. In this connection, debtor countries' that successfully negotiate Paris Club reschedulings of official debt should not be penalized by the denial of new official trade financing support. Bilateral U.S. development and budgetary support, which has again begun to flow to Latin America after a hiatus of many years, should be expanded on the basis of the obvious interests the U.S. has in the area. In order to encourage a more positive approach by commercial banks and potential investors in Latin America, Washington also should consider tax incentives to stimulate investment in those countries eligible for the Baker Plan as well as greater regulatory flexibility for those banks making new loan commitments. In a further effort to build confidence, the U.S. government should begin the process of raising the World Bank's capital, or if political opposition is strong, it should reconsider its opposition to a cautious, modest liberalization of the Bank's gearing ratio.

Conclusion and Recommendations

How would the institutional approach we propose work in practice? The essential element is a medium-term program of structural change and growth resumption together with commitments of new money from the creditors over the same period. Disbursements of new money would be conditioned on the debtor countries' ability to meet specified targets over the period. Procedures for monitoring performance and modifying such targets have to be worked out. Obviously, finding the right degree of flexibility and toughness will not be simple.

The roles we envision for each of the participants are as follows:

- *commercial banks* commit to maintain and increase trade financing, and banks commit new-term financing tied to conditionality of the medium-term program;

- *World Bank* becomes the key coordinator of the medium-term program, both its formulation and implementation; provides increased financing by means of enlarged SALs (Structural Adjustment Loans), partial guarantees of commercial bank loans, increased co-financings, and increased project financings;
- *Inter-American Development Bank* supports World Bank role as outlined;
- *International Monetary Fund* provides key input on issues such as balance-of-payments and foreign exchange policy; cooperates closely with the World Bank in the formulation and implementation of medium-term program; and in effect prevents a net repayment by debtor countries to the Fund by increased lending through a new facility;
- *developed countries/central banks* make commitments to maintain open markets for the debtor countries' exports; offer increased levels of export credit and direct bilateral aid; provide bridge financing and rescheduling of old debts as appropriate; avoid actions by regulators that would penalize commercial banks for their participation in the program; and implement liquidity facility to purchase portions of participating banks' existing debt on an extended repurchase basis (for example, debt sold by a bank must be repurchased by the bank over an extended period such as ten years); and
- *debtor countries* make a commitment to implement politically sensitive structural changes in return for medium-term financing commitment.

No part of this program will be easy to implement, but these roles do appear politically feasible. A credible medium-term approach of this nature presents the best prospect of enlisting bank support, particularly if it is supported by bank regulators. Such a role for the banks is vital, in turn, if other participants are to play their assigned roles. This also holds true for the U.S. Congress, which will probably be asked to approve an increase in the World Bank's capital. The Congress will be suspicious of what appears to be a bank bail-out, but such a medium-term package of financing commitments and adjustment targets may help allay such fears.

Will the debtor countries make meaningful changes in their policies? All too often such policies emphasized heavy state intervention and restrictions on foreign investment and private enterprise. Changes in the right direction have been made in some countries—Mexico, for example—but many of the new policy initiatives are still in embryonic stages of development and internal political support for further progress is weak in many countries. A new approach along the lines suggested should help consolidate domestic political support for such reforms.

The final unknown concerns the U.S. government. Is Washington prepared to change its policy at this time?

Appendix: List of Participants and Discussants in IMF Lecture Series

Fernando Arias
Vice President; Economist
Bank of America

Thomas R. Atkinson
Vice President
General Motors Overseas Corporation

Jane Bardon
International Economist
Office of the Assistant Secretary for International Affairs
Department of the Treasury

David Beckmann
External Relations
The World Bank

Richard Behrend
Bureau of Economic and Business Affairs
Department of State

Patrick J. Brennan
General Manager
Gulf Bank of Kuwait

Frederick Broda
First Vice President
Swiss Bank Corporation

Herbert Cahn
Special Adviser, U.S. Projects
Banco do Estado de São Paulo

Dardo A. Cartier
Senior Vice President and General Manager
Banco de la Nación Argentina

Wolmen Carvalho
General Manager
Banco do Brazil

Donald Cassidy
Mellon Financial Services

John C. Cooper
Senior Vice President
Marine Midland Bank, N.A.

Kevin Corrigan
Vice President, Western Hemisphere
The Chase Manhattan Bank, N.A.

Robert Count
Vice President
Credit Agrico

Andrew Crockett
Deputy Director
Research Department
International Monetary Fund

J.H. Ebbeler
Director, Public Affairs
Eli Lilly and Company

Gary Eisen
Economist
BP North America, Inc.

Tamara Geacintov
President
ALIMA, Inc.

Michael Glover
Financial Economist
Office of Monetary Affairs
Department of State

Donald P. Gregg
Assistant to the Vice-President
for National Security Affairs
The White House

Dan Haendel
Office of General Counsel
(International Affairs)
Department of the Treasury

Bruce F. Henderson
President and Chief Executive Officer
UBAF Arab-American Bank

Richard L. Johnston, Jr.
Vice President
The Chase Manhattan Bank, N.A.

Suhas Ketkar
Vice President
and Latin American Economist
Marine Midland Bank

Ken Klein
Xerox Corporation

Roger Kubarych
Chief Economist
The Conference Board

Charles Larkum
External Debt
The World Bank

Nicholas McCausland
Vice President
Manufacturers Hanover Trust Company

Richard A. Melville
Executive Vice President
Fiduciary Trust Company of New York

Gary Gene Moser
International Economist
Office of Management and Budget

John Mullan
Barclays Bank

F. Carl Reinhardt
Vice President
Allied Bank International

Orlando G. Rodriguez
Vice President
Marine Midland Bank

Donald W. Ropa
Staff Vice President
International Trade Policy
RCA

John B. Ross
Vice President
Bank of America

Robert W. Russell
International Monetary Fund

Frederick Seeley
Senior Vice President, Latin America
J. Henry Schroeder Bank & Trust Company

Daniel Sharp
Director of International Relations
Xerox Corporation

Ronald K. Shelp
Vice President, International Relations
American International Group

Dorothy Sobol
Senior Fellow in Economics
Council on Foreign Relations

Daniel Speckhard
Examiner, International Affairs Division
Office of Management and Budget

Lawrence A. Veit
Manager and International Economist
Brown Brothers Harriman & Company

W. Robert Warne
Director
Office of Regional Economic Policy
Bureau of Inter-American Affairs
Department of State

Gordon R. Williamson
Director of Industry Relations
IBM Corporation

Albert Wojnilower
Chief Economist
The First Boston Corporation

Alan Zuschlag
Associate
National Foreign Trade Council, Inc.

About the Contributors

Lawrence J. Brainard is head of international economic and political analysis at Bankers Trust Company, and since 1975 has served as advisor on East-West commercial relations to the Atlantic Council, the Dartmouth Conference, the Office of Technology Assessment of the U.S. Congress, and the National Security Council. He has published widely on economic issues relating to Europe, both East and West, on international capital markets, and on developing countries.

Robert S. Browne is currently a private consultant on international economic problems, specializing in African development issues. He has worked in the U.S. economic assistance program in Asia and was the first American executive director at the African Development Fund, where he represented the United States, United Kingdom, and Yugoslavia. He is co-author of the *Lagos Plan vs. the Berg Report* (1983).

Irving S. Friedman is currently chairman of the Washington Capital Markets Group based in Washington, D.C. He was a Department Director of the International Monetary Fund for over fifteen years and was the Economic Advisor to the president of the World Bank for nearly a decade. He is the author of *Inflation, a World Disaster* and *The World Debt Dilemma: Managing Country Risk.*

Irving Louis Horowitz is Hannah Arendt Distinguished Professor of Sociology and Political Science at Rutgers University, and president of Transaction Publishers, a social science complex located at Rutgers. His work in international development includes *Three Worlds of Development: The Theory and Practice of International Stratification* (Oxford 1965, 1972); *Equity, Income and Policy: Comparative Studies in Three Worlds of Development* (CBS Praeger, 1977); and *Beyond Empire and Revolution: Militarization and Consolidation in the Third World* (Oxford, 1982).

D. Gale Johnson is the Eliakim Hastings Moore Distinguished Service Professor of Economics. He is currently affiliated with the University of Chicago, and has served as economist and consultant for a large number of governmental departments and agencies. His numerous publications include: *Progress of Economic Reform in the People's Republic of China* (1982, edited by G. Edward Schuh); *The Role of Markets in the World Food Economy* (1983); and *Prospects for Soviet Agriculture in the 1980s* (1983, with Karen Brooks).

Pedro-Pablo Kuczynski is co-chairman of First Boston International and a managing director of the First Boston Corporation. From 1980 to 1982, he was Minister of Energy and Mines of Peru. He has also served at the World Bank, the International Monetary Fund, and the International Finance Corporation. He is the author of *Peruvian Democracy under Economic Stress: An Account of the Belaunde Administration, 1963–68.*

Robert J. Myers has been president of the Carnegie Council on Ethics and International Affairs in New York City since 1980. He has served in Asia with the U.S. Army and the Department of State. He was publisher of the *Washingtonian* and *The New Republic* prior to joining the Carnegie Council.

Alvin Rabushka, a senior fellow of the Hoover Institution of Stanford University, specializes in the domestic public policy areas of taxation, the federal budget process, constitutional limitations on taxing and spending, aging, and housing and also on the political economy of free enterprise economies as found in several postwar developing countries, most notably Hong Kong. His numerous publications include *Hong Kong: A Study in Economic Freedom* and *From Adam Smith to the Wealth of America* (1985).

Henry B. Schechter is deputy director, American Federation of Labor–Congress of Industrial Organizations, Department of Economic Research; and director, Office of Housing and Monetary Policy. He has also been director, Department of Urban Affairs. He is the author of many articles on housing, finance, urban development, industrial policy, and global economics.

Sally Shelton-Colby is vice president in the Economics Department of Bankers Trust, with responsibility for political analysis in Latin America. She served from 1979 to 1981 as ambassador to Barbados, Grenada, and eight other Caribbean nations and territories. A Fulbright scholar, Ambassador Shelton-Colby has been a fellow at the Center for International Affairs at Harvard University, and has taught at the John F. Kennedy School of Government.

Lance Taylor is professor of economics at the Massachusetts Institute of Technology. Active as a development economist since 1968, he has worked as a consultant or visiting lecturer in more than twenty countries, including

Mexico, Brazil, Egypt, Nigeria, and India. His most recent book is *Structuralist Macroeconomics* (1983) and he is currently coordinating a program on the economics of stabilization for the newly founded World Institute of Development Economics Research in Helsinki.

George M. von Furstenberg is Rudy Professor of Economics, Indiana University. He has been chief, Financial Studies Division of the Research Department, International Monetary Fund; and, earlier, was an economist for the American Enterprise Institute. He has published extensively.

John Williamson is a senior fellow at the Institute for International Economics in Washington, D.C. He has been an economic consultant to the U.K. Treasury, and an advisor to the International Monetary Fund. His publications deal with international monetary issues, and include *The Open Economy and the World Economy* (1983) and *The Exchange Rate System* (1983).

Index